VIOLENT
ADVENTURE

VIOLENT ADVENTURE

Contemporary Fiction by American Men

MARILYN C. WESLEY

University of Virginia Press   Charlottesville and London

University of Virginia Press
© 2003 by the Rector and Visitors of the University of Virginia
All rights reserved
Printed in the United States of America on acid-free paper

First published 2003

1 3 5 7 9 8 6 4 2

Library of Congress Cataloging-in-Publication Data

Wesley, Marilyn C.
   Violent adventure : contemporary fiction by American men / Marilyn
C. Wesley.
      p.   cm.
Includes bibliographical references and index.
   ISBN 0-8139-2212-7 (alk. paper) — ISBN 0-8139-2213-5 (alk. paper)
   1. American fiction—Male authors—History and criticism.
2. Masculinity in literature. 3. American fiction—20th century—History
and criticism. 4. Adventure stories, American—History and criticism.
5. Violence in literature. 6. Sex role in literature. 7. Men in literature.
I. Title.
PS374.M37 W47 2003
813′ .509041—dc21

2002155967

FOR JAY AND JORDAN

CONTENTS

CONTENTS

PREFACE

I bore two sons into a world where Hans Solo replaced John Wayne as a national hero and the lost war in Vietnam was mediated by GI Joe dolls and Rambo movies. I packed their Spiderman lunch boxes with peanut butter sandwiches and turned them over to *Julius Caesar* and *Huckleberry Finn* hoping for the best, but every time I watched them climb aboard the school bus I worried. Not always a lot, and perhaps not even consciously, yet enough to inspire this project decades later. Because I was a graduate student interested in literature, my concerns then, and my motivation for this study, can be condensed into these questions: *What do the stories we tell them teach our boys about being men?* And, more specifically, *What does a culture of male violence teach our boys about being violent men?*

In a 1926 book addressed to "recreation workers," Paul Hanly Furfey described the interests of a "gifted" thirteen-year-old boy named Dan. Among his activities—"Standard Games," "Intellectual Diversions," "Manipulative Play," "Scouting"—Furfey included the following laudatory comments on "Fighting Games":

> Every boy enjoys a fight. The fight to a finish *au Tom Brown* is
> uncommon in these effete days; but the same old fighting instinct
> lives on. Dan and a chum have formed an alliance for several
> months now against two other boys and they clash with the oppo-
> sition during school recess with much joyful squealing and perfect
> good nature. Besides this guerrilla warfare there are sometimes
> intergrade clashes accompanied by more bruit than bruises. Or the
> gang devotes a spare hour to the persecution of some unfortunate
> who has incurred their displeasure. Or perhaps the janitor is the
> unhappy victim. (106–07).

What is striking to me in this account is not the particulars of Dan's aggression, but the sense that it is prescribed and celebrated by the author (and may even be tacitly encouraged by the school) as a requisite component of masculine non-"effete" recreation, that it acceptably progresses from what may be a contest to what is labeled a "persecution," that it seems to endorse the creation of classes of victims. One guesses from the tone of Furfey's words that an "unfortunate" may be a boy who does not meet the norms sought by the "alliance" of chums and that class and economic restriction condemn the "unhappy" janitor. The vocabulary casts aggressive "instinct," injury, warfare, and cruelty as inevitable, universal, high-spirited male playfulness.

Several books about boys' development published in 1998 and 1999 challenge the cultural assumptions shaping the 1926 paragraph. James Garbarino, William Pollack, Dan Kindlon, and Michael Thompson, psychologists writing in the aftermath of the spectacular school slayings of 1997–98, describe the kind of aggression Furfey celebrates as an inadequate response to boyhoods shaped by shame, cruelty, isolation, and dissociation. Kindlon and Thompson, for example, tell the story of Adam, who was "being picked on at school, heckled on the bus" and provoked into fighting. A "twelfth-grade bully" led the taunts of "Hey, White Trash! . . . You don't belong here with *us*!" . . . "Why don't you go back to your side of town!"

> "But I never throw the first punch," Adam explained to his mother. "I don't show them they can hurt me. I don't want to embarrass myself in front of everybody." . . . "I get a little down . . . but I'm very good at hiding it. It's like I wear a mask." . . . "I tend to let it boil inside until I can't hold it any longer, and then it explodes." (4)

In Adam's case the experience of the boys' culture of aggression led to depression. But violence directed at the self or others is also a real possibility. As Pollock reports, for males fifteen to twenty-four years of age, two of the three leading causes of death are homicide and suicide (332–33). Garbarino, who bases his book on interviews with adolescent male killers conducted between 1996 and 1998, argues that youth violence of "epidemic" proportions is "spreading across America" (ix).

These books demonstrate that we have begun to challenge the myths of natural boyhood violence promoted in earlier periods. Instead of valorizing bullying, as Furfey assumes we will, the account of Adam implies we are now expected to sympathize with victims. And we are encouraged to analyze the psychological relations and societal conditions that connect masculine development with detrimental aggression. As the two brief quotations also suggest, *how* the story of masculine identity and violence is presented is crucial. We belong to a community that is becoming wary of mass media representations that not only dehumanize aggression and fail to show its consequences, but also associate violence with glamour, success, and popularity. This wariness is necessary because, as Garbarino puts it, too many boys "succumb to the cultural stereotypes of a socially toxic society that defines manhood in terms of aggression, power, and material acquisition" (238).

The story of masculine experience has traditionally been a narrative of adventure—the narrative of a hero's movement and conquest, his discovery of the world, and the assertion of his own important place within it, often at the cost of violent struggle. In *The Adventurer* Paul Zweig reminds us that tales of male heroic action are historically the most ancient, universal, and prevalent forms of narrative. And although the settings, styles, and uses of stories of masculine exploit have varied from time to time and place to place, it may very well be, he argues, "that man risking his life in perilous encounters constitutes the original definition of what is worth talking about" (6). Certainly, as Richard Slotkin's ambitious historical survey of American adventure fiction confirms, the connection of this genre to ideals of manhood and aspirations to power is firmly entrenched, and the adventure tradition, a major means of promulgating male white Anglo-Saxon identity since the earliest days of New England settlement, is still evident in many forms of popular adventure—from televised cop shows to movie techno-thrillers.

But although evolving forms of adventure narrative traced by Slotkin and John G. Cawelti in such forms as cowboy fiction, war stories, and mysteries continue to focus on the masculine development through violent heroics that defines the earliest examples of the genres, in recent decades alterations in social attitude have produced some evident changes. Movies, for example, reveal the pressure to accommodate postfeminist expectations through plots in which contemporary women get to slay their own dragons. In addition, as ethnic voices are increasingly audible, men who do not share the rewards of the dominant group may choose not to duplicate its fundamental stories.

Nonetheless, as this study argues, the genres of adventure fiction in some of its present forms—the Western; what I will define as the contemporary epic; along with the detective, the initiation, and the war story—continue to exert significant influence in fiction by American men. Yet many, especially those who have inherited the social privilege of centrality, have been moved to redefine important features, themes, and forms of its subgenres. And, as the chapter on revisions of conventional mystery by two prominent black writers demonstrates, sometimes outsiders have seized the tradition in order to adapt it to alternative use.

Because it is centered on imagining the successful emergence of manhood, in the genres of adventure fiction violent incident most often structures the inevitable contests that convert a beset protagonist into a victorious hero. However, it is precisely the inevitability of this mode of conversion that contemporary revisions of adventure formulas question. Reading widely in novels and short stories written by a broad spectrum of American men who have adapted recognizable adventure genres, I became increasingly aware of an important—but largely unnoticed—pattern of the relation between masculine identity and narrative aggression: the ways in which narratives of boys and violence promote a change in the expectation that violence produces male power.

The authors treated in *Violent Adventure* demonstrate the attempts of my own generation to address the issues of violence, masculinity, and representation in the shadow of Vietnam. Although each makes use of the adventure genre, by no stretch of the critical imagination could the works of contemporary American writers Tim O'Brien, Thom Jones, Tobias Wolff, Pinckney Benedict, Richard Ford, Cormac McCarthy, Ernest Gaines, Walter Mosley, Russell Banks, and Don DeLillo be labeled (and, as is frequently the case, dismissed) as formula fiction. This group includes holders of such tangible marks of literary achievement as a MacArthur Award, the National Book Critics Award, recognition by the American Academy of Arts and Letters, the William Faulkner Foundation Award, the Jerusalem Prize, the PEN/Faulkner Prize, the O'Henry Short Story Prize, inclusion in the Best American Short Story annual series, and Guggenheim Fellowships. Yet this group also shows evidence of broader appeal—books that have been made into successful Hollywood films, an author featured on Oprah's Book Club, and former President Bill Clinton's favorite mystery writer.

Evidently engaging both general and literary audiences, the works studied also fall into the category of popular literature through treatment of subject—*popular* in Cawelti's sense of making use of prevalent narrative conventions, and *literary* in his sense of raising discomfiting questions about them (*Adventure* 8). Besides being widely known for writing in genres that focus on male violence, like Tim O'Brien's prominence among writers treating the war in Vietnam and Walter Mosley's popularity as a writer of detective fiction, many of the authors featured are specifically associated with violence. For example, reviewing a 1998 novel by Richard Bausch, Donna Rifkind characterized his oeuvre as "fiction [that] charts the valleys and shadows of violence" (8). A 1992 overview of Pinckney Benedict's second collection of short stories is entitled "The Elemental Violence of Pinckney Benedict's peculiarly American Myths of Character." A 1993 *Nation* review describes the stories of Thom Jones's *The Pugilist at Rest* as treatments of a "situation [that] races along its violent or otherwise 'wired' premise to its baleful conclusion" (254), and a 1996 *Houston Chronicle* article blames Jones's acquisition of "the 'new machismo' label" on the predominance of his "tough-guy stories" (26). On the occasion of the reissue of *Blood Meridian,* the *Chicago Tribune* substantially reprinted in 1997 an earlier article entitled "Innocence Meets Violence in American Literary Tradition." On the basis of the content of McCarthy's novels, which "have always been drenched in blood" (16), Sara Mosle warns in the title of a *New York Times Book Review* feature in 1998, "Don't Let Your Babies Grow Up to Be Cowboys." McCarthy himself expressed a belief that may explain both the predominance of violence—and its significant interrogation—by contemporary writers of adventure fiction. "There's no such thing as a life without bloodshed," he declared, and to ignore it "will enslave you and make your life vacuous" (Woodward 36).

As my concluding chapter points out, violence is a structural property so predominant in narrative that any number of texts could illustrate significant revisions of adventure genres. The novels and stories I do consider were selected because in each case they make use of the conventions of an important genre of adventure in such a way as to challenge popular assumptions about the significance of violence for masculine identity. But that is not all. Representing the achievement of many diverse writers—liberal and conservative, black and white, from different geographic regions and class affiliations—these texts may also suggest emerging collective and crucial concerns.

Perhaps not quite a movement, the books of this study represent a significant tendency of men writing in differing styles from various perspectives to challenge the themes and styles of the violent under-pinnings of masculinity. I have come to understand this preoccupation in terms of Kenneth Burke's theory of dramatistic authorization. The "symbolic action" of narrative, Burke argues, provides "equipment for living" by representing "typical, recurrent categories" as replicable pat-terns that "imply command" of recognizable situations (254). The pop-ularity of male narrative violence, I believe, implies its address to the control of central concerns of men's lives and of male-dominated soci-ety: the development of masculine identity, the intergenerational rela-tions that shape masculinity, and the maintenance of societal institu-tions that regulate power.

Motivated by apprehension about the culture that was shaping my own sons, I began this project with the expectation that the fiction would, at worst, be too bloody in the manner of the charge frequently leveled at popular culture or, at best, elaborate some of the feminist-inspired critiques of male gender roles by the academic men's movement of the 1980s. I found neither the motifs I was seeing at the movies—the masculine protest and rejection of feminized authority so well described in Susan Jeffords's 1989 *The Remasculinization of America: Gender and the Vietnam War*—nor the rejection of conventional narratives of Amer-ican heroism forecast by Mark Gerzon's 1982 *A Choice of Heroes: The Changing Faces of American Manhood* or Myriam Miedzian's 1991 *Boys Will Be Boys: Breaking the Link between Masculinity and Violence*. I was surprised in my extensive review of male texts written in the 1980s and '90s by how many relied on familiar genres of adventure—the stories of boys trying to become men, and the stories of men trying not to be boys—to raise questions about masculine empowerment struc-tured by themes of violence.

Real acts of violence are widely varied. Similarly, representations of violence may exhibit differing preoccupations, purposes, styles, and subjects, but according to Slotkin's convincing study, the nation that became the United States has invested over three centuries of stories in the propositions I will define as the ideology of *constructive violence*. Doubtless, some of the violence perpetrated as a result of this extensive indoctrination may have been helpful, even necessary, for individuals or the state. But my review of narratives by current authors revealed a strikingly different theme shared by many: the interrogation of violence and the social expectations it regulates. In *The Political Unconscious* Fredric Jameson ascribes literary production to the need to reveal and try to resolve the conflicts within the fantasies that define us. In *Violent Adventure* I explain the revision of the genres of masculine adventure by contemporary male writers as interventions in the mistaken belief that male violence begets masculine power. The predominance of narrative revisions of this belief in contemporary fiction demonstrates the problematic centrality of violence to narrative and to masculinity rooted in vexed issues of power.

I began my doctoral training in American literature and literary theory during my sons' boyhoods with an evening extension course in psycholinguistics. The professor, a consultant for the FBI, taught the interpretation of threat messages of the self-designated Symbionese Liberation Army and the analysis of the journals of the Texas Tower murderer. He taught the class of county sheriffs, FBI agents, and would-be day students how to talk to hostage takers and how to select the SWAT team to shoot them if words failed. At the same time, an emerging academic feminism taught me that if the personal is political, then so are the stories.

This book, then, inspired by my concerns about my own family, also comes out of a scholarly realization that narratives and violence, that sex roles and stories of violence are significantly connected—and deeply influential. And that it is necessary to ask *how*. After another round of school violence in Santee, California, in 2001, I became even more convinced that as a society we must divert some of our massive investment in the abhorrence of shocking content to the determination of how male narrative violence shapes and challenges the expectations that contribute to real violence. Completing this preface after the horror of September 11, 2001, I am even more certain of the urgency of that project.

Instead of uncritically condemning violent representation, let us learn what it has to teach.

I wish to thank the young men who inspired these concerns, my sons, Jordan and Jay Hayes, to whom this book is dedicated; Christa Baiada, my research assistant; the Stevens-German Library of Hartwick College for research assistance; Hartwick College for leave time and the financial support afforded by my appointment to the Cora M. Babcock

Chair of English; Cathie Brettschneider of the University of Virgina Press for believing in the project; and, as always, my husband, Norman Wesley.

Articles based on material from this book have appeared in the following journals:

"Truth and Fiction in Tim O'Brien's *If I Die in a Combat Zone* and *The Things They Carried." College Literature 29.2* (spring 2002).

"Power and Knowledge in Walter Mosley's *Devil in a Blue Dress." African American Review* 35.1 (2001).

"The Hero of the Hour: Ideology and Violence in Richard Harding Davis." *American Literary Realism* 32.2 (winter 2000).

"The Paradox of Virility: Narrative Violence in a Modern Anthology." *Journal of the Short Story in English:* Les Cahiers de la Nouvelle 33 (autumn 1999).

VIOLENT
ADVENTURE

INTRODUCTION

Constructive Violence and Adventure Narrative

"Here it is, I'm afraid," observes a gunman in Richard Bausch's aptly named 1992 novel *Violence,* "the absolute worst night of your lives" (67). Before the convenience-store robbery he is committing is over, four people have been shot to death, a woman has been raped, and the protagonist has passed into an extreme state of anxiety that forces him to recognize violence as an endemic condition of himself and his family, as well as his world. Told in a single chapter from the third-person omniscient point of view, at a pace slow enough to divulge all the psychological uncertainty and wavering attempts at adjustment by the focal character before, during, and after the hold-up, the novel relentlessly minimizes the excitement and resolution associated with climactic acts of violence in popular entertainment to expose the fear of powerlessness that formulaic representations of violence usually suppress.

But even as it sabotages their familiar modes of coping, *Violence* solicits the identification of its contemporary audience. "You know what a nightmare you're in?" demands the gunman. "I'm talking to you" (68)—an interpellative address that extends beyond the hostages in the store to confront the readers of Bausch's novel, for whom violence continues to be a predominant social and personal concern. By 1978 the *New York Times* was reporting violence as "one of the country's worst public health threats" because the United States was, without even a close contender, the most violent industrialized nation in the world. Homicide was cited as the second most frequent cause of death of those aged fifteen to twenty-four, and two million Americans could expect to be criminally assaulted within the year (Toufexis 185). From 1985 to 1993 the murder of young men fifteen to nineteen years of age increased 150 percent (Butterfield 325). From the mid-1980s to the mid-1990s,

1

the rate of youth homicide increased 168 percent (Garbarino 7). In 1991 death by murder among young males fifteen to twenty-four was occurring at a rate of 37.2 per 100,000, an incidence ten times higher than that of Italy, the next most violent nation, and sixty times that of Great Britain (Butterfield 329). By the end of the 1980s, the shocking statistics on crimes against women were widely disseminated. The FBI disclosed that a woman was raped every six minutes and that one of every ten would be raped during the course of her life.[1] Noting that a woman is beaten every fifteen seconds, and that for four women a day such attacks are fatal, Surgeon General Everett Koop declared "battery . . . the single most significant cause of injury to women in this country" (Mithers 189–90).

Although the news of recent improvements in the rates of violent crime reported in some cities may suggest reasons for optimism,[2] evidently, America is a very violent society. But it is also a society prone to simple explanations of complex problems. And, unfortunately, what George Sorel observed in the early 1900s and Hannah Arendt repeated in 1969 continues to be relevant: "The problems of violence still remain very obscure" (Arendt 35). This obscurity owes a great deal to two influential and reductive theories about male violence. In 1966 Konrad Lorenz posited a natural predisposition for human aggression analogous to the inborn violence of animals.[3] Lorenz's thesis of biological determinism had the appeal of simplifying a complicated and destructive history, but by placing culture and ethics under the control of instinct, it foreclosed examination of social factors at work in that history.

In a similar fashion, one of the most prominent current explanations of violence blames excessive media representation. By 1998 there had been some 3,500 studies considering the relation of violence to media.[4] One 1995 poll by the Opinion Research Council concluded that 82 percent of the public thought television too violent,[5] and another survey conducted the same year found that 21 percent of Americans believed television violence was the *primary* cause of adolescent violence, although experimental data suggest that early exposure to televisual brutality may actually contribute somewhere between 5 and 10 percent to adult aggressiveness.[6] It is ironic that a theory of innate aggression, which largely ignored the impact of culture, has given way to a sweeping belief in a "culture of violence" that obscures almost everything else.

The problem of violence is too often conceived as a combination of both these determinants—destructive instinct and deleterious culture—an explosive mix of masculinity and media. The popular explanation goes something like this: Because males are innately brutal, violent stories and images serve a natural appetite for bloodshed in a way that acts as a safety valve for masculine violence or, worse, stimulates that appetite to produce real action, so that representations of violent acts are understood as a direct cause of the increasing level of violence in society. Besides demeaning men, this tautological simplification impedes potential understanding. Considering symbolic violence in terms of instinctive reflex, either biological or media-generated,[7] tends to foreclose examination of more complicated meanings that may be negotiated by the figuration of male violence.

Contemporary writers of genuine literary accomplishment are in fact writing books chock full of fighting, war, and criminality in patterns familiar from male adventure. But they are not writing about aggression to make American men more violent. Rather, they write about violence to expose the destructive assumptions it generates. By analyzing—instead of condemning—the uses of violent representation in texts by a range of American men, *Violent Adventure* discovers significant revisions of customary beliefs about masculinity and power.

Generic Violence

Contrary to the familiar truisms that "might makes right" and "to the victor goes the spoils," some influential political thinkers have insisted on the reverse—that violence does not and cannot generate power. In *Power and Innocence: A Search for the Sources of Violence,* psychologist Rollo May contended that resorting to violence actually signals the failure of personal power. After exhausting all other recourses to agency through self-assertion and even aggression, a frustrated individual is apt to indulge in "the ultimate explosion known as *violence*" (43), an ineffectual expedient of empowerment but an efficacious expression of rage. "If other phases of behavior are blocked," May explained, "then explosion into violence may be the only way individuals or groups can get release from unbearable tension and achieve a sense of significance" (44). Philosopher Hannah Arendt went even further in her declaration that although "violence appears where power is in jeopardy" and "can destroy power; it is utterly incapable of creating it" (56). And historian/philosopher Michel Foucault asserted that although "the play of power

3

relations does not exclude violence," violence itself does "not constitute the principle or the basic nature of power" ("Subject and Power" 220).

Nevertheless, many subgenres of the male adventure tale—the war story, the boy's life account, the Western, the mystery/detective story, and what I am calling the contemporary epic—endlessly replicate the ideological premise that acts of violent destruction construct power. The constructive link between power and violence is forged by the developmental narrative of the young man, the story of the unfolding identity of the male hero—boy, cowboy, detective, soldier, or national representative. His story of the emergence of the masculine "self" through violence also promotes the social values of the system that authorizes the power to which he aspires. Typically, in tales of popular adventure, the soldier learns to fight courageously to support the threatened solidarity of his unit, the cowboy's shoot-out is the salvation of a nascent community, and the detective's brutality is employed in defense against a challenge to weakened principles of law and order.

In a genre defined by heroic acts in the face of danger, it is not surprising that the "adventurer becomes the child of his own deeds" (Zweig 70) and "through risk and trouble" gains his true self (24). But the male self-construction so characteristic of traditional adventure also came to typify the modern novel. According to Peter Brooks, by the nineteenth century, the bourgeois novel of masculine capitalistic "aspiration" was predominant: "Male plots of ambition" served "the self's tendency to appropriation and aggrandizement, moving forward through the encompassment of more, striving to have, to do, and to be more" (39). This heroic "self," which links serious and popular forms, is, according to Martin Green, largely an effect of modern colonialism. For him, elements of adventure expressed the principal ideological tenets of an historical epoch worthy of study precisely because its violence provides insight into the operations of power. By encoding the military and economic motives of Western imperialism, narratives of "domination" express "that body of historical fact which Simone Weil called force" (340).[8] In America, codes for such expression, traditionally available as tales of war and exploration, were further elaborated during the 1890s by pulp magazines into such subgenres of adventure as the Western and the detective story, extending the definitive features of "action" and "hypermasculinity" to a broad new male audience (Brown 359).[9] The contemporary novels of *Violent Adventure* use inherited adventure formulas to revise private and public expectations about violence.

As Richard Slotkin's massive study of one subgenre demonstrates, typically adventure fiction oscillates between the destructive violence of an antagonist designated as an outsider to the community and what I am calling the "constructive violence" enacted by the young male protagonist who is seeking a "power" that confirms community values. But whereas the traditional forms of adventure generally present violence in a manner that obscures the grounding of power in the conflux of discursive, social, political, and economic agencies accessible to ordinary people in actual circumstances, current adaptations of adventure subgenres by a surprising range of male writers subvert conventional patterns of violent content and generic form to foreground issues of cultural and material power relations.[10]

Although they may differ by region, politics, race, and style, the many contemporary male writers of this study all make use of narrative subgenres of popular male adventure to similar effect. Tobias Wolff's *This Boy's Life* and Pinckney Benedict's *Town Smokes* modify the traditional male initiation narrative; Tim O'Brien's *The Things They Carried* and Thom Jones's *The Pugilist at Rest* are war stories; Richard Ford's *Rock Springs* stories adapt the generic Western to a present-day setting, while Cormac McCarthy's *Blood Meridian* transforms the historical Western; Ernest Gaines's *A Gathering of Old Men* and Walter Mosley's *Devil in a Blue Dress* revise the classic and the hard-boiled detective story, respectively; and Russell Banks's *Continental Drift* and Don DeLillo's *Libra* rewrite the traditional epic for recent politics. But while they each employ conventions of plot, characterization, and closure typical of the adventure genre, none of these texts adopts its prevalent ideology of violent construction. Instead, the authors retain violent representation of action and institute violent dislocations of structure to reform the traditional conventions even as they make use of them.

These texts conserve the thematics of masculine development focused through a plot of violent male action that defines the adventure genre to demonstrate that violence does not produce power; nor does violence promote the satisfactory insertion of the young man into a supportive identifying community. In contradiction to the ideological bridge between hero and social norms effected through the representation of constructive violence in traditional narratives of the development of the hero, the deployment of violence as subject and form in the novels and short stories of these contemporary writers questions the existence of a supportive community or contests the values of the society that is supposed to provide standards and guidance. The contemporary narrative violence treated in *Violent Adventure,* then, challenges the unexamined convergence of masculinity and power in conventional adventure.

Formula stories develop out of wide use in particular social and historical contexts. Permeated "with the symbols of danger, uncertainty, violence and sex," they substitute "moral fantasies" for the apprehensions they arouse, explains John G. Cawelti (*Adventure* 16, 38). In place of the "limitations" imposed by real experience, they provide an imagined "world more exciting, more fulfilling, or more benevolent" than readers or viewers actually occupy (38). According to Slotkin's three-volume study, a central form of American cultural expression has been the male narrative of frontier violence in which "progress depends on the exclusion/extermination of a congenitally regressive type of humanity"—the story of destructive action that produces "the aggrandizement of a privileged race or people" (*Gunfighter Nation* 21). This major generic pattern, originating in folk expression and eventually repeated in mass-market production, promulgates "a set of tacit assumptions about the human experience, on human and divine motivations, on moral values, and on the nature of reality" (*Regeneration* 20). Such collective assumptions are ideology, which, in Louis Althusser's well-known formulation, is an "imaginary relation" to actual circumstances ("Ideology" 165).

What turns the personal wishes described by Cawelti into the national ideology theorized by Slotkin is, of course, the constant reiteration and broad distribution brought about by the repetition of customary formulas. So understood, genres are not merely convenient collections of narrative conventions; they are communal institutions that mediate between individuals and history by providing standardized templates for the replication of shared values. Therefore, reconfigurations of the compensatory fantasy of violence may be understood as intervention in the shared construction of power negotiated by culture.[11] Generic formulas of violent construction retain popular utility when, as in the present period, discourses of power, identity, and community are felt as increasingly unreliable. The texts of this study, however, demonstrate the dangerous inadequacy of violence as an ideology of masculine power and the frightening deficiency of communal patterns of class, gender, and race derived from it.

Christine Bold avers that this nation's generic fiction has provided "allegories of American life" (291) evolving in response to changing historical circumstances.[12] And the grand patterns of American history—the imperial conquest of a native American continent, the massive system of slave labor, the continuous influx of immigrants, the class exploitation of capitalist industrialization, and a series of large-scale modern wars—have ensured the consistent pressures of assimilation and economic competition that have made the violent construction of power an attractive illusion. These historical circumstances also provided a changing ensemble of stereotypes to be cast as the inferior "enemies" of the privileged majority in its enduring narration of what Slotkin calls "regeneration through violence" as a ready response to new situations. Even the inversion, nostalgia, and impersonations of the frontier myth Slotkin finds in current culture imply an ongoing process of revision that blends "old formulas with new ideas and concerns" (*Gunfighter Nation* 6) in the constant hegemony of the narrative trope of constructive violence that is documented in his extensive study from the colonial period to the Gulf War.[13]

In light of this persistence, and although I certainly consider striking examples of each, my focus is neither the brutality nor the immorality of violence. Indeed, in chapter 1 and chapter 2, I note the negative effects of even bloodless and altruistic representations. Instead, *Violent Adventure* concentrates on expectations about violent construction of male power that not only harm young men but also damage the social relations that are supposed to sustain them.

Because the father-son relationship, or its symbolic counterpart in other intergenerational male relations, is, according to influential psychological theories of Freud, Lacan, Erikson, and others, supposed to function as the younger man's conduit into the larger community, an alternative pattern of inadequate parental relations illustrates more than the deficiency of particular fathers. In contrast to the expectation of masculine formation encoded in generic formulas of constructive violence, the blocked development portrayed in many of the texts of *Violent Adventure* indicates a serious deficiency of social institutions and values. By rewriting the conventions of constructive violence, recent male narratives question the organization of power regulated by society, and the failed father in many such texts signals a failure of community.

To provide a background to the deviations from conventional formulas, *Violent Adventure* considers two precursors to contemporary masculine adventure stories. Section 1 begins with an illustration of the typical operation of constructive violence in the adventure narratives of a turn-of-the-century popular hero. Writing in the fin de siècle "gilded age" of American imperialism, Richard Harding Davis, renowned as a war correspondent, also authored mass-market fiction that exhibits in specific historical circumstances the development of the male in relation to a community that his violent endeavors reflect, define, and literally expand. In *Soldiers of Fortune,* Davis's most representative novel, the ideology of constructive violence not only naturalizes the expansionist policies of the period, it also redefines the social practices of class, gender, and work. Yet, as Davis himself seemed to realize, the modern masculine experience he witnessed in the mechanized German army of World War I threatened to foreclose the ideological possibilities his texts celebrate in previous military practices. Davis's realization intimates that because narrative violence emerges from the conditions of its own epoch, the expectations it promotes are subject to change. And in the next chapter I turn to a collection of adventure stories in the process of just such alteration.

The second chapter treats what I define as the "Paradox of Virility" evident in a representative group of modern masculine texts, a widely distributed anthology of short stories spanning the late 1920s to the early 1940s. Despite the implied assertion of its subtitle, *Stories for Men: A Virile Anthology* demonstrates that although violence is the inevitable solution to problems of power, it proves inadequate to thematic necessities of masculine identity and male development. Whereas the practice of violence is plotted as a necessary response to the conditions of modernity, it generally destroys rather than develops protagonists, and it also manifests the strain within competing definitions of masculine identity in the modern era. The paradoxical collocation of constructive violence, paternal induction, and stalled development introduced by the modern "virile anthology" finds more radical expression in the generic adaptations of postmodern narrative examined in the rest of the study.

Although several of the contemporary adventure texts—like Tim O'Brien's *The Things They Carried,* Cormac McCarthy's *Blood Meridian,* and Don DeLillo's *Libra*—are postmodern in style, all are postmodern in effect, if one defines the practice of postmodernism broadly as the subversive revision of the effect of narrative. Each text employs some of the conventions of a traditional subgenre of masculine adventure only to explode the expectations that recollection invokes. In each chapter I begin by briefly commenting on the features of the traditional genre that influence the contemporary treatments. I then proceed to contrast these conventions to each author's representation of violence in content and form. Less concerned with the continuities between the past and the present that support ideology, I uncover discontinuities and identify their revisionary consequences.

The second section, "The Failure of Development," examines from the perspective of predominant psychological and social theories the subgenres of the boy's life narrative and the Western adventure. Chapter 3 interprets adaptations of the boy's life convention by Tobias Wolff and Pinckney Benedict as challenges to the tradition that a young man grows up to inherit a fully formed, patriarchally transmitted culture. In initiation stories by each author, dysfunctional fathering, fruitless quests, and impotent displays of adult violence impede masculine maturation, while in chapter 4, the contradictions of violent practice in Western stories by Richard Ford and the exaggeration of violent figuration in a cult novel by Cormac McCarthy threaten even the illusory integrity of the maternal order theorized by Jacques Lacan.

The third section, "The Interrogation of Community," treats the conventions of war narratives, detective fiction, and what I am defining as the contemporary epic. In all of these adventure genres, the evaluation of society as a source of order is a central preoccupation. The texts examined in chapter 5, "Young Goodmen at War," decenter the ideological narrative of war, which traditionally authorizes political values by depicting the authenticity of pain and death through accounts of a soldier's courage. Thom Jones's *The Pugilist at Rest,* in which competing Freudian objectives hinder masculine development, provides the bridge between the personal failure examined in section 2 and the public failure at the center of Tim O'Brien's texts. In contrast to Richard Harding Davis's violent representations of imperial war to construct personal and social authority, and in conjunction with the subversive practice of some American war literature, post-Vietnam writers Tim O'Brien and Thom Jones introduce ethical considerations of public and private integrity that formulaic narratives of military violence conceal. Chapter 6, "Detecting Power," traces Ernest Gaines's revisions of the classic detective genre in *A Gathering of Old Men* and Walter Mosley's alterations of hard-boiled detective formula fiction in *Devil in a Blue Dress,* two African American texts that redefine empowerment through knowledge by discovering social force in the black community rather than defending conventional white authority.

Chapter 7, "White Epics," analyzes novels by Russell Banks and Don DeLillo as antiheroic revisions of the identification of the national hero with social order, the requisite feature defining the epic. In *Continental Drift* and *Libra,* the central characters, believing in the ideology of constructive destruction, are nonetheless unable to violently construct heroic identities. Their violence is read as the failure of "white mythology" defined by both American culture and Jacques Derrida. Traditional genres of masculine adventure, well represented in Davis's fiction, rely on the ideology of constructive violence to negotiate what appears in the characteristic closure of the text as a resolution resulting in the empowered "identity" of an integrated male adult "self," whereas the postmodern adaptations of this study destabilize this illusory integrity by thwarting conventions of violence.[14]

The concluding chapter differentiates between the destruction of real violence and its shadowing constructive effects. Analyzing the semiotic role of violence in narrative and social practice, the study concludes by emphasizing the importance of the textual significance of violence—the dream behind the devastation revealed through the violent action of literature—in violent acts of contemporary life.

PART ONE
VIOLENT CONSTRUCTIONS

THE HERO OF THE HOUR

Richard Harding Davis

The politics of violent adventure are particularly evident in the works of Richard Harding Davis. As a reporter of foreign wars and a writer of best-selling fiction, Davis enjoyed extraordinary celebrity in the 1890s and early 1900s, when Charles Dana Gibson's fashionable drawings of his lifelong friend made Davis the American prototype for masculine appearance and Davis's own novels and stories cast his personal tastes and dreams as the standard for male aspirations. Booth Tarkington observed that Davis's "stalwart good looks" were as familiar to a generation of young men "as those of our own football captain; we knew his face as we knew the face of the president of the United States, but we infinitely preferred Davis's. . . . Of all the great people of every continent [he] was the one we wished to see" (Lubow 1).

In fact, Davis's literary plots, characters, and moral values remained juvenile enough throughout his career to inspire the enthusiasm of a vast team of youthful admirers. He was, in the judgment of Van Wyck Brooks, "one of those magnetic types, often otherwise second-rate, who establish patterns for living for others of their kind" (190). Brooks's comment, however dismissive, does serve to introduce Davis's genuine accomplishment: shaping the spirit of frontier adventure and heroic competition promoted by American boys' books along with the soldier's code and admiration for technological proficiency that was the staple of British boys' books into the perfect ideological vehicle for American imperialism. The "soldier of fortune" in Davis's novel of that title is an amalgam of popular types—the cowboy hero and Horatio Alger, with a dash of Robinson Crusoe's mechanical ability, and a large portion of the chivalry depicted by Sir Walter Scott[1]—so that masculine identity as represented in and by Richard Harding Davis is an ideal concept constructed through public narrative and personal image. If ideology, as Louis Althusser has proposed, represents illusory "relations" to "real conditions of existence" (162), then Davis's work is an excellent place to begin a study of the cultural construction of the American male and the relationship of that imaginary ideal to historical reality and literary violence. And if, as Michel Foucault contends, relations of power are realized through discourse, then we may observe in Davis's central pre-occupation with male aggression the ways in which the trope of constructive violence develops the ideologies of the hero and the state central to his writing. We may also consider the effect of such representation, especially on the concepts of labor, race, gender, and class.

According to Cawelti, the formulas of popular narratives emerge from the need to conform basic psychological requirements to specific social and cultural conditions (*Adventure* 6), and certainly the imperial plots of Richard Harding Davis grow out of an isolable historical congruence between the powerful narcissistic needs of the author-hero and the economic and political context. Sigmund Freud locates an important source of narrative in the imperious desires of "His Majesty the Ego," expressed as the writer's "ambitious wish" to "elevate the subject's personality" ("Creative Writers and Daydreaming" 752, 751). Davis's strong need for such elevation is evident in an early episode of personal heroics that occurred when he was entering Lehigh University. After Davis flunked out of Swarthmore, his academic future was assigned to an uncle who was a Lehigh mathematics professor, and following a year of tutorial preparation, young Richard began his first year at his second college. Because he had already affected the British clothing and mannerisms that were to become his journalistic trademark, Davis—the only freshman sporting a cane—was probably an easy target for the institutionalized hazing of new students. What most of the class accepted as a "good joke," young Davis reports to his father, he took as the occasion for a moral campaign against a practice he considered "silly" and "undignified . . . besides being brutal" (*Letters* 22, 21). As a result, he was set upon by a group of sophomores. "You're not able to haze me, and I can't thrash twelve of you, but I'll fight any man you bring out," Davis challenged. The consequence of his pugilistic stand was that his own classmates nominated him for a coveted position of student leadership, as he explains in a letter home: "So, you see, Dad, I did what was right, and came out well indeed. . . . I am now the hero of the hour, every one in town knows it, and every one congratulates me and, 'Well done, me boy' as Morrow '83 said, seems to be the idea, one gets taken care of in this world if you do the right thing, if it is only a street fight" (*Letters* 25–26). While I applaud Davis's willingness to confront the kind of bullying that my preface condemns, I am more struck by how early and how clearly he defines the self-serving advantage that was to become his central subject.

Soldiers of Fortune

Claiming the moral high road to justify violence that secures personal gain and public recognition, evident in this youthful episode, is the characterological pattern of all of Davis's subsequent "heroes of the hour," both in his fiction and his nonfiction. But finding the fights that could occasion such self-aggrandizement is dependent on limiting the scale of the warfare in which the protagonist participates. Davis's hagiographic biographies of the careers of *Real Soldiers of Fortune* (1906) make it evident that the political skirmishes of the late nineteenth century provided suitable occasions for the achievement of personal agency and its public rewards. Major General Henry Ronald Douglas MacIver, for example, took on leadership roles in India during the Sepoy Mutiny, in Italy with Garibaldi, in Mexico in the service of Maximilian, and with such rulers or would-be rulers as Napoleon III, the Khedive of Egypt, and the King of Servia. As Davis describes MacIver's practice, "Whenever in any part of the world there was fighting, or the rumor of fighting, the procedure of the general invariably was the same. He would order himself to instantly depart for the front." There he would ask to be put in charge of a foreign legion to fight in behalf of the sovereign's or the insurgent's interests as an "entering wedge," and on the basis of his mastery of this "band of undisciplined volunteers," he would maneuver a commission in the official army. "In almost every command in which he served that is the manner in which promotion came" (*Real Soldiers* 4).

The opportunistic mercenary is a "soldier of fortune" by Davis's laudatory definition in the same volume, "the kind of man who in any walk of life makes his own fortune, who when he sees it coming leaps to meet it, and turns it to his advantage" (75). Davis's characterizations always celebrate the man who can match his own ambition to the general tendency of the colonial struggles of the period. Leaping to meet the opportunities of political disorders "Under Eighteen Flags" (*Real Soldiers* 2),[2] MacIver accumulated neither wealth nor security, but his many citations do attest to the achievement of ample recognition of "His Majesty the Ego." In tones of admiration, Davis describes the awards the old soldier displayed to the young reporter:

> On his bed he would spread out wonderful parchments, with strange heathenish inscriptions, with great seals, with faded ribbons. These were signed by Sultans, Secretaries of War, and filibusters. They were military commissions, titles of nobility, brevets for decorations, instructions and commands from superior officers. Translated the phrases ran: "Imposing special confidence in," "we appoint," or "create" or "declare" or "In recognition of services rendered to our person," or "country" or "cause," or "For bravery on the field of battle we bestow the Cross ____" (6–7)

For the Davis hero, the imperative action is to choose up sides, back the winners, and collect the benefits.

The Hero of Mathematics

Davis's insistent repetition of this plot suggests that there is no inevitable or easy fit between the needs of the individual and the prerogatives of the dominant system. It is, however, the burden of formula fiction to forge such an alliance—at least in the imagination. The adventure story works to conceal the divergence of male experience and masculine ideals through its narrative of the success of the hero, but it does so in relation to the conditions of specific cultures: "New periods seem to generate new adventure formulas," states Cawelti (*Adventure* 40). The historical context of imperialism provides the particular occasion for the alignment of private need with public opportunity that is the hallmark of Richard Harding Davis's fiction. By securing the sponsorship of the dominant order, the Davis hero, like the decorated soldiers the author admired, acquires social sanction, while the affiliation of the hero with the social order valorizes the actions of that system. This reciprocal enlargement of man and society is accomplished in Davis's most famous novel, *Soldiers of Fortune* (1897), through violent confrontation.

Hector St. Jean de Crèvecoeur observed in the early eighteenth century that "we never speak of a hero of mathematics, a hero of knowledge of humanity; no this illustrious appellation is reserved for the most successful butchers of the world" (253). But Davis's late-nineteenth-century protagonist supports the accomplishments of the first category with the rhetoric of the second. In *Soldiers of Fortune,* when protagonist Robert Clay ponders his career, he credits the vocational influence of both his lost parents: "How the mind of the mathematician, which he had inherited from [his mother] the Boston schoolmistress, had been swayed by the spirit of the soldier, which he had inherited from his father, and which led him to the mines of South Africa, to little wars in Madagascar, Egypt, and Algiers" (96). For Clay, employed by an American capitalist to open copper mines in the imaginary South American country of Olanco, the profession of engineering weds technical knowledge to military adventure. And out of this union, imperial labor is born as an important theme of the novel.

To establish the renovated worth of the kind of work he admires, Davis's paean to the civil engineer adapts the heroic conquests of the soldier to express the economic accomplishments of the colonizing "heroes of mathematics." Leading the "lives of pioneers and martyrs . . . fighting Nature at every step and carrying Civilization with them. They were doing better work than soldiers, because soldiers destroy things, and these chaps were creating." Without "banner and brass bands," engineers were doing battle with the geography of foreign lands, despite the "attacks" of hunger, exposure, and fever, knowing all the while that "whatever they decide to do out there in the wilderness meant thousands of dollars to the stockholders" (*Soldiers* 12–13).[3]

This joining of engineer and soldier predicts the plot of *Soldiers of Fortune.* The merit of American expansion and the importance of the Davis protagonist are regularly asserted through the stylized fights of popular adventure. For example, Clay asserts his superiority over General Mendoza in the manner of the American cowboy through a demonstration of his prowess with a pistol (60–62). In the same vein, his intervention in the politics of a foreign nation in defense of his employer's capital investment is presented as the rescue of a helpless woman, a staple of melodramatic motivation. And in the end, Davis's "heroes of mathematics" actually turn into soldiers. At the climax of the novel, Robert Clay and his ad hoc army of engineers and native workers fight to establish the priority of American "progress" defined by capitalist investors over American "exploitation" imputed by native Olancon citizens.

This armed struggle is justified in the novel by redefining the Olancons as economic "others." For Clay, the morality of imperial exploitation rests on the racist assertion that the native population has been "too lazy" to develop its own natural resources (29):

> ". . . you cannot blame us. The mines have always been there, before this Government came in, before the Spaniards were here, before there was any Government at all, but there was not the capital to open them up. . . . [I]t needed a certain energy to begin the attack. Your people let the chance go, and, as it turned out, I think they were very wise in doing so. They get ten per cent of the output. That's ten per cent on nothing, for the mines really didn't exist as far as you were concerned before we came, did they? They were so much waste land and they would have remained so." (50)

It is telling that investment is termed "attack" here. For it is violent aggression that underwrites the growth of the hero and the validity of the capitalist enterprise he champions.

Not only does Davis's application of constructive violence reconfigure the race politics of the novel, it shapes gender expectations and class relations as well. The recognition of the importance of the new mode of masculine heroism is so important in *Soldiers of Fortune* that it also generates a new style of heroine. The doubling of the role of the female protagonist in the characters of the Langdon sisters parallels the strategy of the renovation of the male hero. Just as the characteristics of the old model—the soldier—are adapted to a new system, so too is Hope Langdon a modernization of the Victorian pattern that her older sister, Alice, represents. The crucial distinction is the two heroines' differing capacities for the appreciation of the heroic labor of Robert Clay.

Without knowing Alice, Clay has fallen in love with her newspaper image, which he carries in his watchcase, as the symbol of the class and culture to which he aspires. When she is to be a visitor to the mining operation he has built for her father, Clay imagines the occasion as a kind of "honeymoon" (41). But the real Alice fails to conform to his idealization when she is bored by the expedition. Hope, on the other hand, proves a fascinated student of her father's investment. Unlike Alice, who droops in a shed during the excursion, Hope rides about on a horse, taking an active interest in all aspects of mining. After Alice has suggested that Clay should reach for loftier goals, Hope reassures the crestfallen engineer of the value of his accomplishments: "I think it is a grand work, a noble work, full of hardships and sacrifices. . . . You should be very proud," she tells him (211).

Soldiers of Fortune, serialized in *Scribner's Magazine* before its publication, eventually sold 521,000 copies. Men read this popular work as a tale of adventure, but women appreciated it for the love story of a new kind of American heroine. Hope, who rides and fights alongside the men, is the narrative version of the athletic Gibson girl, the counterpart to Davis as the virile Gibson man. While Alice represents the authorizing sanction of the home society, Hope's participatory energy transforms the authorization of domestic culture, the special province of the Victorian woman, for use in the wider world of American imperialistic enterprise at the turn of the century. As in the Victorian novel, the subject of love really has to do with the consolidation of values, but Davis needed to create a different kind of heroine to accommodate the valuation of a different kind of world.

Colonial imperialism relocates the center of interest beyond the borders of the home community, according to Fredric Jameson, and as a result, the postcolonial hero is plagued by a kind of "spatial disjunction" ("Modernism" 51). Davis's compound hero—comprised of Clay and his buddies—experiences this absence of a locatable center as a nostalgia for the home culture succinctly expressed by MacWilliams's devotion to a "home" that only exists in a sentimental melody: "The song of which he was especially fond was one called 'He never cares to wander from his own Fireside,' which was especially appropriate in coming from a man who had visited almost every spot in the three Americas, except his home, in ten years" (*Soldiers* 88).

The women in the novel operate traditionally to connect the hero to the culture of which they are the representatives, but Hope extends this function to foreign locations. Like any prince created by story, Clay wins his princess and marries her at the end, thus securing his attachment to the society he has left behind to pursue his adventure. In this fashion the modification of the heroine accommodates masculine identity to the changing conditions of imperial venture. And it is violence that is the vehicle of these transformations. Although Hope remains an object of male protection throughout and does not participate in the extended final battle, she is present at the initial coup d'état and at the subsequent defense of the palace. The efficacy of her association with violence is to be judged in her brother's reaction to her after the battle has begun—"she seemed to have grown suddenly much older, and he looked to her to tell him what to do" (260)—and her own reflection on her changed condition—"Hope felt selfishly and wickedly happy" (282). In *Soldiers of Fortune,* then, brutal aggression introduces new meanings for both feminine gender and masculine employment.

Yet the class system in *Soldiers of Fortune* is so influential that labor is subject to social evaluations that contradict even Davis's fulsome revision. In *The Reporter Who Would Be King,* a 1992 biography of Davis, Arthur Lubow argues that a central issue of the fiction is the need to create a pattern for male maturation. But for Davis it is the degree of *authority* rather than *development* that is at issue, and his buddy figures define gradations of distance from authorization. In a key exchange, after the working-class engineers have dined with the wealthy Langdons who employ them, MacWilliams, a rough hero with less social status by birth or education than Clay, reminds the smitten hero, "We're not in that class, and you're only making it harder for yourself when they're gone." Mr. Langdon, the American capitalist whose daughters represent culture to the isolated men, is situated as the source of "civilization" as well as financial reward (*Soldiers* 147). But it is the authority of his money, rather than his culture, that is the true basis of his power. Therefore Reginald King, who has culture without financial force, can be dismissed as less heroic than Clay; and young Teddy Langdon, as one who has not yet learned the practice of capital authority, looks to Clay, a true hero of mathematics, as a mentor.

Mr. Langdon, who early in the text acknowledges the protagonist's skills, and, during the crucial battle scenes, backs out of the action to allow the male hero to promote his boss's financial interests, is a particularly benign version of the Freudian father. Davis's well-received short story, "The Bar Sinister," in which a pedigreeless terrier secures his legitimacy by winning the dog show competitions his registered parent used to win, is a fuller treatment of the father-son fantasy behind the Davis text: "I go hurrying around the country winning money and cups . . . and taking blue ribbons away from my father" (55). Nevertheless, the patriarchal rewards Clay evidently desires are not secured in the novel through his work—or anything like the democracy of labor—but through his violence. Clay's defense of Langdon's investment is a series of gestures of confrontational competence through which he allies himself with paternal economic authority idealized as class value. Clay's own authority as the agent (rather than the origin) of American business, lacking the direct support of either culture or money, is based finally on his capacity for efficacious aggression.

Bloodless Victory

Just as violence promotes Clay's private interests, it provides the foundation for all forms of public order and value in *Soldiers of Fortune,* as the following quotations demonstrate:

> Clay took a step forward and shook his finger into the officer's face. "Try to break that concession; try it. It was made by one Government to a body of honest, decent business men, with a Government of their own back of them, and if you interfere with our conceded rights to work those mines, I'll have a man-of-war with white paint on her hull, and she'll blow you and your little republic back up there into the mountains." (59)

> "If I were the President, I'd have Mendoza shot to-morrow morning and declare martial law. Then I'd arrest everybody I didn't like, and levy forced loans on all the merchants, and sail away to Paris and live happy ever after." (205)

> The sailors had no idea as to where they were going, or what they were to do, but the fact they had been given arms filled them with satisfaction, and they huddled together at the bottom of the car smoking and whispering, and radiant with excitement and satisfaction. (227)

Such direct endorsement of aggression through heroic speeches and authorial interjections is nevertheless oddly inconsistent with the formal treatment of violence in Davis's fiction. The best example comes from *Captain Macklin,* the 1902 novel in which Davis revisits the subject of the soldier of fortune. In the style of General MacIver, Royal Macklin, having suffered dishonorable discharge because of a schoolboy prank after three diligent years at West Point, has joined a mercenary army to pursue his military destiny. But his first battle with Honduran rebels concludes with the storming of the gates and the triumphant taking of a field kitchen:

> In the confusion which had ensued in the barracks when Garcia opened the attack the men who ran out to meet him had left the gates of the barracks yard open, and as I stood, uncertain what to do, I saw a soldier pushing them together. He had just closed one when I caught sight of him. I fired with my revolver, and shouted to the men. "We must get inside those gates," I cried. "We can't stay here. Charge those gates!" I pointed and they jumped from every corner of the place, and we raced for the barrack wall, each of us yelling as we ran. A half dozen of us reached there in time to throw ourselves against the gate that was just closing, and the next instant I fell sprawling inside the barrack yard.
>
> We ran straight for the long room which faced the street, and as we came in at one end of it the men behind the cots fired a frightened volley at us and fled out at the other. In less than two minutes the barracks were empty, and we had changed our base from that cock-pit of a fountain to a regular fortress with walls two feet thick, with rifles stacked in every corner, and, what at that moment seemed of greatest importance, with a breakfast for two hundred men bubbling and boiling in great iron pots in the kitchen. I had never felt such elation and relief as I did over that bloodless victory. (167–68)

Of a piece with Davis's doctrine of seizing the small-scale chance and following it up with energetic application of aggression, in this passage the green soldier proves his worth by leading his men to victory. But although shots are fired by Macklin and by the enemy, there is no bloodshed. In fact, part of the pride of the narrator is the lack of gore a reader might expect in a scene of military conquest. The bloodless victory and the capture of a breakfast might, in the hands of another writer, introduce satire or irony; yet the enthusiasm for the "fortress" shelter and its bountiful provision reiterates Davis's characteristic association of the institution of war with the satisfaction of personal needs. Although Davis's narratives of battle occasionally mention the wounds of war, and even the deaths of soldiers, they do not dwell on lurid details, so this scene is representative of the peculiarly nonviolent rhetoric of his pervasive thematics of violence.

In his study of *The American 1890s,* Larzer Ziff contrasted Richard Harding Davis to Ambrose Bierce on the basis of their similar preoccupation with "the violence of life, of which war was only the evident epidermis" (184). Davis is for Ziff the moral innocent to Bierce's jaded cynic, a fact that puts them at opposite ends of what he entitles "The Poles of Violence." Ziff implies that Davis's dedication to "active Christian morality" (174) somehow makes his stories of heroic adventure less violent than Bierce's satires of an amoral universe. But I am arguing that it is not necessarily the type or amount of carnage that should concern the critic. The most important effect of narrative violence derives from its ability to pattern our expectations, and in Davis's writings, constructive violence, however "bloodless," structures the racial hierarchies, the evaluation of work, the construction of gender roles, and the political values endorsed by the hero's affiliations.

It is precisely because thematic violence can so effectively order the codes of private and public identity that gore is so minimal a feature of the Davis text. Popular fiction, according to Cawelti, works to establish reassuring familiarity, to institute ideological certainty by casting our "genuine hopes and needs" in "plausible and attractive" form (Eagleton 15). Graphic representation, however, by invoking experiences of pain and powerlessness can destroy the illusion of the harmonious alternative constructed by the popular text. Davis's fantasy of masculine validation through aggressive agency, which he plots as always consistent with moral sanction, might have been disturbed by the depiction of violence in terms of distress.

The Intervention of History

It is ironic that the only flaw Davis discerns in his strategic ideology emerges from the same juncture of technology and aggression his early celebration of the engineer endorses. For, in the end, Davis's achievements as war correspondent and writer of popular fiction, bound to a scale of battle limited to the capacity of the individual, are rendered obsolete by the invention of mechanized warfare. His characteristic need to discover in armed confrontation the opportunity for personal mastery colors two contrasting descriptions—Davis's news reports of troop movements of both the Boer War in 1900 and World War I a decade and a half later. At midpoint in a celebrated career, by the South African campaign, Davis had already reported on the Cuban insurrection and the Spanish-American War and had established the urbane style that was his trademark, even at the front.

According to Fairfax Downey in *Richard Harding Davis and His Day,* the correspondent arrived in Capetown with three servants, one of whom did little but polish the reporter's boots. Among Davis's amenities was a tent with windows and a ventilation system, a folding bed, tables, chairs, lanterns, and even a portable bathtub. In addition, he was accompanied by his recent bride (178). Davis eventually and hyperbolically supported the Boer cause: "It has been a Holy War, this war of the burgher crusader, and his motives are as fine as any that called 'A Minute Man' from his farm or sent a Knight of the Cross to die for it in Palestine" (Downey 182).[4] But despite his ultimate sympathy for the Boers, his lifelong sympathy for men and manners British dictated his initial loyalty. Before his endorsement of the burgher crusade, Davis had filed this admiring account of the British advance across the Tugelda River Basin:

Hundreds of teams of sixteen oxen each crawled like great black water-snakes across the drifts, the Kaffir drivers naked and black, lashing them with whips as long as lariats, shrieking, beseeching and howling, and flinging themselves upon the oxen's horns to drag them into place. Mules from Spain and Texas, loaded with ammunition, kicked and plunged, more oxen drew more soberly the great naval guns, which lurched as though in a heavy sea, throwing the blue-jackets who hung upon the drag ropes from one high side of the trail to the other. Across the plain, and making toward the trail, wagons loaded with fodder, with rations, with camp equipment, with tents and cooking-stoves, crowded each other as closely as cable cars on Broadway. Scattered among them were fixed lines of tethered horses, rows of dog-tents, camps of Kaffirs, hospital stations with Red Cross waving from the nearest and highest tree. Dripping water-carts with as many spigots as the regiment had companies, howitzer guns guided by as many ropes as a May-pole, crowded past these on the trail, or gave way to the ambulances filled with men half dressed and bound with zinc-blue bandages that made the color detestable forever. Troops of irregular horse galloped through this multitude, with a jangle of spurs and sling-belts; and Tommies, in close order, fought their way among the oxen, or helped pull them to one side as the stretchers passed,

each with its blue bandage stained a dark crimson. (Downey
180–81)

The content and metaphors of this passage develop the hierarchical
relations appropriate to the mobilization of the forces of imperialism.
First appear the representatives of nature, the animals made to bear
the provisions for the controlling army; then the subjugated race, the
"naked and black" Kaffirs bent to the same task; and finally the British
forces, many mounted above the throng, positioned, according to the
diction, with the power to either fight or aid. The natural world has apparently been subdued and modified by the authorizing force of the
great guns being dragged in the train, with the wounded, twice noted,
to demonstrate the effective capacity of such artillery. Of course, the
correspondent himself, from a perspective well above this panorama,
transcends that which he describes. And this literal position of superiority is supported by the specification of Texas horses and cowboy lariats and the odd comparison to Broadway trolleys. In effect, Davis sub-
ordinates the power of the British Empire to his own enlargement—as
the reporter who organizes its mise-en-scène—and shifts its impact to
his readers' appreciation of things characteristically American.

In direct contrast to the description of the movement of German
forces cited below, for Davis this scene of British military force is meta-
phorically related to tamed nature and confined to human scale. The
domesticated animals imply human control. Even the writhing "black
snakes" of the moving columns are more suggestive of the phallic power
enjoyed by the mounted men and their great guns than of the alien force
of nature, which like the related "black" men has been relegated to
service of the Crown. Further, the domestic details of hospital tents,
cookstoves, and water wagons, so reminiscent of Davis's own elaborate
war kit, imply that the engine of war shelters rather than threatens the
men who run it. Within such a context, in the push and pull of objects
and events, particular men can still assert the significance of their own
participation.

Despite his preoccupation with similar elements in the later report,
Davis's famous World War I description of the march of the German
army into Brussels has an opposite effect:

The change came at ten in the morning. It was as though a wand
had waved and from a fete-day on the continent we had been

25

wafted to London on a rainy Sunday. The boulevards fell empty. There was not a house that was not closely shuttered. Along the route the Germans were advancing, it was as though the plague stalked. . . . For two hours I watched them, and then bored with the monotony of it, returned to the hotel. After an hour, from beneath my window, I could still hear them; another hour went by. They were still passing. Boredom gave way to wonder. The thing fascinated you against your will, dragged you back to the sidewalk and held you there open-eyed. No longer was it regiments of men marching, but something uncanny, inhuman, a force of nature like a landslide, a tidal wave, or lava sweeping down a mountain. It was not of this earth, but mysterious, ghostlike. It carried all the mystery and menace of a fog rolling toward you across the sea. The uniform aided this impression. In it each man moved under a cloak of invisibility. Only after the most numerous and severe tests at all distances, with all materials and combinations of colors that give forth no color, could this gray have been discovered. That it was selected to clothe and disguise the German when he fights is typical of the German Staff, in striving for efficiency, to leave nothing to chance, to neglect no detail. . . .

The might of the German army is suggested by a sublime and dangerous nature beyond control. Like the eruptions of volcanoes, or landslides, or tidal waves, modern war is compared to unnatural devastations; its effect is magical; it is "uncanny," beyond human understanding rather than domesticated to human needs. When Davis introduces the necessary satisfaction of those needs by the German system, his rhetoric stresses its inexorable efficiency and mechanistic incongruence to the men it exploits instead of serves:

For three weeks the men had been on the march, and there was not a single straggler, not a strap out of place, not a pennant missing. Along the route, without for a minute halting the machine . . . the cooks prepared soup, coffee, and tea, walking beside their stoves on wheels, tending the fires, distributing the smoking food. Seated in the motor-trucks cobblers mended boots and broken harnesses; farriers on tiny anvils beat out horseshoes. No officer followed a wrong turn, no officer asked his way. He followed the map strapped to his side and on which for his guidance in red ink his

route was marked. At night he read this map by the light of an electric torch buckled to his chest.

To perfect this monstrous engine, with its pontoon bridges, its
wireless, its hospitals, its aeroplanes that in rigid alignment sailed
before it, its field telephones that, as it advanced, strung wires over
which the vanguard talked to the rear, all modern inventions had
been prostituted. To feed it millions of men had been called from
homes, offices, and workshops. . . .

It is, perhaps, the most efficient organization of modern times;
and its purpose only is death. . . . And like Frankenstein's monster,
this monster to which they had given life may turn and rend them.
(Downey 251–56)[5]

It is significant that the mysterious power of this display both draws
the reporter from his superior perch in the hotel room down to the confused awe of the man in the street and obliterates the particularized
identity of the singular soldier. The advent of monstrous modernity
threatens the death of the capacity of the individual ego. Instead of the
pushing and pulling, the private efforts of men signaled by the tum-
bling participial and prepositional phrases following the strong verbs
of the British passage, the subject-verb-object construction dominating
the German passage seems to restrict its own modification. The machine of war contains all private impulse. All personal characteristics
are absorbed by the gray fog of a uniform technology into which identity evaporates. The pagan holiday, the May Day celebration invoked in
the first passage, is renounced in the lost fete of the second. An awful
"change" has come. Like the plague, this new style of warfare is lethal
to individual attainment.

In Davis's writings, the veneration of warfare and the approbation of
the violence that defines it is an effect of the definition of battle as a
desirable contest of competitive egos—a struggle on the scale of the
street fight in which an insecure young man may capture the admiration of his peers. The powerful outrage against modern war in the second passage is not so much a political as an emotional response to the
loss of opportunity for individuation.[6] It is perhaps telling that Davis
himself died at the same time that his version of warfare as individual
enterprise was obliterated by the massive scale of the first World War.[7]
By 1916 "the hero of our dreams" in H. L. Mencken's apt phrase (Mar-

tin 54), was dead of a heart attack at fifty-two, and his fiction, which spoke so powerfully to his own generation, was quickly forgotten.

The narrative of male identification through constructive violence, of course, neither starts nor stops with Richard Harding Davis. However, by specifying an imaginary reciprocity between the hero and the capital imperialism of his own day, Davis's texts demonstrate an important relation of story to reality. Davis, according to Ziff, "made an immense contribution to the fantasy of American superiority" (180). By establishing an influential narrative of masculine identity defined in terms of male confrontation, by identifying conquest with the public good, and by making acts of violence the primary means of recognizing value, texts like Davis's formulate ideological patterns—of aspiration rather than accomplishment—that influence the dreams of who we are, who we wish to be, in a society whose power relations we are unlikely to examine in terms of actual operation. The pleasure of the formulaic work, for Cawelti, is a product of intensifying the familiarity of "a world" that has "become familiar by repetition," an imaginary world we learn to enjoy by avoiding comparison with "our own experience" (*Adventure* 10). Although, like Davis's turn-of-the-century fiction, the modern stories to which we now turn try to solve problems of masculine identity through violence, at the same time they reveal the contradictions within that solution.

2

THE PARADOX OF VIRILITY

Stories for Men

In 1936 Charles Grayson collected thirty-five short stories by "contemporary masters . . . each dealing with a different phase of the actions and activities of men" (ix). Published in 1944 under the title *Stories for Men: A Virile Anthology,* these stories, recovered from their original appearances in magazines from 1925 through 1935, provide a window into both popular and literary constructions of manhood just after World War I and into World War II. Although Richard Harding Davis was finally unable to establish labor as the measure of the man in 1897, the "stories for men" center on work experiences defining masculinity. Like Davis's novel, this collection makes aggression the inevitable solution to problems of power, but unlike *Soldiers of Fortune,* in the "virile anthology" violence proves inadequate to thematic necessities of masculine identity and male development. Although the practice of violence is plotted as a necessary response to the conditions of modernity, it generally destroys rather than develops protagonists. The violence of the stories also introduces the strain within competing definitions of masculine identity in the modern era.

The paradoxical collocation of violence, paternal induction, and the impossibility of progress in these representative modern texts characterizes what I define as the "Paradox of Virility," exemplified in stories of the prototypical masculine occupations of criminality, manual labor, and war. In the previous chapter I argue that Richard Harding Davis's description of the machinelike efficiency of the German army in the First World War marks the demise of the strategies of masculinization represented in his turn-of-the-century fiction of imperial adventure. This chapter examines later fiction for alternative narrative patterns of masculine identification and representational violence adapted to the modern condition of mass force.

Criminal Identity

The manly "actions and activities" of *Stories for Men* include poker playing, gambling, boxing, hoboing, bullfighting, cockfighting, motorcycle racing, ranching, sailoring, soldiering, engineering, digging tunnels, flying planes, playing sports, and committing crimes. But among the diverse occupational fantasies that constitute modern manhood the predominant category is criminality, which is significant as incident or background in twelve of the thirty-five stories. There are evident historical reasons for the burgeoning popularity of criminal adventure in this period. The experiences of war challenged conventional conceptions of morality, Prohibition made violation of the law a common experience, and the widespread deprivations of the Depression may have made criminal activity seem like an expedient solution. Cawelti observes that during the 1920s and '30s the narrative representation of crime shifted from traditional admonition to aesthetic celebration of the criminal act, romanticization of criminal motivation, and scientific explanation of the social genesis of crime (*Adventure* 54–58). The depiction of crime in *Stories for Men* suggests another important psychological and social use for the emerging genre: the expression of masculine predicament.

"Dressing Up," a 1929 short story by W. R. Burnett, whose *Little Caesar* (1927) provided one of the movie archetypes of the era, presents the essence of the problem and the solution of modern male identity. Surprisingly, the plot does not focus on the unlawful acts of the criminal protagonist, who is instead primarily engaged in buying and wearing the expensive clothing that symbolizes his imagined ascension to a higher order. He intends to "dress from the hide out," he explains to an unctuous salesman, and you can toss "my old duds in the sewer" (48). Resplendent in silk lavender underwear and fitted out with the kind of munificent wardrobe that the hero exhibits in *The Great Gatsby,* he summarizes his new status: "Here I am, old Blue, riding the Century, dressed up like John Barrymore" (52). The second significant action in the story is a brief account of his murder, retribution for betrayal of another criminal. This truncated plot encapsulates several key factors of what I will call the paradox of modern virility: (1) the overwhelming and destructive power of forces beyond the individual male self, represented here by the avenging violence of the criminal community; (2) the absolute need for positive masculine identity, represented in the story by the acquisition of haberdashery; and (3) the employment of violence (Blue ruminates about a recent murder he has committed) as a means of self-creation.

The first factor illuminates the key difference between this story and the fiction of Richard Harding Davis. Like Blue, Davis's protagonists seek the transformation of masculine identity and practice violence as a means to that end. But Davis sees a clear and constructive connection between the hero's goals and capabilities and the economic needs of the national and business interests that define the greater forces in which his personal actions are embedded. In fact, his success derives from the mesh of the individual and the authority with which he is affiliated. But in "Dressing Up" the logic of this supportive connection is rescinded by a plot structure permeated by betrayal. Blue betrays his criminal community, they betray him, and the patronizing attitude of the clerks during his sartorial metamorphosis, which signals the impossibility of his transposition into a successful man on their class terms, betrays even his illusions. The physical violence in the story—Blue's previous actions and the revenge that kills him—signals the inexpedience of violent construction. The similarity of violent world and violent man does not symbolize a connection, but instead effects a separation between Blue and the overwhelming forces that surround him. Apparently, personal violence is a stopgap that cannot institute permanent private authority, fix the terms of masculine identity, or protect the limited individual from larger powers.

Violent Predicament

In all of the stories of the collection, individual men are radically disconnected from the greater social and natural powers that control them; yet, whatever the circumstances, they, like Blue, characteristically make use of violence as a means of attempting to transform impossible situations and limited selves. The circumstances of overwhelming control are varied. Besides being invested in the criminal community, power resides in varied mechanisms of social control: *the justice system* in "The Blue Wall" by William Corcoran, a prison escape story; *the econ-*

omy in such stories as "A Cup of Coffee," a Depression study by Louis Paul, which records the desperation of a man who has lost his previous financial security, and "The Bulldogger" by James Stevens, which tells of the heroic work a man endures for the mere chance of financial survival. The *force of collective opinion* is apparent in the importance of the crowd's response in sport stories as widely different as Ernest Hemingway's account of a bullfight in "The Undefeated" and Horace McCoy's depiction of a "duel" by motorcycle in "The Grandstand Complex." And *social expectation* is an important force in James M. Cain's "The Dead Man," in which a young bum unexpectedly confesses to the perfect crime, and F. Scott Fitzgerald's "A Short Trip Home," in which a beautiful virgin is rescued from her willing complicity in a "fate worse than death." The *necessity for social approval* motivates a young man's willingness to kill in Ross Santee's Western initiation story "With Bated Breath," and the *cost of social sanction* is the theme of James Thurber's ironic "The Greatest Man in the World," in which a champion aviator is killed because he is an inappropriate hero. *Overwhelming power* also affects individuals *as a result of war* in William Faulkner's "Turn About" and "Not in the Ritual," by Georges Surdez, a story of the French Foreign Legion. The *overpowering force of nature* is exhibited in "High Air," by Borden Chase, which recounts the story of a drowning during the construction of a tunnel, and in "Fortitude," by Albert Richard Wetjen, which tells of the survival of a first mate and his crew after a shipwreck that confines them to a desert island.

Of course, different kinds of cultural, physical, and economic authority are also manifested in stories that stage contests between individuals. Most notable in this anthology are Steven Vincent Benet's "Elementals," in which a young couple put their lives and love on the line in a wager to gain economic security, and the well-known tale of a manhunt staged for the amusement of a jaded big-game hunter in Richard Connell's "The Most Dangerous Game."

In twenty-five of the *Stories for Men,* violence is a significant element of the situation or the action portrayed, and in addition to defining the power against which the hero struggles, it frequently characterizes an attempt by the protagonist to control his own overwhelming situation. In two exemplary stories, this instrumental violence introduces a final aspect of the paradox of virility as I am defining it: pater-

nal male figures whose relation to youthful protagonists predicts ethical or social progress. "High Air," by Borden Chase, and "Turn About,"[1]
by William Faulkner, both initially published in 1934, exceed the plot
appeal and character interest typical of the collection to establish well-
developed contexts for action and outcomes.

The introductory note to "High Air" identifies its author as a genuine "sandhog," or a worker employed in digging tunnels under rivers.
But in addition to verisimilitude, Chase brings to his story a fully articulated oppositional structure of gendered values. The "pleasant world"
above the river is marked by "sunshine and gentle breezes" (76). This
is the world in which young Steve Redman, under the influence of his
mother, had been going to college to become an engineer. However, as
he confesses to his father, Joe, a veteran sandhog, the lure of the alternative could not be resisted: "something about the tunnel—the high
air." He doesn't know exactly what, but when he was in school it
preoccupied him until he "couldn't stick it any longer" and had to
return (81).

Just as Joe and his estranged wife are literally "apart" in the plot, the
"man-made" (76) environment of the sandhog is symbolically separate
from its feminized alternative: "Only women were missing—the tunnel
is a man's game" (77). The underworld of the tunnel is "different" (76),
even "mad" (81) in its brutal reversal of the "pleasant" conditions of
enervating safety and comfort of the world "above the shimmering
surface of the river" (76). Scorchingly hot, dangerously ventilated, and
physically demanding, it is the supercharged professional arena for a
masculine contest against the overwhelming force of engulfing nature:
"a man's trade: fighting the river; driving a tunnel beneath the threatening flood; pitting his strength and skill against the elements" (84).

The sweaty breathlessness of exertions within the confines of the
tunnel suggests that the occupational penetration of the earth replicates
the male sex role, and the plot introduces the problem of correct technique. Working "the center pocket" (79) together, Steve and Joe enact
conflicting procedures: "His father was of the old school. Caution—
care—precision—they were things for men to worry about. Speed—that
was the order of the day. Drive ahead, make tunnel, keep the shield moving—this was the way of the young sandhog" (83). The contest between
mature prudence and youthful impetuousness, more than a divergence

in sensual style, also symbolizes the shift in definitions of manhood that developed during the change from the late Victorian to the early modern periods.

According to Gail Bederman, in *Manliness and Civilization: A Cultural History of Gender and Race in the United States, 1880–1917,* by the turn of the century the definition of nineteenth-century "manliness" was threatened by the modern conception of "masculinity." The earlier system of identification stressed the moral achievement of manly identity through tight control of the passionate impulses, a vitality that was sublimated into the achievement of middle-class economic status. However, as the financial hegemony of the bourgeoisie eroded because of competition from an increasing immigrant population and a more demanding working class, the source of male selfhood shifted to activities and proclivities previously associated with the satisfaction of unrestrained impulses by the lower classes. Working men's occupational sites and recreational activities became sources of *masculinity,* a term stressing the universal characteristics of maleness rather than the achievement of self-control denoted by *manliness.* In "High Air," the tunnel itself and the Klondike-style saloon in which the sandhogs sweat and gamble between shifts are representative modern locations. By 1930, Bederman observes, the concept of masculinity included the "mix of 'masculine' ideals . . . familiar to twentieth-century Americans—ideals like aggressiveness, physical force, and male sexuality" (19).

"High Air" is interesting precisely because it dramatizes the problem of that mix, both the collision and the connection of two competing systems of masculine value. The construction of the tunnel proceeds by the energetic physical work of pick-and-shovel digging representative of the laboring classes in tandem with the bourgeois ideal manifested through the careful construction of a retaining structure. Thus a precarious balance of pressure between the "high" compressed air piped into the shaft and the dangerous force of the river itself is maintained. It is a balance that also suggests the difficulty of achieving masculine identity. When Steve's youthful impulsiveness causes him to slice through the protective surface of the tunnel wall, causing the deadly decompression of a "blow," father and son face the emergency together. Jumping into the pocket with his son, Joe struggles alongside Steve to staunch the escaping pressure as the "gaping hole" sucks all their ballast and tools into the "growing vacuum" of a lethal "whirlpool of muck" (85–86). Finally, Joe takes desperate suicidal action. Lacking any object to block the flow, the father leaps into the "twisting hole" and the "swirling sand packed tightly about him" to bind the break with his own body (87), an act of altruistic but horrific violence that saves the day.

While the rape imagery of the story may signify mutual male terror of maternal vaginal voracity, the conclusion acknowledges contradictions about masculine development. Steve's precipitous activity has been motivated by the need to prove his manhood to his father, who thinks he is "still a kid," he complains to a coworker (84). Nevertheless, although Joe, as the omniscient narration emphasizes, "had worked at a man's trade" and "wanted to die like a man," in his last words he charges his son to tell his mother "I sent her boy home" (87). This emphatic differentiation between *man* and *boy* introduces the complicated paradox of virility the "stories for men" cannot resolve. The father's sacrificial violence does not solve the problem of the boy's gender identity, for if he goes home to his mother he will never be able to claim adult male status.

Although violence is apparently an attribute of the adult male, it evidently also destroys the "man" it "saves." At best a temporary stay against overwhelming counterforce, the instrumental violence of the alternative professional world of men is the only means to masculine maturity, and yet it cannot produce manhood. Further, such violence does not alter the divergence between the two styles of masculine identification embodied in the related and opposing "Red" men. Yet, although literally destructive of the relationship it supports, the father's violent sacrifice is coded by the story as an act of paternal love. Since to be virile is to possess the qualities of an adult male and to be capable of functioning sexually in the male role, it is ironic that the son's pursuit of virility is foiled by the very violence presented as necessary to its achievement. Both essential and impracticable in the double project of controlling overwhelming external power and claiming manhood, the instrumental violence of "High Air" operates paradoxically, and the affectionate bond between father and son, mentor and novice, further complicates this paradox.

The motif of male induction, in which a boy is guided toward development by a concerned older man, introduces expectations of social or moral progress—a sense that there are lessons to be learned about an existent order represented by the father figure.[2] In "High Air" Joe's sacrificial concern certainly implies the value of paternal example, and he seems to model a possible masculine order that combines Victorian control of passion and modern access to elemental masculine experience; yet, paradoxically, he is actually destroyed, like Blue, by the threatening forces that surround him. In "High Air" the literary formula for masculine identity posits the essential connection of virility and violence by promising the possibility of the former while demonstrating the impossibility of the latter.

In a comparable story, William Faulkner treats the same combination of instrumental violence, paternal induction, and the possibility of progress. In "Turn About" the fatherly figure is Captain Bogard, an American flyer who almost literally stumbles across a drunken young British naval officer asleep on a European thoroughfare in 1918. The masculine professional activity is warfare. Taking Claude Hope under his care, the experienced pilot transports him to the "aerodrome" (166) to sober up. Offended by the callowness of the teenager, who babbles enthusiastically about a competitive game he is engaged in with a shipmate, the captain decides to teach the youth a lesson in manhood before returning him to his own duty: It would be unfortunate for the sailor to have been "in this mess for four years and him not even to see a gun pointed in his direction" (168).

The story, related from the third-person limited omniscient point of view, favors the American perspective. Claude is depicted as an effete and incongruous schoolboy at oblivious play in a serious man's world. His obvious lack of manly status is emphasized by the diction: "erect on his long, slim, boneless legs, he looked like a masquerading girl" (158). Claude is denominated as girl-like three times in the first two pages, as a "child" twice in the first section, and as a "boy" throughout. In contrast to his scornful companions, the other airmen under his command, Captain Bogard is compassionate about Claude's presumed deficiencies: "He's just a kid," he explains (164). Assuming direct exposure to the violence of the First World War will be a salutary antidote to the problem of masculine immaturity, the old hand takes the new kid on a bombing mission to Berlin and back. Discounting his obvious skill with a machine gun, the Americans suppose that when Claude continues to lean outside the cockpit throughout the mission, he is being sick with fright, but he is actually observing a dangerous condition of which the Americans are unaware. Claude is extremely impressed with the apparent courage and craft of the flyers, for only he has noticed that they have flown and landed with a malfunctioning bomb suspended beneath the right wing. "[F]rightened," he had attempted to alert the Americans, but realizing that they "knew" their "business" better than he, Claude marveled in silence at their "skill" (171).

Just as Claude misreads error as mastery, the Americans, relative newcomers to the English war, misread Claude's youthful enthusiasm as inexperience, as Captain Bogard learns when he pays a reciprocal visit to the motor launch manned by Claude and three other young Englishmen. The Americans have misunderstood the actual mission of the ubiquitous small British boats, thinking them "aquatic motorcycles" (159) zipping about like a "male marine auxiliary to the WAACS" (162). Perhaps, they surmise, the flimsy craft deliver "messages" or (162) "ice" to larger vessels.

What the motor launches actually deliver are large torpedoes. Each exposed crew must bring its thirty-foot open boat extremely close to an enemy ship, manually release the single torpedo by cranking a small windlass, and rapidly scuttle out of the path of detonation. "You mean you aim the torpedo with the boat and release it and it starts moving, and you turn the boat out of the way and the torpedo passes through the water that the boat just vacated?" Bogard demands incredulously just before he witnesses the explosive demonstration arranged in consideration for his own tutorial hospitality. And sometimes, as Bogard discerns, after the torpedo is activated, it does not move forward out of the bay as it must, a good example of what young Hope cheerfully describes as the perilous necessity of running "a war with makeshifts" (173).

The last section of the story reveals that Claude's launch was eventually lost during a mission and that Captain Bogard had almost perished during a raid behind enemy lines. Without the protection of scout planes, and after obliterating an artillery depot, with "the remaining two bombs, he had dived the Handley-Page at a chateau where the generals sat at lunch" while wishing "all the generals, the admirals, the presidents and kings—theirs, ours—all of them" could be his targets (183). Bogard's unprecedented and reckless action, for which he receives a commendation, indicates that he has adapted the example of Claude's brave and heedless style of instrumental violence.

The title "Turn About" describes the actual maneuver of the motor launch, acknowledges the captain's revised opinion of Claude's status, and also emblematizes the modern reversal of the traditional conception of "manliness." In contrast to "High Air," in which abandoning the principle of Victorian self-control is disastrous, in "Turn About" the paternal captain learns that unexamined aggression—the boyish heedlessness and simple enthusiasm modeled by Claude—may be the only appropriate response to the unrestrained destructiveness of modern war. Virility rather than morality is the order of the day. Faulkner's story structures this transposition of male values through the episodic reversals of motifs of the two mirrored missions. For example, although the airmen assume Claude will get sick, it is Bogard who becomes ill. Similarly, the Americans assume Claude's intoxication is an effect of indulgent irresponsibility. But when he administers a bracing drink to the shaken captain, one begins to suspect that the British schoolboy crews of the torpedo launches consume alcohol in order to adapt to their dangerous missions, another example of the "makeshift" that makes the war possible. As Bogard's impetuous final mission suggests, manhood, conditioned by modern destructiveness, is a matter of action rather than care.

In contrast to "High Air," "Turn About" supports modern masculinity over Victorian caution, but like "High Air" it also endorses instrumental violence. The only difference is that in Faulkner's story, the terms of masculine identity are misunderstood by the father figure rather than the son figure, and it is the son, not the father, who is literally destroyed by the overwhelming violence of the external world. As in "High Air," the motifs of male family affection, initiation, and learning introduce the possibility of social bonds and even moral progress. Yet violent action fails to secure either.

Modern Masculinities

As historian George L. Mosse observes, the ideological relation of violence, power, and masculinity is central to modern social experience. Although varying within communities and periods, the concept of masculinity was consolidated in conjunction with the development of the modern world as a constellation of physical and moral traits that consistently embody the established values of a given social group (8). In his study of the evolution of stereotypical masculinity, Mosse insists that a manly ideal of force and restraint "played a determining role in fashioning ideas of nationhood, respectability, and war" (15) and "was present and influenced almost every aspect of modern history" (4). And Angus McLaren claims that "confrontational homicide was located not beyond, but within the boundaries of normal masculinity" during the period between 1870 and 1930 (131). It is not surprising, therefore, that in the adventure narratives of that period violent action conjoins agency, authority, and emergent masculine identity. What is surprising is that *Stories for Men* documents the peculiar maladaptation of narrative violence. Reflecting changing social definitions of masculine identity in the period between World War I and II, the "Virile Anthology" employs plots of instrumental violence that repeatedly dispute the possibility that such violence can be genuinely constructive.

And, if W. M. Frohack's 1957 study of *The Novel of Violence in America* is credible, the paradox of virility continues to be central to male literature of the postwar period. According to Frohack, the experience of the Second World War created a general atmosphere that made stories of passive heroes "intolerable to read" (3). A new mood was better served by the "the novel of destiny," in which the "hero finds himself in a predicament such that the only possible exit is through inflicting physical harm on some other human being. In the infliction of harm he also finds the way to his own destruction. But still he accepts the way of violence because life, as he sees life, is like that: man's fate. Thus the pattern of this kind of novel is in a sense tragic. The hero may be defeated, but he is not frustrated" (6–7). The paradox of implied value and actual destruction of the modern anthology is redeployed as existential tragedy in novels from the 1930s through the 1950s.

Despite a variety of historical circumstances and changes in interpretations of the essentials of manhood, fiction by American men, like that of Richard Harding Davis and *Stories for Men,* has continually connected violence to masculinity. To identify the paradox of such representation in *Stories for Men* reveals the peculiar fact that the very literature that celebrates the definition of masculinity through violent action may also suggest its failure. This paradox of virility recoverable in *Stories for Men* is fully exploited by the recent texts of male adventure to which we now turn. In revisions of initiation, Western, war, detective, and epic stories, the contemporary writers of this study represent violence as graphic disturbance in order to question its codes. Their fiction challenges the ideology of masculinity and violence—the human relations it fails and the social forms it fosters.

PART TWO

FAILURE OF DEVELOPMENT

3

BOYS' LIVES

Tobias Wolff's This Boy's Life *and*
Pinckney Benedict's Town Smokes

In addition to action and conflict, literary adventure also includes the expectation that the naive protagonist will develop. For as Anthony Burgess observed, the "principle that human beings change" is probably a basic requirement of genuine fiction (viii). And although not all heroes of adventure are literally little boys or even young men, their conventional trajectories, the often violent struggles to become—to learn, to progress, to achieve—are rooted in the developmental patterns laid down in the initiation genre to which we now turn. Stories by Tobias Wolff and Pinckney Benedict wed the coming-of-age theme to the masculine movement and male violence typical of adventure fiction.

During the nineteenth century, cut loose from the farm labor required of youth in previous decades, male children in emerging towns and cities enjoyed what E. Anthony Rotundo calls "boy culture" (32), a special freedom from the supervision of mothers and fathers. Through often violent play among themselves, boys developed a code of conduct and values that included physical prowess, stoic endurance, competitiveness, bravery, admiration of dominance, emotional self-control, respect for mastery, loyalty to the group, and independence from adults (41–46). From the more formal attachments of the next stage, which Rotundo calls "youth culture," the young man learned to shape the rough-and-tumble of boyhood games into the authoritative control available through social organization; he "learned to maintain and extend institutions, to make and administer policy, and persuade and campaign in pursuit of . . . goals," skills that adapted him well to the roles of middle-class Victorian manhood (71).

But the passage of boy to man has been less easy of late. An important focus of the groundbreaking men's studies movement of the 1980s,[1] in the aftermath of the killings at Columbine High School, the difficulty of present-day male maturation has again engaged popular consciousness. Citing several recent studies of masculine development—*Raising Cain* by Dan Kindlon and Michael Thompson, James Garbarino's *Lost Boys,* Michael Gurian's *Wonder of Boys,* William S. Pollack's *Real Boys,* and Susan Faludi's *Stiffed*—journalist Stephen S. Hall has charged that America is enduring a new "national crisis of boyhood" (33). Similarly, texts by Pinckney Benedict and Tobias Wolff mark a turning point in the representation of male initiation. The problem of boys' development that finds expression in the violence of their books is the failure of a society in which mature manhood is imaginable.

When Leslie Fiedler observed several decades ago that American writing was a vast book for boys, he was scolding a culture that lauded heroes and authors who never grew up. Contemporary fiction by men is still concerned with the youthful male protagonist suspended in a space short of adulthood, and this psychological, social, and moral suspension continues to be a reason for criticism, not celebration. There are, of course, many models for the anticipation of a young man's coming of age. The traditional *Bildungsroman,* a vast popular literature for boys dating from the 1880s to the present, classical fairy tales, and Freudian psychoanalysis all provide organizing conventions for narratives that do assume the transition from adolescence to adulthood. But although Wolff and Benedict write in the shadow of this transitive tradition,[2] their narratives of father-son violence raise doubts about the possibility of male maturation and the meaning of American manhood. Their protagonists' violent initiations indict a culture that fails to foster masculine development.

A popular literary handbook defines the *Bildungsroman,* the apprenticeship novel that "recounts the youth and young adulthood of a sensitive young protagonist who is attempting to learn the nature of the world, discover its meaning and pattern, and acquire a philosophy of life and 'the art of living'" through a string of related German synonyms: the *Entwicklungsroman,* or novel of development; the *Erziehungsroman,* or novel of education; and the *Kunstlerroman,* or the novel that deals with the formation of the artist or the writer (Holman and Harmon). All of these definitions assume two common features: (1) that young people can and will progress, and (2) that there is a stable social organization ready to guide, receive, and in the case of the artist, be modified by the young. Nineteenth-century American literature addressed to youth confidently emphasized the first feature, but twentieth-century American literature about maturation disputes the likelihood of the second.

Social historian Michael Kimmel notes the nineteenth-century pre-occupation with professional success that transformed the "crude aggressions and the raw boisterousness of boyhood" into the "refined self-assertion" and competitive "self-discipline of manhood" (*Manhood* 55)[3] and popularized two formulas: rags-to-riches biographies of Eastern robber barons and Western outlaws and fiction about boy heroes like Horatio Alger, stories that outlined masculine advancement from obscure privation to renowned prosperity. Yet, while the popular genres of the Gilded Age aggressively promoted male progress, a contradictory literary pattern—the erosion of confidence in the possibility of social maturity necessary to this process—also began to emerge during this period, according to Patricia Meyer Spacks. Although the eighteenth-century narratives of adolescence she analyzes in *The Adolescent Idea* proceed "toward a happy ending in which the protagonist symbolically enters his or her anticipated adulthood," by the nineteenth century, in spite of plots in which "heroes and heroines still grow up and marry," some stories raise "questions about the possible value of conventional maturity," and twentieth-century narratives, she argues, typically move "towards indeterminate conclusions" (295).

Nevertheless, Erik Erikson, the most influential twentieth-century philosopher of adolescence considered by Spacks, finds within this indeterminacy the seeds of a heroic, albeit unruly, struggle for self-completion and social salvation by young men: "[I]n a time of rapid change" whether "the disintegration of the old or the advancement of the new, the meaning of confirmation changes," he explained. The "leaderless youth" of his own period "who have temporarily lost, or never had, meaningful confirmation in the approved ways of their fathers" were seeking "an identity based on defiant testing of what is most marginal in the adult world" through "sporadic riots and other excesses" (Spacks 263).[4] Despite the absence of a "patrimony" of "cultural identity" based on the "experience of social health and cultural solidarity," and in the face of attendant "infantile fears . . . mobilized" in this context, Erikson affirmed the often violent reactions of modern youth as a source of societal reintegration (*Childhood* 412).

Influenced by Erikson's developmental theory, social psychologist

Robert Jay Lifton characterized the evolution from childhood to maturity as the cultural experimentation of a youthful "Protean man" who pursues "a relatively new life style, characterized by interminable exploration and flux, by a self process capable of relatively easy shifts in belief and identification" (*Psychohistory* 39). Further, Lifton identified this Protean man as a source of innovative spiritual renovation for adult society: "While [his] play draws heavily upon childhood experience, it is nonetheless the play of adults, playfulness seasoned by insight. The innovator has always lived in exquisite equilibrium between a refusal to be an adult as ordinarily defined and a burdensome assumption of responsibility for a large segment of adult action and imagination" (*Life of the Self* 149). In the psychosocial accounts of both Erikson and Lifton, delinquent American youth of the 1950s, '60s, and '70s respond violently to an unstable adult society that only they had the capacity to reform. Inspired by existential themes of independent self-construction beyond social norms, such theories encouraged representations of the young male as excluded from but better than his own community. The "angry young man" in British literature and the juvenile "rebel" in American film are two period examples.

At present, however, changing conceptions of fathers' roles, alterations of popular images of men, and more and more widely shared distrust of authority prompt a general sense that masculine maturation is problematic. At one end of the political range of concerns about men's issues is Timothy Beneke, a social critic who writes from the background of antirape activism. Beneke argues that for American boys, forced to try to identify with the distorted models provided by popular culture because fathers are largely unavailable, a confident sense of masculinity is forever beyond their grasp. In its place they substitute various unproductive behaviors to "prove" their manhood, among them the sometimes violent expression of "sexism, fascism, homophobia, and racism" (41).[5] Urging a renewal of paternal responsibility, social conservative David Blankenhorn contends that "a culture of fatherlessness" (2) is the direct cause of youth violence, domestic violence against women, child abuse, and many other problems (chapter 1).

This general concern about boys' development, father absence, and violence is also expressed by contemporary authors Wolff and Benedict. In place of the easy passage of the Victorian period or even the corrective connection between young males and their communities popular from the 1950s through the '70s, the autobiographies and fiction of Tobias Wolff and the fiction of Pinckney Benedict, published in the 1980s and '90s, present an alternative picture of American coming-of-age. *This Boy's Life* (1985), in particular, and *In the Garden of North American Martyrs* (1981), *The Barracks Thief* (1984), and *Back in the World* (1985) by Wolff, and Benedict's *Town Smokes* (1987), especially, and *The Wrecking Yard* (1992) by Benedict, portray the adult community as available but useless. The violence that characterizes it is adopted by both men and boys, not as the sign of productive social alteration, but as an empty signal of unrealizable power, which also finds expression in the representation of ineffectual fathers.

Although the adolescent males in these contemporary works become neither Erikson's existential rebel nor Lifton's protean hero, they do confront the systemic disorder assumed by both psychologists. In works depicting adolescent attempts to grow up, Wolff and Benedict each reveal the attenuation of "un-developing" masculine identity in terms of ineffective violence through revisions of three devices of the coming-of-age tradition: the motif of developmental quest, the characterization of social mentors and father figures, and the theme of social integration.

Journeys to Failure

It is no accident that the adventure of the would-be prince in a fairy tale frequently takes the form of a journey—the premodern narrative figure for movement from childhood to maturity. An inadequate child, often the least promising of multiple brothers, he sets out to correct an injury or repair a lack. On his way he passes tests that give proof of his own masculine adequacy, and he meets helpers who provide gifts from the powerful world beyond his control. At the conclusion of the adventure, secure in his own powers and in conformity with the communal norms modeled through his encounters with those who come to his aid, he returns to the paternal kingdom to rule in the father's stead.[6]

As Eric J. Leed observes in *The Mind of the Traveler,* "travel is the most common source of metaphors used to explicate transformations and transitions of all sorts" (3).[7] And Lifton locates the source of this basic developmental imagery in the body's biological imperative to attain growth and competency: "Thrashing arms and legs are the infant's first self-induced expressions of vitality. Body movement never ceases to retain some of that significance" (*Broken Connection* 58). The male protagonists' journeys in Wolff's autobiographical *This Boy's Life* and the title story of Pinckney Benedict's *Town Smokes* indicate the centrality of the developmental project that these authors represent and critique. Moreover, because representations of the protagonists' movements endorse their capabilities, the exhaustion of possibility these works also present cannot be charged against their youthful seekers.

This Boy's Life is a tale en route. The book begins during Toby's cross-country journey with his mother, Rosemary, to a new life in the far West. He and Rosemary have just crossed the Continental Divide when they spot a tractor trailer, air horn blaring, speeding out of control, about to plunge "hundreds of feet" over a rocky cliff "through empty space to the river below," where it finally lands to lie "on its back among the boulders" (3). The violence of this runaway disaster is juxtaposed with a shared "dream of transformation." Rosemary confidently expects to acquire boundless wealth prospecting for uranium in Utah, and young Toby dreams of maturity and power, "Western dreams, dreams of freedom and dominion and taciturn self-sufficiency" (8). He begins to fashion his new identity by changing his name to Jack, "after Jack London," in the belief that taking the name would convey the "strength and competence" Toby attributes to his hero (8). The disaster that awaits Toby's protracted bid for personal autonomy is not his own fault, for he clearly brings intelligence and commitment to his quest for development. This boy's failure is due to the inadequacy of the helping figures, especially his stepfather, who cannot represent for Toby the beneficial standards of an adult world.

Similarly, the fifteen-year-old unnamed protagonist of Benedict's title story, "Town Smokes," sets out on a developmental adventure after the death of his father provides him with the impetus and the rudimentary tools for such an undertaking. The father's death, after a tree he is cutting down crushes him, implies the limited technological skills of Benedict's adult males. The father figures of his stories are generally helpless in the face of violent natural and economic restrictions. The boy takes from his childhood some unhelpful oral lore and the material heritage of a gun, a knife, and six dollars on a trip to town during a storm that has produced deadly flash floods in the hollows below his mountain home. In these conditions, his father's personal calamity comes to include the possibility of universal destruction. On his trip down to the valley town, the boy encounters two youths who steal the old Colt, the clasp knife, the money, and even his worn sneakers. "We could do you," the thief with a rifle explains, "kill you just as easy as killen that shoat" and no one would know or care (162).

Although the boy has no money, the storekeeper whom he later meets, mistakenly believing the boy's father has perished in the floods, gives him what he has come to town to secure: a pack of Camel cigarettes. These "town smokes" are at once a mark of the boy's maturity and the symbol of its limits. When his uncle rejects his request for tobacco by asking derisively if he also visits prostitutes, the boy replies seriously, "These are things a man does" (152). In fact, limited physical gratification is about the best a man can hope for in the world of Benedict's fiction. At the end of the story, the boy is dragging in smoke from his fourth cigarette in the face of the continuing storm. His only plan for the future is a visit to the emblem of a destructive masculine power he admires but can never possess—the dam that gave way and caused so much damage. The boy has already learned that masculine force is limited to petty violence, which, at best, imitates natural disaster, the symbol for any power exceeding personal capacity. This is the message in his father's last story to the boy just before the logging accident.

One winter, when he was fifteen, the father and the uncle had ventured down to the valley to a farm that raised shorthorn cattle. Although the river was frozen solid along its banks, a narrow channel still flowed swift and dangerous, and the youths managed to drive some of the cows out onto the ice to their deaths. The boy's daddy recalled shaking with laughter when the first one fell through. As the steer disappeared, dark water shot up, and the sound, like a gunshot, stampeded the rest onto the thinner ice. They, too, sank without even the "time to look surprised" (158). This bovine execution exhibits the constrictions of the father's power. Although he can be the occasional agent of havoc, he has none of the moral, social, educational, or financial skills he would need to deploy power responsibly or to secure power from those possessing access to more (like the owners of the cattle). The father's pleasure in gratuitous suffering replicates the antic cruelty of the two youths who rob the boy.[8]

In contrast to the limitations confirmed by Benedict's masculine quests, Vladimir Propp defined the fairy tale hero's encounters with helping figures he meets during his travels as a means of empowerment. In the generic plot outlined in *The Morphology of the Folk Tale,* the questing boy must withstand a test, or greet the agent kindly, or provide some necessary service to the donor, who then grants a boon of strength or wisdom (43–48). But in "Town Smokes," instead of helpful agents the boy meets two young thugs, an event that underscores an absence of education in moral masculine authority through its traditional sources—the royal father and the fairy tale helpers. Since the encounters of the male hero in the traditional tale provide access to cultural supports that the hero has not yet developed, it is clear that Wolff's Toby and Benedict's boys, despite their readiness for the maturational adventure, are bound to a failure determined in advance by limited developmental opportunities. This failure is especially apparent in the lessons the boys learn from their principal mentors, their real and substitute fathers.

Defective Fathers

Unlike the so-called juvenile delinquent of the 1950s, who is defined by his angry rebellion against an adult world, young Toby of Tobias Wolff's *This Boy's Life,* the memoir of his life from the age of ten in 1955 until his enlistment in the army in 1964, demonstrates an unrelenting effort to find acceptance by that world. As presented in his brother's biography of his father, *The Duke of Deception* by Geoffrey Wolff, and Tobias Wolff's own account, the facts are as follows: Never really in love with "Duke" Wolff, the boys' mother, Rosemary, married him to escape her own abusive father. After an inauspicious start, the marriage grew worse. Duke put most of his considerable intelligence into conning his way into and maintaining an impressive career for which he had absolutely no formal training. He also indulged in numerous casual affairs, and at home he was frequently critical of his insecure wife. After eight years, the couple separated. Leaving Geoffrey behind with his father, Rosemary took Toby with her to Florida, then to Utah, and on to the state of Washington, the setting of many of his stories. *This Boy's Life,* beginning with the trip west, is fashioned throughout as a boy's quest for confident masculine identity.

He proceeds by trying to learn from and accommodate to the various brutal father figures Rosemary's unfortunate relationships provide. The first is Roy, who gives Toby a gun but little else before Rosemary runs away from another abusive man. Rosemary's emotional pattern is to move from one destructive partner to the next. And the next, in this case, is Dwight, a Dickensian villain in the modern vernacular, an ugly stepfather who takes on Rosemary's son as a special project. As Dwight informs him, the "trouble" with Toby was the illusion he could "get through life" without working. Still more "trouble" with the boy is that he thought himself "smarter than anybody else" and he didn't think that anybody else was smart enough to know what he "was thinking," or that he didn't think at all (95).

Dwight's response to all this filial "trouble" was what we would today certainly term child abuse. The form it took was not so much actual violence but steady derision and exploitation. Dwight's strategy is to break Toby's spirit with hard work and humiliation. For example, he insists Toby shuck horse chestnuts—shuck them without gloves, because gloves were for sissies—until the boy's hands are chronically bloody from the stabbing spines and permanently orange from the juice of the nuts, much to the amusement of his new classmates. Toby husked the horse chestnuts nightly for most of the first winter stepson and stepfather spent together while Rosemary wound up her affairs in another town; much later, when the shelled nuts had turned moldy, Dwight threw them all away. Dwight also put Toby to work peddling papers, only to eventually steal his earnings; and he even pilfered Toby's prized rifle to trade for what must have been the world's most unlovable dog—not a companion for the boy, but a hunting accessory for the man.

Dwight's project to reform him alters Toby's expectations about himself and his world: "I had come to feel that all of this was fated, that I was bound to accept as my home a place I didn't feel at home in, and take as my father a man who was offended by my existence and would never stop questioning my right to it" (105). Because Toby misses his estranged father and brother, he really wants to please Dwight, who represents, however inadequately, his only chance for paternal relationship. Of course, a bully like Dwight cannot be pleased, so in the end Toby takes what he sees as his only recourse: to steal school stationery and forge the glowing reports of his mediocre record at Concrete High that win him a scholarship to a prestigious prep school. But after being dismissed from Hill School for outrageous behavior and inadequate preparation, he joins the army.

The Barracks Thief, Wolff's novella, seems to take up where the later autobiographical account leaves off: It introduces a protagonist whose defining youthful experiences of paternal abandonment relate him to young Toby Wolff, and it follows him into basic training preliminary to service in Vietnam. The initial scene establishes a context of paternal relation and negative expectation. The father has formed "the habit" of stopping in his young sons' room at night to consider them thoughtfully. In their presence, he feels a "peace" that generates the "fear . . . that by loving his children so much he was somehow endangering them." He also "tried to imagine what form the evil might take" (1).

After the father leaves the mother and is alienated from his family, Keith Bishop, the younger son, turns into a teenager confused by drugs, and later an adult confused by life. But the main story concerns the older boy, Philip. In psychological terms, it is the story of a young man trying to find masculine identity and paternal connection through public symbols because of the private experience of his father's absence. Specifically, the plot centers on related episodes in Philip's training in the army. After basic instruction as a paratrooper, Philip is transferred to Fort Bragg, where as an untried soldier he understands he will feel left out of the small community of veterans until he has been tested by military experience.

One July Fourth he is thrown together with two other newcomers to guard a seedy munitions storage site. When a nearby forest fire brings some locals to warn them to leave the area because they may be in danger, the young men decide not to abandon their post. Out of this shared act of masculine bravado a companionship of sorts develops. Although they don't discuss what has happened, the three young men don't want the experience to end. Staying together afterward, as Philip reports, they could believe for an "hour or two," anyway, "that we were proven men" (27).

Besides Philip, there is Hubbard, whose best friends are killed in a drunken accident on that same Fourth of July; he deserts before being shipped overseas. The third, Lewis, is an isolated loser who is ultimately revealed as the barracks thief of the title. Although he doesn't understand it, Lewis steals to try to establish some form of human connection. Ostensibly, he wants the money to try for a sexual relationship with a prostitute, but his impotence in this instance stands for his general inability to effect contact. In fact, by being a thief Lewis is inadvertently declaring his exclusion. As a respected sergeant puts the matter: "an infantry company was like a family, a family without any women in it, but a family . . . What sort of a man would turn his back on his own kind?" (32).

Critics have noted the experimental shifts from first-person to third-person point of view in the story, a technique Wolff explained during an interview with Bonnie Lyons and Bill Oliver in terms of the similarity of Philip and Lewis and, given this equivalence, what must be Philip's growth of consciousness as a result of Lewis's experience: "Philip feels accused . . . he feels . . . complicity with Lewis . . . As for the thief himself, I wanted to give the sense of a person who has no attachment to the past, who has been tremendously hurt by it but is cut off from his consciousness of it" (14).

Lewis's failure to achieve the familial male fellowship afforded by the military makes him an alter ego of Philip, who is also less than consciously seeking in the army the things he has been deprived of by his father's absence. Lewis, then, is the personification of the "fear" and the "evil" resulting from paternal abandonment presaged by the initial scene. When the soldiers take revenge on Lewis by "blanketing" him, Philip sees in his frightened look a more universal expression, of humiliation as well as fear, which he later observes in his own lost brother and in Vietnamese captives intimidated by American interrogation.

The circuit between a boy's experience of paternal inadequacy and the violence at the heart of Wolff's oeuvre is also a central feature of Pinckney Benedict's short fiction. The young protagonist's attachment to his father in "The Sutton Pie Safe" is never in doubt, but the developmental value of that relation is a question the story, the first in *Town Smokes,* introduces as an important theme of the collection. When the father, Jack Albright, a West Virginia farmer, and his ten-year-old son, Cates, are hunting copperheads, the boy spots a large blacksnake, and, eager for the crack of the cut-down .410, he coaxes his father to shoot, but the father sensibly defends the snake's existence on the grounds of its natural function. At this point, however, an impressive automobile pulls up, from which emerges the attractive wife of a prominent local judge. Her sexual and economic power are obvious in this scene, and the father responds with a discomfort apparent even to the boy. His father seems "embarrassed" that he is not wearing a shirt. At first Albright raises the rifle in a self-conscious "salute," but uncertain that this is appropriate, he waves awkwardly with his other hand (2).

The woman's evident economic and class superiority is further asserted in her offer to buy the antique pie safe that the family hasn't taken much notice of. Finally, the mother accepts the generous offer. But before that occurs the father counters with a maladroit display of his own power. He slaughters the blacksnake, providing the excuse that he is going to make a snakeskin belt for the boy as his own father had made for him. Shirtless, chest stained with the blood of the reptile, and aggressively exhibiting the dead snake, he enters the house, where the two women are talking. The attractive woman keeps her composure and secures her purchase. When Cates is unenthusiastic about the proposed gift, his father destroys the skin, an act Albright describes as an object lesson to the boy. The skinning of the snake and the extraction of a mouse it had swallowed signify to Cates his father's capacity for violence, but the ruin of the skin educates him about its ineffectuality (12).[9]

A similar lesson is learned by Adonijah, the teenager in "All the Dead" who witnesses his stepfather's death as a result of impractical rage at a more powerful man. The boy finds the ironically named stepfather, Makepeace, dying at the base of a statue of a handsome young Confederate soldier. As Makepeace had intimated in recounting its creation, in addition to its overt representation of regional pride, the statue covertly signifies masculine failure. The model had a crippled hand that was not displayed.

Like "The Sutton Pie Safe," this story is focused on the education of a boy by a father figure, a purpose made explicit in Adonijah's memory of an incident that occurred when, like Cates, he was ten years old. After Adonijah had gotten the worse in a fight with another boy, Makepeace had found him sniveling on the ground and had threatened to beat him with a belt. Urging the boy to "keep on his feet" whatever the likely outcome, Makepeace explained that most of the time "it's all a man has that he can take what he takes standen up" (45). Like "The Sutton Pie Safe," this story teaches the same lesson as the *Virile Anthology:* Unproductive violence is a necessary response to threatened male power despite inevitable defeat.

The works of both Wolff and Benedict invoke the tradition of the questing boy's reliance on the paternal community as a source of valuable education for development, but the tutelary examples encountered by Toby and the protagonists of the stories in *Town Smokes* replace the expected achievement of male power with endemic ineptitude. There is considerable geographic and social distance between Wolff's Concrete City, Washington, and Benedict's West Virginia mountains, between Toby's aspirations to an upscale education and Benedict's protagonists' incentives for hardscrabble survival; yet both authors' adaptations of the boy's life genre share a common theme—violence as symptomatic of the absence of a social system that can produce capable adult men.

Social Disintegration

The predominant modern transcription of masculine integration into a functional community is, of course, Freud's Oedipus myth. As the young boy emerges from childhood, his initial resentment of his father's intervention in his sustaining relationship with his mother is replaced by identification with his father's worldly power. A controversial feature of this transition is the impetus supplied by violence—the son's dawning perception of his father's authority surmised through the threat of castration. The positive conclusion of this process is the son's acquisition of social order introjected as the Freudian superego, a result unavailable in "Booze," by Benedict, and "Hunters in the Snow," by Wolff. Both stories treat hunts by adolescent boys or childish men as attempts to achieve contemporary manhood—a state in which actual violence, rather than possible castration, signals local disintegration instead of communal order.

In Benedict's story, Eli watches his friend Kenny use an auger blade to kill a full-grown "quarter ton" (28) rogue boar. Nurtured as symbolic masculine compensation for an impoverished farmer, the renegade hog, Booze, like William Faulkner's fabled bear "Old Ben," acquires the cachet of legend. After Booze's escape from Tobe Fogus's pigpen, the powerful animal evolves from cannibal nuisance to fabulous creature: "The farm seemed changed somehow, a place where a monster had lived" (29). But his numinous impact derives from more than his occasional consumption of house pets and farm animals; by eluding the capacity of a prized Remington rifle, Booze has also apparently ingested the manhood of Eli's father: "My dad had emptied the Remmy and lost his best dog—had given up. He didn't seem to want to try anymore" (27).

In *The Bear* Faulkner turns the ritual contest of male potency into an examination of societal values. As a result of the lessons of the hunt, the young hero renounces the Southern heritage of economic exploitation and slavery. In Benedict's contemporary rendition, however, masculine violence is not transmuted into guiding principle. During the death struggle with the thrashing boar, Kenny Yates's leg is horribly crushed, a mutilation symbolizing impotence. And his porcine adversary winds up as garbage, dragged ingloriously through the fields and dumped into "the pit where we put the dead cattle" (32).

The unheroic denouement of this story indicates the general futility of the asocial struggle for phallic power enacted through violence by all of Benedict's fathers and sons. The boy's adoption of the father's temporary force does serve to separate him from women—Old Tobe particularly prizes the story of Booze devouring Mrs. Fogus—but it cannot provide permanent access to the societal authority Freud's theory of male identity promises. As Lacanian interpretation of the Freudian parable emphasizes, the function of the father is to provide access to the social system in which he participates. His power, symbolically expressed as imagined castration, derives from existing law. As a result of "successful Oedipalization," Kaja Silverman explains, the young man finds himself "'at home' in those discourses and institutions which define the current symbolic order in the West, and will derive validation and support from them at a psychic if not an economic and social level" (141). But the cycle of violence at the heart of Benedict's collection cannot initiate the boy into paternal authority precisely because the father lacks any relation to the public "discourses and institutions" from which power derives.

It is discursive "validation and support" that Wolff's hunters also fail to achieve. The protagonists in "Hunters in the Snow" are inhabitants of the degenerate environment Toby tries to escape in *This Boy's Life.* They are poor and they are sad, and at least one of them, Tub, is literally hungry for something they cannot define but desperately desire. That something is a definition of themselves that they can begin to respect. Like Dwight in *This Boy's Life,* they try to establish that identity through the assertion of constructive masculine violence ritualized in hunting. And, like Dwight, they fail. Their guns afford them self-destruction instead of self-transcendence.

"Hunters in the Snow" concerns a trio of young men who differ psychologically. Tub's obesity and related awkwardness cast him as the victim, the butt of the group. Kenny, the most verbally and physically aggressive, plays sadist to Tub's masochism. Frank, apparently trapped in an early marriage, signals his unfocused desire to change his life in a love affair with a sixteen-year-old baby-sitter, and counters even this vague impulse toward transformation with an incongruous sixties rhetoric of cosmic acceptance: "You can't hurry nature. If we were meant to get that deer, we'll get it. If we're not, we won't" (*Garden* 13).

During the hunt these conflicting attitudes result in Tub's shooting Kenny. At the conclusion of the story, Tub and Frank are drawing together, while Kenny probably freezes or bleeds to death on an incompetent drive to the hospital. Although Wolff admits to reservations about the use of irony—"Irony is . . . a way of not talking about the unspeakable. It is used to deflect or even deny what is difficult, painful, dangerous," he warned in the introduction to *Matters of Life and Death* (x)—"Hunters in the Snow" is a superb example of structural irony used to suggest rather than deny the complexity of experience. During the course of the story, each character reverses his former psychological role by acting out its buried contradiction. But the conclusion of the tale suggests that such reversals only result in opposing simplicities rather than genuine resolutions.

Kenny sets the sequence of psychological reversal in motion when he kills a farmer's dog on the way in from their unproductive hunt. The others never doubt that this is a mean-spirited act meant to counter disappointment with aggression. When Kenny announces, "I hate that dog," and shoots and then, still armed, counters Tub's outrage with the words, "I hate you," Tub responds to his perception of deadly threat by shooting Kenny in the stomach (*Garden* 16). It turns out, however, that the farmer onto whose property they pursued the deer had asked Kenny to put the old and ailing dog out of its misery. Thus, in the course of a violent moment of misunderstanding, Tub and Kenny have exchanged the positions of aggressor and victim.

During the ensuing attempt at muddled rescue, Frank moves from a pattern of passive to active acceptance. When he and Tub stop to warm themselves over cups of coffee, leaving the injured man in the back of the pickup truck in the stormy cold, the heightened tension of the afternoon leads them to an exchange of confidences. Tub confesses that his weight is not a result of glandular dysfunction, as he has adamantly maintained, but the effect of repeated episodes of compulsive consumption, and Frank shares details of his affection for the baby-sitter. This newfound camaraderie makes both participants "feel good," but the suggestion at the end of the story—that Kenny will probably not survive—questions a simplified philosophy of community that ignores the sometimes deadly consequences of complicated social responsibility.

In *The Reproduction of Mothering,* Nancy Chodorow theorizes that inadequately fathered contemporary sons both "appropriate those specific components of masculinity that will be used against them" and develop a sense of what it is to be masculine "through identification with cultural images of masculinity and men chosen as masculine models" (176). Adopting the first option, the son's use of the paternal violence of Benedict's stories replaces the evolution of social ideals in the Freudian developmental narrative. In Wolff's oeuvre, son figures illustrate Chodorow's second option, the pursuit of identity through public images of masculinity. But hunting expeditions and military service prove to be inadequate substitutes for induction into a societal system of values. "There's a logical progression of the kind of life that boys are encouraged to lead and dream of in this country," Wolff remarked. "There's a lot of violence in [*This Boy's Life*]—a lot of male violence." "The boyhood obsession with weapons has a terminus somewhere . . . it ends in war" (Lyons and Oliver 3–4).

The inadequacy of military experience as a source of communitarian values is the theme of "Soldier's Joy" from Wolff's *Back in the World.* This story, which returns to the preoccupations of *The Barracks Thief,* published the previous year, concerns another trio of soldiers in a similar setting, a stateside army camp, on a similar mission—guard duty. The difference is that the emotional center of the story is not the consciousness of the outsider, but the protective fellowship of the already initiated.

Hooper, a twenty-one-year veteran recently busted to private first class, is in charge of two younger soldiers who have been furnished with live ammo with which to guard the camp communications center. Although the ammunition is supposed to be "strictly for show" (102), it represents a temptation neither of the men assigned to the duty can resist. Porchoff, nicknamed Porkchop by the men in his unit, threatens to use it to kill himself because he hasn't found the camaraderie in the service his father's army stories led him to anticipate. His father had recounted "the great experiences his buddies used to have, camping out and so on" during his years in the National Guard. But, as the son complains, "Nothing like that ever happens to me" (115).

In trying to talk him out of the suicide, Hooper reveals that the Vietnam War constitutes his most fulfilling experience: "[I]t was a kind of home. It was where he went to be back with his friends again, and his old self." Being "back in the world" meant "confusion" only the intensity of the battlefield could clarify (116). And that is exactly what occurs. Trac, the other guard, a young man only recently returned from the field, re-creates the destructive clarity of his war experience. In what is apparently a flashback, he shoots and kills Porchoff to resolve the situation. And the two combat veterans draw together at the conclusion of the story to cover up the incident. The death of the isolated soldier implies that the desirable masculine connection created by the violent rituals of male bonding is purchased at too great a cost. The artificial unity of military organization is produced at the expense of genuine social responsibility.

Similarly, the title story in Benedict's second collection, *The Wrecking Yard,* treats the failure of masculine systems of social order. The settings—the wrecking yard itself, a down-home hell for automobiles, and the scenes of fatal collisions—set a colloquial tone of brutalized dissociation. The filial roles of the earlier stories are replicated in this story by the auto salvagers, who play weak sons to the more powerful police in charge of the accidents. Unlike the sons of *Town Smokes,* however, the wrecking crew, whose perspective the story favors, are not initiates but jaded professionals accustomed to inevitable violence: "Guys died in almost every car we got" (21). It is their business to extract paltry gain from devastating loss, so when they encounter a tractor trailer that has careened over a steep embankment, disgorging bellowing injured steers, they chat amiably with the seasoned drivers, minds busy with personal projects—Perry's plan to purchase a car in which a boy has just committed suicide, Weasel's theft of car parts from the junkers that they crush. Only an outside observer registers the horror of the situation: a passerby "jabbering" and "weeping" over the CB radio "about legs and bones and hair. . . . Legs and heads and oh, the animals. . . . Death on such a scale'" (22, 23, 28).

The highway patrolmen are merely wreckers with guns, badges, and attitude, as we observe when a trooper "pokes a thick finger into Perry's chest. 'Listen, wrecker man,'" he threatens. "This is our time. You get back until we're done" (26). Concluding with another episode that rescinds the expectation of its rescue plot, the story leaves a strong impression of mundane and unabatable ruin. The crew from the wrecking yard watches as a search party goes after a young girl who has disappeared over a dangerous bluff with a "daredevil" (36) in a fast car. As a young trooper bears her body up the hill, "long pale legs . . . slung over his shoulder," the dead girl's "head hangs down and her dark hair trails the ground. It is full of dirt and twigs and bits of tree" (37). "What a waste, eh, Lou?" the older trooper says salaciously (38). The men in this story—wreckers, truckers, ambulance drivers, and cops—can salvage, but they cannot save. Varying in degrees of professional authority, they share the general helplessness of all of Benedict's males, fathers as well as sons. Not so much brutal as brutalized, they inhabit a violent milieu that represents a society failing in its powers of human protection.

Throughout the centuries, the literary trajectory from youth to manhood systemized in various "boy's life" narratives has charted the relationships of men to the social systems they inhabit. The European folktale, for example, probably mediated rigid class exclusions inherited from the medieval world; the strategies for economic recognition of worthy waifs in late-nineteenth-century fiction was certainly a response to the rise of industrial capitalism; Freud's myth of complicated patriarchal induction into civil order could have emerged from his own experience of anti-Semitic social exclusion. And in the wake of World War II and the ensuing race for nuclear arms, modern psychologists Erikson and Lifton must have been comforted by theorizing the homeopathic violence of the juvenile delinquent. Tobias Wolff and Pinckney Benedict, however, adapt the initiation genre to problematize assumptions about contemporary manhood.

"Maturity and masculinity come together in a confident definition which masks a host of contradictions," asserts John Fiske. Men define themselves in terms of "individualism or power and control," but "society frequently denies males the means to develop these qualities." Because the "material experience" of men does not measure up "to their ideologically produced expectations," the concept of "masculinity . . . is socially and psychologically insecure" (201, 202). And, given this situation, responsible community appears to be unachievable, as the works of Wolff and Benedict reveal. Although their contemporary boys evidently possess potential, inductions into paternal violence signal a degenerate social system unable to integrate the young man into a society that can satisfy his need for private identity and public order. This definitive separation of masculine violence from civil order is further revealed in the works of contemporary Western fiction by Richard Ford and Cormac McCarthy, which also exhibit the failure of young men to thrive as a reflection of communal defects.

4

LACANIAN WESTERNS

Richard Ford's Rock Springs *and*
Cormac McCarthy's Blood Meridian

The Western adventure occurs at a special point in the emergence of "American civilization." Previous "savagery and lawlessness" are threatened by an "advancing wave of law and order" but retain enough power "to pose a momentarily significant challenge" according to Cawelti (*Six-Gun Mystique* 65). As a result, the hero of Western adventure is poised between the competing alternatives of East and West, cast as justice and outlawry. In the traditional Western narrative, he manages to negotiate a changing ideological landscape by dramatizing appealing aspects of both binary terms. He is frequently called upon to defend nascent justice by using the violence practiced by the outlaw, and much of his popular appeal is a result of his ability to support the morality associated with the bonds of community while practicing the transgressive individuality attributed to the bandit. Enjoying this intermediate status between the responsibility of the socialized adult and the freedom of the unruly child, the Western hero is, regardless of age, a successful version of the archetypal boy.

Contemporary texts by Richard Ford and Cormac McCarthy, however, expose the psychological and social irresolution of the Western genre. In stories set in the Western middle ground between boyhood and manhood, *Rock Springs* (1987) and *Blood Meridian* (1985) use male violence as theme and form to portray the failure of masculine development. Whereas Tobias Wolff and Pinckney Benedict expose the predicament of the young man unable to complete his development because of the absence of appropriate Freudian fathers, the boys in *Rock Springs* and *Blood Meridian* are stalled in an emotional position that does not anticipate patriarchal empowerment. Overwhelmed by the inefficacy or the sheer destructiveness of the violence they encounter, the protagonists of these narratives may be understood through their attachments to the integrative projection of childhood that Jacques Lacan has theorized as the Imaginary mother. In Ford's text this preoccupation suggests the developmental impossibility facing individual young men, while McCarthy employs this theme to challenge the assumptions of national myth.[1]

"A Border Between Two Nothings"

The title of Richard Ford's collection of short stories, *Rock Springs,* the name of a working-class town in Montana, places them within the narrative space of the Western, the genre "defined by its setting" (Cawelti, *Six-Gun Mystique* 62). In a modern age bereft of either genuine wilderness or promising institutions, Ford's stories recast the Western drama as a point in male development, the perceptual predicament of a young man transversing the border-state between idealizations of a mother's affectionate integrity and a father's constitutive violence. Whatever the protagonist's actual age and circumstance, the focus is the boy's negotiation of the issues this position generates. Like the traditional Western hero, Ford's composite boy wants to put his violent heritage in the service of an emergent civilization, but he never manages to balance the gendered divergences experienced in his relations with mothers and fathers, and the memories that comprise the stories replay moments when his dilemma is most evident.

The title of the story "Great Falls," the name of another Montana town, invokes the symbolic Western location to establish the dramatis personae of *Rock Springs:* the father, the mother, and the boy. In this story, the father, Jack Russell, is an airplane mechanic, a fisherman, a duck hunter, and a part-time professional poacher. As his son, Jackie, recalls, he could "catch a hundred fish" during a "weekend" (30) and a "hundred ducks" in twenty seconds (31)—illegal game that he sold to a local caterer. Jack's proficiency in slaughter connects him to the Western ideology of male violence as a means to masculine empowerment, but the flaw in this position is intuited by his son: The "true thing" he knows about his father is that he didn't "know limits" (30). Ford's major thematic preoccupation is the boy's alignment to the problem of "limits" defined through the gendered roles of his parents. In the action of the story, the father has brought Jackie back early from hunting to confront the man with whom the mother leaves the marriage. The father comes near to killing Woody, the other man, but finally does not do it. As he explains to his rival, he would like to find a way to "hurt" him but cannot think of any and feels "helpless" as a result (42).

The key to the deficiency of Ford's men is precisely this kind of choice. They understand that violence is expected, so choosing the pacifistic option, accepting moral "limits," typically unmans them. The father in "Great Falls" wants to know if Woody considers him a "fool" (42). Abdicating the masculine resolution of a Western "showdown" is also a motif in one other story. In "Sweethearts," Arlene's first husband, a man who does transgress lawful limits, stops by to have Arlene and her second husband drive him to jail to begin a three-year sentence for issuing bad checks. Russell, the second husband, cares for his young daughter and makes breakfast for Bobby, the first husband. For the first three pages of the story, gender role reversal and ambiguous pronouns make it unclear as to whether the narrator, who is eventually revealed as the second husband, is a man or a woman. His maternal care does, however, place Russell's consideration as the antithesis of Bobby's lawlessness. At the end of the story, outside the jail, Bobby reveals that he has a gun and wants to kill Arlene, but a shoot-out with the watching deputy is avoided by Russell's deflection of the Western script Bobby is trying to set into motion. Similarly, in "Fireworks," the protagonist thwarts possible conflict with a competitor by simply refusing to meet with his wife's former husband. The men in *Rock Springs* try, usually without much success, to maintain effective limits, because when the expected male confrontation does occur, the outcome is disastrous. In "Optimists" the boy sees his father slay a provocateur with one deadly punch, an act that also destroys the family relationship. Male violence in these stories is presented as unresolvable masculine dilemma: To avoid violent action is to be "helpless" and unmanly, but to act violently, as in the modern anthology *Stories for Men,* is destructive rather than constructive.

Unlike the father, whom the son understands, in the *Rock Springs* stories the mother remains an attractive mystery throughout. In "Great Falls," for example, the mother is effectively lost to the boy. On the day after she has left with Woody, she arranges a meeting to say good-bye to her son. He perceives her abandonment as a turning point that precipitates the uncertainty that characterizes him. Although everything may be "fixed by staying," to leave and not return "hazards life" because things can get out of control (48).

"*Great* Falls," certainly an ironic superlative title in view of the father's helplessness and the boy's loss, concludes with a series of questions about the pivotal event that the narrator has never been able to answer. He wonders why his father would not allow his mother to come home, why the other man would risk his life for a woman he apparently doubted, and why his mother had left. Although Jackie had never been able to answer the questions, their enigma might be approached, he suggests, through the philosophic observation that concludes the story. There is some "low-life . . . coldness" in everyone, a "helplessness" that prevents an understanding of life and that makes people behave like wary "animals—watchful, unforgiving, without patience or desire." And it is this destructive condition that turns "existence" into a "border between two nothings" (49).

One of these "nothings" between which the psyche of the boy is suspended is evidently a missing mother. In eight of the ten stories of the collection, an absent mother is a fact of life, and that primary absence is a condition the protagonists can never fully come to terms with. Besides the loss of the mother reported directly in "Great Falls" and "Optimists," in "Rock Springs" and "Sweethearts" the father abdicates traditional aspects of masculinity to care for a mother-abandoned child; in "Children" both the boy narrator and his foil have been left behind by mothers; in "Going to the Dogs" the focal character, whose wife has left him, seeks comforting from two women willing to mother him; in "Winterkill," in which feminine solicitude is a more important value than sexuality, the story begins with reference to the narrator's impossible project of going home to his mother; and in "Communist" the forty-one-year-old narrator recalls a troubling event when he was sixteen years old, which he continues to ponder, noting that he and his mother didn't ever really talk again (235). In the gendered terms of the Western genre, the woman associated with the civilizing community that establishes limits in the wild West is simply unavailable.

In six of the ten stories a man is out of work, and in "Optimists" the pressure of the imminent loss of the father's railroad job is the underlying motivation for the murderous response the story recounts. Thus, the other defining negation affecting the boy is the father's characteristic economic marginalization, which makes his legendary capacity to assert power through violence actually ineffectual. This failure is treated most extensively in "Communist," the final story in the collection. In the story, the deceased father is replaced by Glen Baxter, a Vietnam vet, who takes the boy and his mother, Aileen, to hunt Canada geese. In retrospect, the boy, Les, recognizes his first hunt as a kind of initiation, a realization that "something important" would "happen" to him on a "day" he would never forget (219). What happens is that at the very point when Les is being inducted into the male ideology of violent power, the polarized meaning of the masculine and feminine ethical positions are enacted for him by Glen and his mother. Aileen, who is disturbed by the hunt because of her objection to killing the "special birds" who "mate for life" (219), is eventually captivated by the beauty Glen's expedition has made it possible for her to witness, the migrating geese turning silver in the setting sun (228).

Using his dead father's shotgun, Les proves a proficient hunter, a capability that reminds him of other lessons his father had provided through teaching him to box: to "tighten" his fists, to "strike" from his shoulder, never to hit while "backing up," to snap his fist inward, to hold his "chin low" and, to move toward a fighter as he falls in order to be in position to punch him "again." Most significant is the instruction not to shut his eyes when he is hitting an opponent in the face and "causing damage," because he will need this sight to "encourage" himself (226).

This education in pugilistic violence is supposed to instill masculine competence and clear-sighted evaluation, but that ideal is annulled by the problem of violence as unnecessary destruction and the absence of "limits" introduced by the boy's description of the father in "Great Falls." This problem finds expression in "Communist" when the mother discovers that Glen has shot a last goose by "mistake" and that it is still swimming wounded. She demands that Glen finish it off because that's the "rule" (230). Glen insists that it "doesn't matter" (231). In "The Short Happy Life of Francis Macomber," Ernest Hemingway memorably coded the uncompleted kill as a failure of masculine potency. To this allusion Ford adds the onus of the failure of human sympathy. The already troubled relationship of the couple ends with the mother's accusation that because her lover does not possess a "heart," there is really "nothing to love" in him (231).

"Communist" opposes two Western ideals: male violence, which signifies an absence of rules, and female love, which portends the possibility of moral integrity. The absence of masculine limits produces the killer's irresponsibility. But the incident also implies the failure of violence to produce genuine empowerment. When Glen comments on the beauty of the geese and observes to Les that he doesn't know why he shoots them, Les admits a definitive confusion: "Maybe there's nothing else to do with them" (228). That is, for the adult male, violence, the only option, is evidently ineffective. Already implicated in the violence of such "helpless" fathers, Ford's boys also recognize the necessary morality assigned to absent mothers and long for an apparently impossible combination that includes the failed possibilities of each.

This contradictory attempt to retain the imagined integrity of the unavailable mother while practicing the destructive violence of the ineffectual father is staged as oedipal drama in the story "Children," a title that suggests the truncation of masculine development as a consequence of this dilemma. The young male narrator and his boxing pal, Claude, participate in a scheme to keep secret from his mother the fact that Claude's father has a lover. Sherman, a railroad man of Indian blood who has twice been to prison for brawling and theft, has been sleeping with the young girl at a local motel (71). When the boys take her fishing, the story intimates that she may come to harm. After a confrontation with his father, Claude says that he thinks they ought to "kill her . . . just to piss him off" (75). The father-son rivalry culminates in Claude's sexual connection with the girl who belongs to his father, but the possible violence is deflected. At the crucial instant when Claude thrusts his knife at the girl, ostensibly for her to use to remove the hook from a fish, he is excited by two possibilities: that they could kill her and "Who'd know about it?" or that she could kill him when he gives her the knife (92). She averts the crisis by calmly tossing Claude's knife into the creek, taking off her clothing, and having intercourse with him.

Claude exemplifies the boy who is beginning to follow the trajectory of Freud's Oedipus complex, in which fear of castration by the powerful father causes the boy to renounce his attachment to his mother and bury his resentment toward his father in order to gain masculine authority on his father's terms. If his son gives him any "trouble," Sherman warns, "I'll break you up" (77). The father's implicit transference of access to the girl (Claude asks if his father is "giving" her to them as a "reward" [74]) signals the benefits available at the conclusion of this negotiation. But the story also introduces an alternative pattern. The narrator's relationship with the girl, Lucy, takes on the features of what E. Ann Kaplan calls "romantic" love rather than genital conquest. While Claude fishes to demonstrate his masculine prowess, the narrator and the girl sit together on a blanket to share confidences and a gentle kiss.

Lucy's significance may be understood through Jacques Lacan's interpretation of Freud's account of masculine development. During the Lacanian oedipal process, the boy loses not the mother but the illusions of coherent selfhood that the mother has fostered by her nurturance of the child through the stage of identity Lacan calls "Imaginary," although the desire for this fundamental integrity always remains an important component of the Lacanian unconscious. According to both Freud and Lacan, the provocation for the oedipal passage is the realization of the mother's "castration," which for Lacan is the understanding of her lack of power within the social system. However, the exclusive relationship of mother and child temporarily excludes the power arrangements the father's presence introduces. Therefore a competent female can lend meaning to the boy's projections of wholeness, and thus it is the "phallic" mother of his infancy rather than the castrated mother figure of his later experience who is the object of the pre-oedipal boy's yearnings.[2] Lucy, who simply takes the symbolic phallus Claude is trying to claim and invalidates its authority, enacts the role of empowering mother to the narrator, who is fixated on the elusive fantasy of maternal integration.

In her analysis of the narrative patterns of rock videos, Kaplan defines the type that corresponds to the preoccupations of Ford's boy narrators as "romantic" because of the "yearning quality" depicted toward a love relationship: "The address is to the absent or loved one, or the video plays out the pain of separation" (59). For Kaplan the appeal of such productions derives from their representation of the Lacanian "transition between the pre-Oedipal and the phallic phases" (94), the intermediate position of the narrator of "Children," who does not share his friend's phallic pretensions.

After the boys have helped the girl get a bus out of town, Claude brags that he is "strong" and "invincible" and that he doesn't have anything on his "conscience." Although Claude's egotistic claims suggest he has not fully experienced the dissolution of self concomitant to the Lacanian Symbolic order, and his denial of "conscience" indicates he has not realized the superego that concludes oedipalization as Freud has defined it, he evidently aspires to the only masculinity structured by the generic Western—that of the violent male. The narrator, in contrast, is understandably leery of a paternal disorganization founded on ineffectual violence. Not preoccupied with Claude's illusions of genital conquest, he describes himself regretfully as lacking the consolidation of even a specious phallic identification: "What was *I* good for? What was terrible about me?" (98).

The boy's longing for the absent phallic mother who is capable of supplying the limits the father's violence lacks is the characteristic concern of Richard Ford's *Rock Springs* stories. The title, with its connotations of both masculine obdurateness and feminine nurturance, may symbolize this desire. Perhaps the appeal of the oedipal allegory found in the formula Western is that the hero—the cowboy as the American boy—can participate in the abrogation of limits, the unlimited power promised through male identification, at the same time he supports the communal creation of civilization by the feminized order of the settlement. But unlike Freud's oedipal young man, the cowboy hero never has to choose. Like The Lone Ranger, after saving the town, never fully identified, he can get back on his beautiful phallic horse and ride away. Themes of preoedipal longing signal the need for order in the face of adult male violence in *Rock Springs,* but unlike traditional Westerns, Richard Ford's stories recount the costs of such holding actions in his protagonists' lives. "I think of the characters . . . as being rather unfixed, I think of them as changeable, provisional, unpredictable, decidedly unwhole," the author confided in an interview (Lyons 43). The narrator of "Children" further articulates this sense of displacement and incompletion: "Outside," he explains, is an "empty" "place" that didn't even seem to "exist," somewhere you could occupy for a "long time and never find a thing you admired or loved or hoped to keep. And we were unnoticeable in it" (98).

This quotation conveys a preoccupation with "lack" within the project of masculine development that Ford dramatizes and Lacan theorizes. Lacan's formulations relate to the complex negations of Ford's family drama, because unlike the social scientists and psychologists cited in the previous chapter, Lacan, like Ford, problematizes the concept of developmental progression. Nevertheless, there are important differences. The Lacanian subject is shaped by two contiguous occurrences. The first, the Imaginary, is the intuition of an integrated personality, an illusory selfhood that is shattered by the second, the Symbolic, the realization of subjectivity within the social order imposed by linguistic practice. Although Lacan narrates these conditions as the chronological events of infantile experience he borrows from Freudian theory, they are conceived as inseparable and permanent conditions of the human psyche. That is, for Lacan, culture and community are not, as in the Western, projected in terms of feminized spaces to be loved and left. Inevitably conveyed through the structure of language, they are the foundations of paternal power, which in Western adventure is supposed to be generated by male violence.

Unlike both the Freudian father and the Lacanian paternal signifier, which derive their authority from culture and language, the Western male archetype is defined outside the feminized community through aggressive intervention. Although communal order with its accompanying loss of phenomenal identity is the inevitable fate of the Lacanian subject, the generic Western structures the failure of socialization. The revelation of that failure is the project of both *Rock Springs* and *Blood Meridian*. And if the development of the young male is apparently doubtful within the negations of Ford's family relationships, it is patently impossible within the phantasmal parental void of Cormac McCarthy's novel. *Blood Meridian*, by situating its unnamed protagonist in a field of phenomenal saturation, exposes asocial violence as a ruinous basis for both personal manhood and communal integrity.

The Masculine Imaginary

What happens when a boy is reared by wolves? In the myth of the founding of Rome, a society of war and law emerges, but McCarthy's *Blood Meridian; or The Evening Redness in the West*, a tale of war without law, tells the story of a boy who joins an itinerant band of wolfish scalp hunters,[3] whose predatory violence does not presage any kind of civil order. McCarthy's Western novel, based on historical accounts of the Texas-Mexico border in the decades before the Civil War, does not present the Western hero in the generic role of mediator between the "civilization" of the town and the "wilderness" of the outlaw (Cawelti, *Adventure* 193).[4] The central issue of the traditional Western, according to Cawelti, is the victory of the "good violence" exercised by the hero in defense of emergent culture over the "bad violence" perpetrated by "villains" with "evil aims" (*Six-Gun Mystique* 15). *Blood Meridian,* however, is a different kind of Western that repudiates constructive violence.[5] In it there are only villains, and theme and form establish the awful preponderance of "bad violence" as the dominant feature of a historical period of American conquest through a narrative of boyhood staged as the Lacanian Imaginary without the concurrent Symbolic order.[6]

McCarthy's revised Western excises any source of moral authority through the enigmatic figure of "the judge" derived both from the stock Western character and from actual history. Judge Roy Bean is the figurative grandfather of this motif. Having appointed himself justice of the peace in 1882, he held court in his Texas saloon. A convicted rustler as well as the only "law west of the Pecos," he represents not only the difficult struggle to establish law in a new territory but the contradictions of the concept of "law" in a lawless region.

In "'What kind of indians was them?': Some Historical Sources in Cormac McCarthy's *Blood Meridian,*" John Emil Sepich reports that McCarthy's character was based on the real Judge Holden described in Samuel Chamberlain's account of Captain John Joel Glanton's gang of bounty hunters: "[A] cooler blooded villain never went unhung; he stood six feet six in his moccasins" and had a face "destitute of all hair." A speaker of many languages and an expert in botany, geology, and mineralogy, "the best educated man in Northern Mexico," the actual judge was, paradoxically, also the "ravisher" of children (Sepich 125–26).

In addition to exaggerating the judge's bizarre appearance, McCarthy mystifies his combined violence and erudition. What Chamberlain calls an "appetite" for "blood" (Sepich 125) McCarthy styles as seeming capricious viciousness, which is really fundamental philosophy. In one instance the fictional judge purchases a pair of pups from a ragged child only to immediately toss them into the river. Perhaps the most appalling example occurs after white raiders harvested the "long locks" of the Indians to leave the dead "rawskulled" in "bloody cauls" (157). When the judge discovers one living Apache child among the mutilated tribe, he carries the half-burned boy before him on his saddle. Two days later the judge is observed dandling the child on his knee one minute and apparently murdering and scalping it in the next. The destruction of such obvious victims as the dogs and the Apache boy indicate that the judge's brutality is motivated by more than the economic reward offered for Indian scalps.[7] To McCarthy's judge, murder is the instrument of effective "ritual," which always involves the "letting of blood," and death is merely "agency" (329).[8]

The judge's blood rituals are attempts to define himself through the assertion of power over everyone and everything else, which also find expression in his scientific observations of the Western landscape. The judge's constant measuring, sketching, recording, and collecting supports the ambition of total control. Because "nature" can subdue mankind, he seeks its subjugation. Only when every "entity is routed out" and exposed to him, he explains, will he become "suzerain of the earth" (198). Toward that end he must control all "pockets of autonomous life" (199). What abides beyond his "knowledge," he declares, "exists without" his "consent" (198). To attain the ultimate power to which he aspires, "nothing" must be allowed to exist on earth except through his "dispensation" (199).

Imperial Eyes, Mary Louise Pratt's landmark analysis of the travel discourses of European colonialism, equates eighteenth-century studies of natural history with the imperialist exploitation of the very territories the naturalists were exploring, often in the same expeditions as soldiers and merchants. Despite so-called scientific objectivity, natural history functioned, she charges, as an adjunct to imperialism by itemizing the exploitable wealth of a "new" region and by introducing the pattern of acquisitive knowledge that made projects of global economic power imaginable. The portrayal of the judge crossing the "virgin" West with his journals and specimens harks back to a type that precedes the cowboy. He is the fictive American heir of the European naturalists whose totalizing descriptions helped convert world into empire,[9] but whereas their domination served the economic expansion of the home society, his serves the egoistic aggrandizement of the homeless self.[10]

The judge's narcissistic naturalism has parallels with Linnaen science and Lacanian psychology. Linnaeus, Pratt argues, arranged all plant life through its conformity to or difference from twenty-six "basic configurations" (25). "One by one the planet's life forms were to be drawn out of the tangled threads of their life surroundings and rewoven into European-based patterns of global unity and order. The (lettered, male, European) eye that held the system could familiarize ('naturalize') new sights/sites immediately upon contact, by incorporating them into the language of the system" (Pratt 31).

Linnaeus's system, as Pratt interprets it, is similar to Lacan's theory of the Symbolic order, into which the young man is incorporated through the oedipal process. Both Linnaen taxonomy and the Lacanian Symbolic are hierarchical regimes patterned after the similarities and differences structuring language, and both operate to reproduce the authority of the dominant male class. But the judge, separate from any order except that of his own devising, a burlesque of Linnaen science, is also a parody of Lacan's Law of the Father. According to James M. Mellard, "The Symbolic order, like language, permits human relations to occur on a plane of mediation that is exemplified in the figure of the judge, the ruler, the arbitrator, the authority" (17). Yet McCarthy's judge is the antithesis of the social mediator. Because the judge has no source save his own will, his titular name is in fact a mockery of the masculine system of Symbolic authority. His self-serving violence, which assigns all externals to the illusion of his own absolute power, and his strange reciprocal relation with the boy demonstrate a more complex position in the male maturational drama.

Just as the judge's private desires differ from the public effect of natural science, the protagonist's experience with the judge differs significantly from the achievement of Symbolic order. Lacan dramatizes a boy's entry into culture as the emergence from the private world of the mother into the public realm of the father. But in McCarthy's novel the maternal solicitude that lends support to Imaginary integration does not exist, and a paternal order independent of egotistical will is inconceivable.[11] *Blood Meridian* begins with the significant fact that the boy's mother died at his birth in 1833, and his father, a besotted former schoolmaster, does not even teach him to read or write. In these details McCarthy thwarts the two rudimentary necessities for Lacanian maturation—a supportive mother figure and a father figure who embodies the communal system inscribed in language.

In McCarthy's novel, the figuration of the asocial judge denies the possibility of his Symbolic representation of the Father, the Lacanian personification of the patriarchal system of culture. The absence of a mother for whom the boy can imagine a romantic attachment precludes the interpretation of the judge as the "imaginary father,"[12] whose competition for maternal relation institutes oedipalization. Because he displays the control that the unformed protagonist requires, the judge is cast instead as a grotesque projection of the phallic mother. Indeed, the judge in *Blood Meridian* plays a phallic mother run amuck. The novel depicts what happens when, rather than an integrating mother, a castrating father operates as the dyadic authorizing figure of the boy's mirror stage, for such is the role of the judge in the psychic life of the immature protagonist known only as "the kid." As a result, the judge and the kid are locked into a circular relationship of dangerous dualism, from which the boy gains neither the sense of personal integration of the normative Imaginary phase nor the induction into social regulation of the Symbolic order.

The most important episode of the Lacanian Imaginary is the mirror stage, in which the protection of the mother inspires the child's vision of himself as complete, an identification symbolized by his image in the mirror—a representation of self that appears whole, but is only an ideal created through the agency of reflection.[13] Based on dualistic and unstable mirroring, the scopic events of this period are experienced as repetitious similarities rather than definitive differences. In *Blood Meridian* this destabilizing reflection is characteristic of the strange relationship between the judge and the boy.[14] Although there is no communication acknowledged between them until the end, they observe each other throughout: "The kid was watching the judge" (79), and "Watching him" across the dim and smoky room "was the judge" (325).

At the conclusion of the book, the boy and the judge finally speak to each other about the effects of their participation in reciprocal and destructive mirroring. Watching the boy, the judge asks if it was always the kid's belief that if he didn't "speak" he wouldn't "be recognized." Ignoring the kid's claim that the judge *had* "seen" him, the judge explains that although he had "recognized" the boy the time first he "saw" him, the kid was a "disappointment" to him and remained so. "Even so at the last I find you here with me," he concludes. But the boy demurs: "I ain't with you" (328).

For Mellard "the Imaginary order is evidenced in the subject's awareness of 'two-ness,' of others caught in either a narcissistic or an aggressive relation with the ego of the subject" (28). The dyadic relation of the judge and the boy is both narcissistic from the point of view of the boy ("You seen me") and aggressive from the perspective of the judge ("You were a disappointment to me"). "Aggression is produced in response to the mirror stage" through the "rivalry over which is the self and which is the other, which the ego and which the replica," as Jane Gallop explains (62). For Lacan, "Aggressivity is the correlative tendency of a mode of identification that we call narcissistic," and this inevitable aggression "determines the formal structure of the ego and the register of entities characteristic of his world" (*Écrits* 16). Thus the threatening mirroring of the boy and the judge represents relationship in a world dominated by the need of the ego to secure its power. Nevertheless, according to Gallop, "Lacan's writings contain an implicit ethical imperative to break the mirror, an imperative to disrupt the imaginary in order to reach 'the symbolic'" (59). McCarthy's "psychodramatization" (Lacan, *Écrits* 9), however, denies the possibility of a culturally constructed revision of the extreme egotism represented by the judge.

As Lacan defines it, the appeal of the scopic drive that dominates the Imaginary situation is that it "most completely . . . eludes castration" (*Fundamental Concepts* 78). That is, the boy seeks the supportive reflection of identification sustained through the gaze of the mother in order to counter the "castration" from illusory integration threatened by the father. In Lacan's revision of Freud's oedipal story, the threatened castration by the "father" representing culture forces the boy into the Symbolic order of definitions and laws that contradict his false sense of personal value. But McCarthy's vicious judge, the opposite of the integrating mother, is also an inversion of the potentially castrating father. In Freud's description, it is the threat, not the act, of castration that moves the boy out of narcissistic dualism into the system of social authority internalized as the superego. Yet the judge is himself stuck in the mirror stage of aggressive narcissism and has no law to transmit, so when the boy begins to differentiate himself from their mirroring relation, the judge makes good on the threat of paternal castration by apparently killing him. The judge destroys what he cannot control after the kid makes two significant moves away from scopic reciprocity near the end of the novel.

First, despite the dominant violence of his surroundings, the boy futilely attempts to fashion his own moral order, as evidenced by his promise to aid the mother figure he discovers among a company of murdered penitents. Coming upon their mangled corpses, he spies what appears to be an old woman at prayer. Without recognizing that she has been dead a long time, the kid pledges to save her. The second deadly move occurs during the interview with the judge when the boy asserts his separation: "I ain't with you." In the Imaginary register of the violent judge, those "not with him" are against him, and what he cannot incorporate as reflection of his own ego he systematically destroys.

As the boy's death implies, the emotional extremes of the Western Imaginary are not in *Blood Meridian* a preliminary to any kind of social order. The anonymous kid evidently dies without ever being named; that is, without ever assuming his place within the Name-of-the-Father of the Symbolic organization of language and community.[15] McCarthy's work suggests that pervasive violence begets only violence. Without a paternal order to move into, the kid's attempt "to break the mirror" cannot result in his entrance into the communal salvation he naively promises to the effigy of the absent mother.

The Violent Sublime

The boy's developmental failure makes *Blood Meridian* an anti-oedipal parable. Although it does not endorse the anarchic supervention of social regimens that Gilles Deleuze and Felix Guattari theorize in *Anti-Oedipus,*[16] the novel's form inscribes an eternal Imaginary through repeatedly enacting the undifferentiated pulsations of experience they endorse. Repudiating the rising action and climax of the conventional novel, McCarthy's tour de force endlessly replicates free movement across vast prairies, hostile deserts, and dangerous mountains. And his rhetorical intensity simulates for the reader the protagonist's peculiar psychological predicament.

"They rode . . ." is the formulaic commencement of countless paragraphs and chapter divisions in *Blood Meridian,*[17] and, as in the following example, it establishes the rhythmic metonomy that organizes the novel: "They rode" through windy mountain passes and forests of pine, the "shoeless mules slaloming" through dry grass and pine needles, through the shaded "coulees" of northern "slopes" with their light dustings of snow. "They rode" through the fallen leaves of dark trails and "they rode" through the narrow passes "shingled" with ice. Crossing a high ridge at sundown where wild doves rocketed "down the wind" to veer between the horses and drop "into the gulf below," "they rode" into a forest of dark firs, the "little Spanish ponies sucking" at the weak "air" (136).

Even this condensation of a lengthy passage demonstrates the poetic effects Longinus is assumed to have described as "the sublime"—the audacious and passionate use of poetic language that "flashing forth at the right moment scatters everything before it like a thunderbolt." The description of nature, the rhythm, the imagery, the synaesthetic appeal to the senses, the striking diction of "slaloming" mules and ice-shingled leaves contribute to a poetic texture denoting, according to Longinus, a "plenitude" that demonstrates rhetorical "power" (77).

The effect of this sublime passage, that literally moves its characters upward, also connotes transcendence in the Romantic tradition of natural description.[18] But McCarthy rescinds the transcendental promise through both structural repetition and the contravening violence that always follows description in his novel. At the very crest of the passage, Glanton, the leader of the band of outlaws, encounters a bear "with dim pig's eyes," and violent mayhem ensues. When his horse rears up, Glanton draws his gun. The horse behind him falls as the Delaware riding it struggles to regain its footing by hitting the horse's head with his fist. At this point, the bear swings toward Glanton "stunned . . . beyond reckoning, some foul gobbet dangling from its jaws and its chops dyed red with blood." When Glanton shoots the animal in the chest, it snatches the Indian off his reeling horse, meeting the next shot, the body still hanging from its bloody maw. Throughout this melee, the forest resounds with the shouts of men and the loud "whack" of their efforts to beat the "screaming" ponies into "submission." As Glanton gets ready to fire a third round into the bear's arcing shoulder, the enraged animal rolls over him, a "sea of honey colored hair" reeking of "carrion" (137).

This second passage is also sublime in its heightened effects—the precise description, the graphic imagery, the exploitation of senses— but its fullness of expression of all aspects of violence promises repetitious horror rather than climactic transcendence. The unresolvable intensity illustrated by this passage, typical of the Imaginary order, structures the entire novel. *Blood Meridian* endlessly varies the same poetic sequence of extreme sensation leading to violent actions. In the same way the judge contracts knowledge to murder, the structural pattern of the novel reduces human experience to sensational violence. This paradoxical reduction, a repeated figure that fills the whole field,[19] obliterates any other possible organization through the exhibition of obsession. And just as the sublimity of style does not lead to transcendence, the repeating pattern denies the possibility of progress.[20] For order, which depends on the differentiation of the Symbolic system, cannot be born of the endless similarity imposed by the reiterative structure of this novel. Although the sublime depiction of violence may appeal to a hunger for sensation, the replication of intensity is, in effect, cloying. In the Imaginary condition, to which identity is confined, violence leads not to meaning but to chains of endless sensation drained of significance.

McCarthy, who uses standard Western conventions in his novels of *The Border Trilogy,* at first seems to be evoking in *Blood Meridian* the cinematic sweep of the typical Western setting, with open plains and vast "snow-covered peaks" (Cawelti, *Six-Gun* 67). This definitive setting, according to Cawelti, signals the hero's "epic courage and regenerative power" (68) to destroy the old ways and secure a "settled society," action that "almost invariably requires a transcendent and heroic violence" (Cawelti, *Adventure* 193–94). But it is precisely the ideology of transcendence through a violence conceived as heroic—the illusion that the aggressiveness of the hero can install an advancing civilization—that *Blood Meridian* disputes. By representing the brutal events of a particular era, McCarthy substitutes a degrading history for a progressive myth. His allusion to a figurative Western landscape connoting promise is rescinded by the violent abridgement of signification in repetitive scenes of exploitation. The depravity of the judge, the death of the boy, and the sterility of the setting all inscribe the absence of a moral order.

Critics charge that the Edenic setting of the mythologized Old West and the idealization of the Western hero obscure the violent elimination of its native inhabitants (Jewett and Lewis 44 ff.). McCarthy's settings, however, filled with appalling historical violence, obviously reverse this omission. But they do something more. Tzvetan Todorov describes the process *Blood Meridian* turns into story: "in some remote place where the law is only vaguely acknowledged. . . . Far from central government . . . all prohibitions give way, the social link, already loosened, gives way, snaps, revealing not a primitive nature, the beast sleeping in each of us, but a modern being, one with a great future in fact, restrained by no morality and inflicting death because and when he pleases" (*Conquest* 145).

The Psychotic Western

In form and theme McCarthy's phantasmal novel dramatizes Lacanian psychosis. The kid's story enacts this condition because he experiences the inability of a father figure to embody social order ("the foreclosure of the Name-of-the-Father in the place of the Other") that "gives psychosis its essential condition" and "structure" (*Écrits* 215). As Lacan explains it, in the static situation of the psychotic, "the lack of the Name-of-the-Father in that place which, by the hole that it opens up in the signified, sets off the cascade of reshapings of the signifier from which the increasing disaster of the imaginary proceeds" (*Écrits* 217), a description that accounts well for the repeating nontranscendent structure of *Blood Meridian.* According to Lacan, psychosis exhibits "the subject's topographical regression to the mirror stage" as an instance of "a relation to the specular other . . . reduced to its fatal aspect" (*Écrits* 209), a psychological location duplicated in the retrogressive Western setting of *Blood Meridian* and its protagonist's deadly encounter with the destructive judge.

If the psychotic condition, as Lacan contends, provides the novelist with "situations [that] are his true resource" (*Écrits* 216),[21] McCarthy's novel is a stunning realization of novelistic potential. Enjoying cult status since its publication in 1985, *Blood Meridian* has already provoked much excellent commentary. To read this enigmatic and nihilistic text once more, this time in light of Lacanian theory, is useful because Lacan stresses the necessary connection between private experience and public meaning that the extraordinary exaggeration of the novel also brings into focus.

For Lacan it is the almost unimaginable failure of the institution of community as an organizing system that is the cause and content of psychosis—and, I am arguing, it is that failure that provides the central theme of McCarthy's narrative. The generic kid's inability to mature into the Western hero is rooted in a context of extreme violence, a landscape of ethical sterility presented as a place and time that contradicts a Western mythology of incipient civilization. Nothing less than the disclosure of the political unconscious of the Western genre and the romance of Western history, *Blood Meridian,* a psychotic parable of the violent past, serves as a warning to the violent present: Social value cannot develop out of personal or public aggression. McCarthy's plot and structure speak to the absence of a culture and community that model and promote genuine power in the lives of American men. Masculine maturity cannot proceed from violence, and social system does not develop out of the abrogation of communal order.[22]

Richard Ford's *Rock Springs* and Cormac McCarthy's *Blood Meridian* challenge the formula Western.[23] The Imaginary encounters of their protagonists in private relationships and public exploits uncover the defects of male violence in the developmental transaction of American boys and refuse to vindicate them through the solace of Western adventure. Ford's realism depicts in ordinary, contemporary Western life a parental failure of power and order that cannot nurture the adult development of his sonlike characters, while McCarthy's sublime re-presentation of Western history emblematizes a politics of destruction that cannot be rewritten as progress. In the next chapter, we will observe that Thom Jones and Tim O'Brien similarly unpack the mythic representation of war as moral victory.

PART THREE

INTERROGATION OF COMMUNITY

5

YOUNG GOODMEN AT WAR

Thom Jones's The Pugilist at Rest *and*
Tim O'Brien's The Things They Carried

Stories of war link the ideals of particular communities to the promise
of male maturity and masculine empowerment that is at work in all
adventure fiction. Richard Harding Davis, as we observed, presented
war as a reliable means to both personal authority and public righteousness, but the post-Vietnam writers of this chapter disrupt formulaic presentations of military violence to challenge that construction.
Thom Jones's postmodern stories depict violence in order to explode
its conventional employment as an expedient in the development of
the young soldier, and they thwart narrative expectation to interrogate
the society that supports the war. Similarly, Tim O'Brien's postmodern
dislocation of the traditional formula of war as masculine initiation
challenges the role of story in war—the fabrication of a narrative
"truth" that validates the politics of the war maker.

Violent Excess in *The Pugilist at Rest*

Like Richard Ford, Thom Jones portrays the psychological conflicts
that make masculine development impossible, and like Cormac McCarthy, he connects that impossibility to historical conditions outside the
control of the individual. But unlike Ford's and McCarthy's protagonists, whose passages to maturity are truncated well before they absorb
the imperatives of a Freudian father, Jones's hero encounters conflicting values in the thick of the oedipal transaction. The Freudian plot, the
parable of Oedipus, represents the process through which a young man
is socialized into the dominant values of his community. For Freud the
successful dissolution of the Oedipus complex also signals the acquisition of the superego, the personal equivalent of the communal standards modeled by a powerful father. In *The Pugilist at Rest* (1993), Tom,

the protagonist of the three Vietnam stories it contains, engages in masculine violence as a boxer and as a soldier in an attempt to establish some connection to his functionally absent father and, through him, to complete his oedipal transition into a meaningful system of values.

This Freudian plot of social closure is, however, contradicted by the story's Freudian form. In "Break on Through," the epilepsy he suffers and the amphetamines he pops before battle distort Tom's experience. Shaped by his perception, events are represented through a visionary warp reminiscent of the dream process described by Freud as the expression of unrealizable desire. The resulting contradictions between ideological expectation and military experience can be understood as the Freudian oppositions of plot and form theorized by Steven Cohan and Linda Shires. In *Telling Stories,* Cohan and Shires argue that pressure for oedipal alignment organizes the search for literary closure around meaning consistent with cultural norms, but at the same time, the dream process of some storytelling "jams the apparently straightforward equation drawn" (29). Although the story works by establishing connections, its narration may also introduce an "explosion or dissemination" of meanings that exceeds final signification (26).[1] That is, formal organization structured like the Freudian dream can actually "break" or disrupt the Freudian plot. In the appositely named "Break on Through," Tom's developmental project is opposed by the dream structure of the story. The protagonist's oedipal desire for a closure both literary and social is blocked by the depiction of his war experience as an open-ended nightmare.[2] And that this nightmare has cultural and ethical implications is symbolized by the surprising manifestation of a Hawthornian devil in the middle of a battle in Vietnam.

In Nathaniel Hawthorne's classic initiation tale, Young Goodman Brown seems to enter the dark forest of contradictory meaning under the aegis of the devil, whose scepter is a walking staff that is transformed into a snake. At the start of "Break on Through," Tom describes encountering a strange "apparition"—a man with the "face of Lucifer." Taking off his "doeskin glove," the awful figure reveals an "eagle's talon" in place of a hand. When he turns his back, lifting his coattail like "someone flashing me the moon," Tom glimpses a "muscular, and purple" tail "thick with spines" just as the phantom strides "into the fog on cloven feet" (29). And immediately after his vision of the devil, Tom spots a python on the path before him. Like Young Goodman Brown, Jones's focal character enters the dark forest—in his case, an NVA (North Viet-namese Army) ambush in which he experiences the contradictions of meaning that are the central issue of the collection of stories. As in Hawthorne's tale, the protagonist's sense of received order is opposed by an alternative vision, which in "Break on Through" finds expression through the depiction of violence.

That the central issue of Hawthorne's story is the alignment of the son with paternal authority is signaled when the devil convinces the boy to accompany him on the basis of his long friendship with both Brown's father and his grandfather. The parallel oedipal project in "Break on Through" is expressed through Tom's memories of his fam-ily. In a series of battle flashbacks, he recalls his grandmother as a maternal provider. Mag, a German immigrant who ran a small grocery store, sold food on credit during the Depression, when hunger was prevalent and money was scarce, seeing to it that her neighbors were always provided for. But in contrast to Tom's heritage of maternal care, a nurturing bond with his father remains out of reach. When Tom vis-its "the old man" in the "psycho ward for the criminally insane" shortly before the father's suicide, the ex-prizefighter fails even to acknowledge his son. The only thing he has any interest in is how much Marlboros cost on the street. "They're screwing me in the hospital canteen," he complains (52). Nevertheless, it is this remote paternal figure whom the abandoned son tries to emulate through becoming a boxer. "*Uncle John, how good of a fighter was my dad?*" young Tom had demanded. He was "*very good*" and "*had guts,*" the uncle had replied. And although he always fought drunk, his moves were "*slick.*" "*Number five in the world . . . I don't think the son of a bitch was afraid of anyone*" (49–50).

Tom tries to complete the incomplete oedipal process of identifying with his father's power through similar practice of his father's violence. In the system of equivalence set up by the plot, we can represent this attempt as *son = violence = father,* a move that would set Tom within the recognizable social order predicated by oedipal identification and patriarchal power. The meanings of the violence that Tom experiences, however, initially as a boxer and later as a combat marine during heavy enemy fire, exceed the limits of this simple equation. In Thom Jones's fiction, violence as a category of male behavior is charged with many meanings and contradictory significances.

First, in "Break on Through" violence signifies the professional competence of the trained soldier. Tom is at pains to recount his proficiency in employing "smoke," a hand grenade, and a rifle during a lethal struggle with three enemy soldiers. And after dispatching them with impressive efficiency, he prepares for the others who may follow by precisely placing a mine and so skillfully camouflaging it that it is undiscoverable. The second significance of violence is born of the difficult fraternal care of one soldier for another, a concern illustrated by Tom's effective ministrations when a fellow soldier's thumb is almost blown away. After cleaning the wound, Tom draws the torn flesh together and stitches it over the exposed bone. Although he is evidently upset by the sight of the damage, Tom perseveres in dressing and taping the injury.

Yet violence also denotes antisocial impulses. In a hallucination, Tom reconstructs a semifinal Golden Gloves match he boxed in Chicago. Boasting about the effectiveness of his style, he asserts that it was "so easy" to set up his opponents, he nearly pitied them. But sympathy is not his dominant inclination. The rest of the passage emphasizes how much he enjoyed toying with his unsuccessful adversaries, "liked making it last, making their pain and fear endure" because he "wanted them to know how it felt" (52).

Mixing competence and madness, healing and hurting, the discrepant violent practice of "Break on Through" cannot contain or be contained by regulation or expectation. This paradoxical failure is epitomized by Baggit, a convicted murderer released from death row to join Tom's unit, who eventually earns the Medal of Honor. Likewise, another member, Dang Singh, is both "easy" and "lethal," at the same time a sympathetically portrayed youth and an ace torturer. According to Cohan and Shires, "in order to forge an equivalence of . . . binary oppositions" and secure closure, conventional storytelling can only proceed by "privileging similarity and denying difference" (29). But the irreconcilable differences demonstrated by violence in all of Thom Jones's stories explode the very codes of relation that narrative seeks to establish. Baggit's violent conduct is a case in point. On the one hand, Baggit's military proficiency brings him into familial relation with the men of his unit when he saves the life of the protagonist by killing the NVAs who would have shot Tom. On the other, he repudiates family alliance by brutally abusing the mother and father figures whom he seeks out in a friendly Vietnamese village.

Through both character and incident, violence is figured in "Break on Through" as an indeterminate system that can at once create and destroy social orders. The violent competitions and competencies of its members organize the military unit into a band of brothers supervised by a sergeant who serves as a source of paternal authority and a captain who serves as a source of paternal reward, but as Baggit's excessive brutality in the village suggests, violence may also destroy the filial order it constructs. Further, Baggit's continuing story shows that the imposition of oedipal alignment that functions through the temporary family in Vietnam is dysfunctional in the outside world.

After he returns to Los Angeles after being injured in battle, Baggit sends two signals of the conflicting effects of male violence. When the unit receives a clumsily written postcard, the narrator believes Baggit is saying "thanks for saving him." After the village incident, another soldier had brutally beaten Baggit, a move the others believed pulled him back him from a moral and mental "abyss" (63). The redemptive violence of masculine bonding is celebrated throughout Thom Jones's work, but his stories also demonstrate that violent competence is only constructive within the sanction of the limited male worlds of war and boxing. Baggit's second message—the one that rescinds the promise of personal and communal integrity granted through violence—is implied from his appearance on the front page of the *Los Angeles Times*. Barricading himself in a California beauty parlor with "his estranged old lady," Baggit had committed the murder-suicide that destroyed his family and ended his life (64).

Jones's narrative may be misread as the conventional war story of male buddies and the incompatibility of soldiers and society, but I believe that the invocation of Hawthorne takes us deeper into the issue of masculine identity. In "Young Goodman Brown" the visionary perspective introduced by the devil, the anti-oedipal father, overturns the hero's accommodation to the settled norms of community. In like manner, the hallucinatory experience of "Break on Through," a feature of the protagonist's epilepsy common to several of the stories, introduces an alternative to received values.

In "The Black Lights," for example, the Tom character is undergoing treatment in a mental hospital for the seizures that have begun as a result of blows to the head in a boxing match,[3] but his salvation through the ministrations of a doctor-father is inconclusive. The ending of the story makes the still delusional patient's eventual normality doubtful.

Dismissed by, rather than aligned with, the paternal institution, he catches a ride in a stolen T-Bird with an AWOL marine hell-bent for escape. As the car speeds away, the narrator reports that he could momentarily imagine himself in Vietnam or as a boxer again: "kill or be killed . . . It was ecstasy" (85). In a related story, "A White Horse," epilepsy obliterates social identity—name, family, responsibilities— from time to time when the protagonist finds himself in foreign countries after a seizure. Having once again skipped his medication, in this story he winds up on a plane on the way to India. The story ends, like "The Black Lights," with the escape from community. Realizing he has no passport, no wallet, no clue to his own identity, the protagonist heads for a hotel, where he believes he may eventually find himself again, but for the time being he prefers anonymity.

David Leverenz argues that *The Scarlet Letter* is marked by "unresolved tensions" concerning issues of masculine identity. Although the early introduction of Hester as an apparently feminist protagonist in that work suggests "revolt against punitive patriarchal authority" (160), by the conclusion of the novel the narrator and the narrative have capitulated to the dominant values of Hawthorne's period. "In the narrator's increasingly Oedipal allegory, a regressive inquisitorial family triangle of cruel, impersonal father; kind despairing mother; and tortured triumphant son all but drives out early expectations for Hester's adult subjectivity against public patriarchy. A sadomasochistic symbiosis of father and son becomes a vision of transcendent, victimized love" (176).

The Pugilist at Rest introduces but rejects a comparable "sadomaschochistic symbiosis of father and son" through violence. Jones's narrators, like Hawthorne's characters, articulate the tensions of masculine identification stalled before the boy's socialization into normative manhood. Like Hawthorne's, Jones's stories are frequently organized as oedipal encounters, but unlike Hawthorne, Jones eschews resolution of the conflicts the oedipal drama would reconcile. The collection presents visionary episodes that typically include violence as contradiction to the social commitments the successful completion of masculine identification would institute. Thus Jones's realistic protagonists continually dream of brutal masculine communities in which violence constructs and dialectically deconstructs the expectations set up by literary and social systems.

Postcards from the Edge

The bedeviling thickets of violent alignment in Thom Jones's *The Pugilist at Rest* find parallels in the characteristic thematic and formal dislocations of Tim O'Brien's *The Things They Carried.* A number of novel factors have converged to produce the extraordinary dissidence of such post-Vietnam writing. The contested scripting of the moral purpose of the conflict in Vietnam by an active protest movement, the (eventual) media presentation of the war in images so unprecedented that they were difficult to organize into a reassuring fiction, the misunderstanding of the enemy's military capacity by generals and politicians, and the subsequent inability of the ground troops to make much sense of the field operations in which they were engaged resulted in an extensive literature on the war in Vietnam characterized by multiple layers of fundamental uncertainty. Accounts by combatants often stress the pervasive sense of unreality produced by guerilla encounters in unfamiliar territory; the irresolution of an equivocal United States withdrawal finds expression in skepticism about the political meaning of military experience in both fiction and nonfiction; and, most notably, some contemporary literature of the Vietnam experience, well exemplified by the prize-winning short fiction of O'Brien and Jones,[4] employs contradictory representations of violence to challenge core structures of ethical value. But whereas Jones concentrates on the impeded development of his protagonist, O'Brien focuses on evading the ideological constriction of "truth" that is the rhetorical objective of war.

The issue of truth in war finds a fitting emblem in the World War I Field Service Post Card issued to British troops unable or unwilling to write original letters. This "first widespread exemplar" of the modern "Form," which Paul Fussell includes in *The Great War and Modern Memory,* was frequently posted after a fight to reassure relatives awaiting news (185). All the embattled soldier had to do in order to communicate was to underline the applicable choice or fill in the requisite blank (fig. 1). What is most striking about the form is its restriction of what can be communicated to binary choices that omit all other possibilities. The combatant is either "quite well" or being properly cared for by the authorities. Period. There is no provision for alternative interpretation. To be morally offended, confused, lost, frightened, hungry, lonely, elated at victory, suffering the widespread symptoms of the mental condition then known as shellshock, even moderately ill, or slightly wounded is literally impossible. And in the event of hospital-ization, the possibility of death is obviously out of the question.

This WWI "postcard from the edge," a device that prescribes the story of battlefield experience, aptly introduces Elaine Scarry's contention in *The Body in Pain* that narrative representation is an integral component

---

NOTHING is to be written on this side except the date and signature of the sender. Sentences not required may be erased. If anything else is added the post card will be destroyed.

I am quite well.

I have been admitted into hospital
{sick} and am going on well.
{wounded} and hope to be discharged soon.

I am being sent down to the base.

I have received your
{letter dated _____
{telegram " _____
{parcel " _____

Letter follows at first opportunity.
I have received no letter from you
{lately
{for a long time.

Signature}
  only. }

Date _____

Verso text from a WWI Field Service Post Card

of war. The story of war is the exposition of a special kind of violence: deliberate violence that in turn provokes narrative deliberation. For war is the calculated action of a society rather than the random accident of an individual, and although war is aggression against singular mortal bodies, its effect, according to Scarry, depends on collective fictive interpretations. War, she explains, is a violent contest in which each side tries to out-injure the other to bring about "perceptual reversal" from the premise that "physical damage" is "acceptable and ideological and territorial sacrifices" are "unacceptable" to the opposed proposition that more physical damage is so unacceptable that sacrifices of territory and belief can be tolerated (89). Fighting a war seems to be a matter of personal experience—the effect of weapons on bodies. But winning that war is actually an effect of the alteration of a society's predominant perceptions about its own purposes, the influence of narrative on minds.

Because war is a contest between two competing sides, Scarry contends, it imposes a rigid binary structure (like the choices imposed by the Field Service Post Card) that I am calling *the war narrative.* War in its narrative aspect transforms all possible relations into the distinction between friend and enemy, and all possible evaluations into issues of winning and losing. In contrast to the variety that characterizes human experience, war, understood in this way, introduces "a self-cancelling duality . . . that by the very force of its relentless insistence on doubleness, provides the means for eliminating and replacing itself by the condition of singularity" imposed by winning (87). This predictable conflation of epistemological possibility Fussell dubs "the *versus* habit: one thing opposed to another, not with some Hegelian hope of synthesis involving a dissolution of both extremes . . . but with a sense that one of the poles embodies so wicked a deficiency or flaw or perversion that its total submission is called for" (*Great War* 79).

The semiotic "translation of opened bodies into verbal issues" (Scarry 96) achieved through war is the result of standard narrative process, which highlights and organizes discrepant events into temporal plots implying relationship, development, and significance. The narrative depiction of "the enemy" is one of the first steps in waging war, and, Scarry posits, it is the public translation of the destructive events of war into a story of victory and defeat that finally ends it. Thus, war stories are not secondary reflections about war but part of its essential operation. Narrative completes the ideological project of war in one of two ways.

Either war stories resolve contested issues by certifying the currency of belief with the specie of blood. Or stories challenge tenuous beliefs by exploiting the same authenticity of spent gore to refuse ideological closure. Although the popular story of military adventure, as exemplified by Richard Harding Davis's *Soldiers of Fortune,* uses violence to endorse prevalent beliefs, American war literature has, at its best, depicted the violence of war to challenge popular assumptions.

Violent Contradiction in American Literature of War

The genre of the American war story descends historically from the epic depiction of Greek gods and Roman heroes through the exploits of extraordinary British leaders to the confusions of ordinary young men so evident in stories about the war in Vietnam. This trajectory, outlined by Northrop Frye as the declension of "mythic," "romantic," "high mimetic," "low mimetic," and "ironic" modes, classifies male protagonists according to their "power of action" through their superiority or inferiority to "other men and to the environment" (*Anatomy* 33). In the formulaic war story, the control (or its lack) so crucial to Frye's categories is established as a result of a character's ability to employ or withstand military violence.

Another taxonomy that predicts heroic preeminence is the class system of the old world, which also informs the system of military rank. Throughout history aristocrats have borne arms in the service of their own prerogatives; when commoners fought, it was to support the goals of their leaders. Following that tradition, the European war stories inherited by the men who became Americans were stories of aristocratic superiority modeled by exemplary officers on the occasion of battle. Their violence—illustrating "good breeding" witnessed by devotion to duty and taciturn, but obvious, bravery—is essentially conservative. It teaches the virtue of adherence to masculine standards set by the ruling classes, and it justifies their political agendas. Herman Melville's reference to British hero Admiral Nelson in *Billy Budd: Foretopman* is an instance of this legacy. But the example of Nelson's "shining deeds" (246) might, Melville declares, be obsolete: "nowadays . . . a certain kind of displayed gallantry . . . be fallen out of date as hardly applicable under changed circumstances" (245). One of the tacit questions raised by Billy's stoic sacrifice to the discipline demanded by British military order of his day is its value within the context of American experience.

The American experiment was founded on an alternative vision of violence, that of democratic rebellion—creative rather than conservative, voluble rather than dignified; its leaders tacticians instead of gentlemen, and its stories a celebration of transformation instead of tradition. From this point of view, the narrative depiction of war celebrates violence as a tool for change, the pattern Richard Slotkin identified as "regeneration through violence" in his study of American frontier myths. But in practice, storytelling preserves old attitudes and introduces new, and American military fiction frequently combines both perspectives, often through the trope of the young soldier's maturation. Popular plots, whether a novel by Richard Harding Davis or a film starring John Wayne, often resolve symbolic alternatives through the tale of a brash young soldier whose initial behavior may threaten the cherished values of a brave leader. Eventually, in such works as Davis's *Captain Macklin,* the young American acquires the authority and manner, and even the causes, of the European officer; while the son figure in the movie *The Sands of Iwo Jima* finally establishes a filial relation with John Wayne, the American (noncommissioned) officer-father. In conventional military adventure, youthful rebellion ripens into service of the state.

There is, however, an alternative tradition within American war literature, the kind of story that pits one vision against the other. In Stephen Crane's *The Red Badge of Courage,* for example, both themes—the conservative violence of the old world warrior and the deviant potential of the resistant American—are plotted but unresolved. Henry Fleming both rejects the romantic lure of customary heroism by running away from conflict *and* adopts it as the stalwart standard-bearer of his company in the midst of battle. Yet these differences are not, as in generic adventure, elided as the progressive account of a young man's development. While Henry's red badge remains an ambivalent symbol of competing ideologies, Crane's treatment of violence moves even beyond the uneasy balance of ambiguity to further definition.

In *The Red Badge of Courage* the representation of violence exceeds both the officer's conformity to social standard and the frightened recruit's rejection. Indeed, the unresolvable opposition of these two ideological positions makes possible an alternative reading exemplified by the famous scene in which Henry discovers a dead man in the forest:

The corpse was dressed in a uniform that had once been blue, but was now faded to a melancholy shade of green. The eyes, staring at the youth, had changed to the dull hue to be seen on the side of a dead fish. The mouth was open. Its red had changed to an appalling yellow. Over the gray skin of the face ran little ants. One was trundling some sort of bundle along the upper lip. (455–56)

The violence of plot incident—the death of the man—is long past, but the shock registered by Henry is present in the rhetorical effect on a reader of the passage. The simple subject-verb pattern of the sentences, the common nouns and verbs, and the repetition of forms of the verb *to be* stress the ordinariness of what is usually perceived as extraordinary in literary experience: death. And yet the violence of war establishes the antithesis of this perception. In battle, death is a common event; the ordinary and the extraordinary *do* change places.

In this passage, the setting in nature ironically exploits the war-born sense of death as a "natural" event, and the sequence progresses through a series of related reversals. First, ordinary expectations based on color are rescinded by the natural deterioration of death—the red of the healthy mouth converted to the yellow of decay. Then the qualities of the human and animal world—marked by the reference to the dead fish and the disturbingly anthropomorphic ants—suffer a transposition that degrades any elevated concept of the human condition. In this scene the soldier's destruction cannot be defined in terms of the social alternatives Henry's military experience puts to the test. The naturalistic depiction of death evades military violence as the occasion for humiliation or the opportunity for honor.

Crane's representation of war in terms of poetic naturalism is inscribed in the gap between contradictory representations. Henry does not in the course of the story turn into the soldier ordained by the tales of Greek heroes or English chivalry he read as a child (10), nor does he abandon that project. Instead, he enacts two irresolvable options, a superfluity of representation that allows an alternative position: Crane's portrayal of violence as naturalistic process and war as institutional practice.

Although the contradictory terms may vary by period and by author, and certainly the emergent critique of war and violence changes, the oppositional exploitation of representations allows for critique. Observable in Jones's Freudian discontinuity, it defines the achievement of Tim O'Brien's later Vietnam literature. But even O'Brien found it difficult initially to evade the expectations imposed by the adventure tradition, as a comparison of his early autobiography and his later short stories reveals.

In contemporary culture Frye's godlike mythic heroes tend to be depicted as cartoon superheroes or characters out of science fiction; romantic heroes—men superior in degree to both their worlds and their companions—are usually relegated to the television or movie adventures of figures like Rambo. But the literature of the Vietnam War centers on realistic protagonists. Occasionally the focus is the high mimetic leader figure, a man of superior rank, skills, or insight, but most often the work concerns the low mimetic everyman, the young initiate to the world of war. In O'Brien's 1990 cycle of war stories, *The Things They Carried,* the divergent depiction of these figures, as well as the rendition of clashing codes of violence, rewrites issues of representation and integrity unresolved in his 1973 memoir, *If I Die in a Combat Zone.*

Equivocation in *If I Die in a Combat Zone*

In effect, conventional codes of violent presentation do not so much describe war as inscribe its reception. Whatever the ongoing underlying causes, an act portrayed as aggressive violence serves to inaugurate the dramatic sequence of the rendition of war itself, which only "begins" when an Archduke Ferdinand is shot or a Pearl Harbor is bombed. In terms of Kenneth Burke's four-stage theory of the "dramatistic process" that configures all story, this act of aggression introduces the "Pollution" that violates the central tenets of a social system and demands correction. This act also allows for the representation of "Guilt," the establishment of who or what is responsible for the violation that must be expiated through "Purification," frequently a violent act of elimination that effects "Redemption," or the reestablishment of the social system (*Rhetoric* 4–5). Therefore, not only does violence in the story of war assign archetypal roles like "brave leader" and "young soldier," but also the conventional war narrative, in conformity with Burke's redemptive sequence, structures the plot events of war to impose their evaluation in advance.

That is to say, before a textual shot is fired, the war narrative is culturally loaded *for* the establishment of sanctioned interpretations of actions and people and *against* the representation of the as-yet-unclassified "truth" about war, whatever that is perceived to be. But, paradoxically, it is precisely the standard of truth as a faithful portrayal of unique experience that is most consistently applied to the literature of the Vietnam War. In his discussion of memoirs of the war, J. T. Hansen observes that all the writers he studied shared the objective of "authenticity," an authority based on "knowledge of the war they experienced" (134–35). Similarly, Don Ringnalda points out that for the former soldiers, who are the most exacting audience for the Vietnam story, the standard of evaluation is "accuracy, factualness, faithful attention to details" ("Unlearning" 65). "It seems," muses Michael Bibby, "that the Vietnam era remains, even a generation after, a period in which 'being there' is paramount" (ix); but, he queries, why "should *this* period, more than others, exert such a call for authentic experience?" (x). Perhaps the widespread absence of moral certainty about Vietnam has created the appetite for the verisimilitude that is the most important criterion for accounts of the war. However, as Lorrie Smith argues, verisimilitude has "no inherent value" if the text does not also examine "the cultural assumptions which animate and give meaning to its images" (90).

From his earliest work, Tim O'Brien, to use the words of one of his more recent titles, has been engaged in the effort to "tell a true war story," but in so doing he has also struggled to evaluate the attitudes that produced and were produced by the Vietnam experience. In repeated treatments of the same subject matter, he has been trying to solve the special problem of "truth" posed by the disparity between literary codes of authenticity in the war story and social analysis of the war. The incidents in *If I Die in a Combat Zone,* his collection of autobiographical essays on his service in Vietnam, do not vary significantly from the incidents fictionalized in the stories of *The Things They Carried,* published seventeen years later. However, whereas the first book relies on the representation of truth patterned by conventional war narrative, the second, by abandoning literary realism, comes closer to presenting an evaluative account of the Vietnam experience. While the first book intends a criticism of war, that effect is discounted by its reliance on representational codes that annul subversive analysis—its characterization of the noble officer and its preoccupation with the theme of courage, traditional devices that repress the disturbing impact of violence in Vietnam.

The verisimilitude of O'Brien's memoir is a result of his evident eagerness to communicate with his reader through straightforward description of sensations and emotions, thematic self-revelation, translation of military argot, and organization based on the usual sequence of military service: induction, basic training, arrival in Vietnam, participation in battle, term in the rear, and return to the States. This effort to engage the reader is so powerful that O'Brien frequently presents his own experiences in the second person, as in this description of a helicopter lift into a war zone:

> You begin to sweat. Even with the rotor blades whipping cold air around like an air-conditioner, you begin to sweat.
>
> You light a cigarette, trying to think of something to say. A good joke would help, something funny. Laughing makes you believe you are resigned if not brave. (112)

Through its representation of easily identifiable physical and emotional effects—the chill of apprehension and the desire for laughter to relieve tension—the passage insists that the alien experience of war in Vietnam is directly transferable. In fact, the convergence of author and reader, insisted upon by grammatical address in which the perspective of an absent "you" substitutes for direct observation of a participant "I," is engineered through the presentation of universal and simple correlatives of shared experience. This sense of apprehensible truth is reinforced through the soldier's engaging confession of weakness.

Whatever genuine differences that may exist between a noncombatant reader and the veteran writer are denied through the narrative production of verisimilitude. And although the insider's language the author uses to introduce the texture of alternative reality might separate his perspective from that of an outsider-reader, O'Brien cancels this effect through careful translation. "Pinkville," he explains is "GI slang for Song My, parent village of My Lai—the Batangan Peninsula or the Athletic Field, appropriately named for its flat acreage of grass and rice paddy" (126). And just as the alien geography of Vietnam can be naturalized for American consumption, so too can the chaotic experiences of the soldier be ordered as events in an identifiable succession of incidents from his introduction to the military to his exit, generally presented as historical movement from month to month.

It has long been acknowledged that realism as a literary form does more than record the texture of a setting or present believable characters. According to Leo Bersani, mimetic fiction also constructs "a secret complicity between the novelist and his society's illusions about its own order . . . by providing [society] with strategies for containing (and repressing) its disorder within significantly structured stories about itself" (247). To present war as literary "truth," then, is to destroy its capacity to challenge the very social expectations that may have produced it.

The formal assimilation of the Vietnam experience in *If I Die in a Combat Zone* is reinforced thematically through archetypal representation of the heroic officer and the young initiate. Although O'Brien includes a variety of leaders—the insensitive Colonel Daud; the dangerous, bumbling ROTC-trained Captain Smith; a racist first sergeant blown away by black infantrymen; the maniacal Major Callicles; and the war-loving lieutenant, "Mad Mark"—his most extensive account of an officer is a tribute to Captain Johansen, especially fulsome on the occasion of Johansen's rotation out of Vietnam. O'Brien describes this tall and handsome officer, brave in battle and scrupulously "fair," as "one of the nation's pride." At the ceremony when he relinquishes command, Johansen expresses his respect for the unit, his sadness at losses and injury, and his pride in the men, who hear his words standing at attention, "feeling like orphans up for adoption" (148). This portrayal records O'Brien's evident admiration through the characterological codes of superiority—those of breeding and bearing—that do not so much describe an individual as enlist him within the ranks of what Martin Green designates as the "aristo-military caste."[5] Thus Johansen's example extends from personal achievement to public principle. As the generic "officer" of traditional war narrative, he embodies the American military project as a form of fair-minded paternal intervention, and the affiliative connection explicit in this passage makes it difficult for the "orphaned" son to write about his valiant father's war as an instance of personal and political moral hypocrisy. Nonetheless, that is exactly what O'Brien is trying to do in *If I Die in a Combat Zone*.

The trope for this subversive project is the representation of violence. O'Brien resists the repression of the disturbing "disorder" of the war in Vietnam by revealing the barbarism and carelessness of American power. Displaying a Viet Cong ear as a battle trophy and destroying a peaceful fishing village because of mistaken coordinates for defensive mortar fire are examples that contradict the restraint and concern for others modeled by Captain Johansen's military authority. But the subversive presentation of a violence out of ideological bounds is weakened by the memoir's preoccupation with the courage war requires. In formula stories of war, violence provides the primary filter, the test of courage, through which masculine character may be evaluated. Even though O'Brien redefines conventional courage as Platonic "wise endurance" (138), his thematic investment repeats the traditional trope of war as the uniquely desirable setting for the ultimate determination of a young man's mettle.

Although O'Brien includes ethical and political objections, his challenge is discredited by the formal realism and the traditional narrative tropes of *If I Die in a Combat Zone,* which transform his memoir into the conventional account of a young soldier within the military tradition. But, in contrast, by abjuring realism and omitting codes of complicity, *The Things I Carried,* written almost two decades later, compels radical critique.

Postmodern Morality in *The Things They Carried*

The title story of *The Things They Carried* invokes and revises two key devices of generic war fiction: the structure of dramatic action and the focal representation of the officer. Buried within this narrative is a conventional plot. A platoon of infantrymen from Alpha Company, led by Lieutenant Jimmy Cross, are on a mission to destroy Viet Cong "villes" and tunnels. The seventeen men—among them, Ted Lavender, Lee Strunk, Rat Kiley, Henry Dobbins, Mitchell Sanders, Dave Jensen, Norman Bowker, Kiowa, and Tim O'Brien, characters who recur throughout the collection—are especially uneasy when they discover a tunnel. Standard operating procedure demands that one of their number, chosen by lot, crawl inside and explore before they blow it up, a maneuver literally dangerous and psychologically unnerving. On the day of the story, Lee Strunk is unlucky enough to have to descend. The others, worried for him and uneasily aware of their own mortality, await his eventual reemergence. Although Strunk returns unscathed, Ted Lavender, the most frightened of the group, is later shot while returning from urinating. A helicopter is summoned to remove his body, and the men respond to his death in a variety of ways: relief, humor, hysterical grief, and the destruction of the nearby village of Than Khe.

But this imposed dramatistic structure of violation and resolution, which makes violent death and chaotic response comprehensible as stages of Burkean Pollution and Purification, is not adopted by the story, which is instead organized as lists of actual and emotional burdens toted by the soldiers. The things they carry include the accoutrements of war, such as steel helmets, which, O'Brien carefully notes, weigh five pounds; the particular objects of their military duties, the twenty-three-pound M-60 of the machine gunner or the medic's bag, which weighs twenty pounds (6–7). They also bear the heavier load of fear and whatever the men rely on to cope with fear, like Ted Lavender's drugs, Kiowa's Bible, and Jimmy Cross's love letters.

In *Writing War* Lynne Hanley contends that modern military narratives are suffused with a "'secret unacknowledged elation' at the thought of war, with the conviction that war is exciting,"[6] and that this style of representation has promoted war as a desirable societal event (4). But by presenting violence in terms of burden rather than battle through deliberately nondramatic structure, "The Things They Carried" deflates the excitement of violence. By stressing the continuous pressure of war through the metaphor of weight to be borne rather than the dramatistic portrayal of military adventure, it also deflects the ascription of moral purpose to the violent events of war.

Similarly, the story, which foregrounds the reactions of the officer, Lieutenant Jimmy Cross, obviates his reception as noble example. Jimmy fights the inexpressible fear the men share by obsessing about a girl he wants to love and substituting the banalities of her letters for the reality of Vietnam. After Lavender's death, Cross digs a foxhole and gives in to uncontrolled weeping. Finally, despite the rain, he burns the letters. Accepting the "blame" for his soldier's death, he resolves to be a leader, not a lover (24). He imagines himself, henceforth, an officer in the manner of John Wayne. In the event of quarrels or complaints, he resolves to square his shoulders like a commander, resolutely form the straggling troops into ranks, "saddle up," and march on (25). Like the rest of the men, the lieutenant responds to the random violence in largely unproductive ways. He doesn't set any superior standard because, like the others, he can find no relevant standard to set. His recourse to the movie model of the officer is, unfortunately, as much a product of fantasy as his accession to the role of lover.

Lavender's death cannot be explained or contained by Cross's pose of heroic responsibility any more than it can be relieved by the unit's destruction of the "chickens and dogs" and hooches of Than Khe (16). In "The Things They Carried," the unplottable violence of the Vietnam experience is structurally contrasted to the assimilable violence of war as popular fiction. In the space between these two opposed representations—experiential disorder, the way the events of war feel to the soldiers in the field, and fictive order, the way popular representations suggest they should respond—emerges the "truth" about Vietnam as a constant process of "humping," or carrying the impossible responsibility of power through a violent landscape.

The proper treatment of this truth, O'Brien suggests, is storytelling. Conditioned as we are to the designations of "fiction" and "nonfiction," it is easy to imagine that truth and stories are opposite categories. "How to Tell a True War Story," however, dissolves this relation to allow storytelling to emerge as the pursuit of provisional comprehension. Two scenes of graphic violence organize this effect. The first is the death of a young soldier, Curt Lemon, who steps on a mine during a happy moment; the second is the destruction of a baby water buffalo by his best friend, Rat Kiley.

In the first scene, just after speaking to Kiley for what turns out to be the last time, Lemon makes an awkward misstep out of the sunshine onto a "booby-trapped 105." The explosive blast lifts his dead body into a nearby tree, and Kiley and Dave Jensen have to clamber up to "peel off" the "dangling" parts. The narrator recalls "pieces of skin and something wet and yellow that must've been the intestines" and terrible "gore" he is unable to forget (89).

The action in the second scene is Rat Kiley's systematic torture of a baby water buffalo. After a first shot through the knee, the animal makes no sound. When it stumbles but regains unsteady footing, Rat aims carefully and shoots off an ear. He then fires again into the small hump on its lower back. "It wasn't to kill; it was to hurt." Next he turns the rifle to the animal's muzzle and shoots it away. During this performance, the watching platoon says little. Although they may be feeling a great deal, they express little "pity" for the injured beast. Rat blows off the tail, then wounds the baby water buffalo in the ribs, the belly, the nose, and the throat. It is still living when one of the men kicks it, and the group finally dumps it into the village well (86).

It is impossible to read these two passages without placing them in a causal relationship that induces emotional and political interpretation. As we observed in the Crane paragraph, the juxtaposition of nature and death is especially shocking. In the first scene, the sunlit American boy is wastefully decimated by a hidden explosive device. Rat Kiley and Curt Lemon have just been playing catch with a smoke bomb, turning war, for a few moments of pastoral innocence, into a carefree game.[7] But the Viet Cong have evidently broken the rules. An invisible enemy, they not only kill Curt, but also cruelly dismember him. Although presented as a kind of hero, Curt is reduced to a substance to be peeled off and scraped away. Just as Crane's color images are means of ironic reversal, Curt's "wet" and "yellow" intestines are converted from organs of life to signifiers of death.

The second scene is apparently a direct result of the first. Rat chooses a symbol of Vietnamese innocence, the ubiquitous water buffalo—an emblem of the culture, not an agent of war, and a "baby" at that—to mimic Curt, the momentary emblem of youthful American guilelessness; and his attack on the body of the animal imitates his friend's fragmentation and evisceration. The biblical motto of vengeance, "an eye for an eye . . . " is literally enacted in a narrative sequence meant to inscribe the sense of just retribution.

Revenge, as David Whillock notes, is a common plot device in film treatments of the Vietnam War that attempt to impose the closure "not possible" in actuality (310). This text, however, will not let the imputed causal attributions stand. At the end of the account of Curt Lemon's death, O'Brien appends a narrative interpolation, explaining that what interrupts his sleep two decades after the event is "Dave Jensen singing 'Lemon Tree'" as they tossed down "the parts" (89). Dave's humor, probably a means of self-protection, nevertheless deflects an automatic assignment of blame. Similarly, previous details about some of Curt's playful "pranks" disrupt his reception as an innocent character. In the condoling letter Rat writes to Curt's sister, he describes a terrifying incident he thinks of as funny. One "spooky" Halloween night, Curt smeared his naked body in different colors of paint. Wearing little more than a "weird mask," he went off to trick-or-treat in a nearby ville, "just boots and balls and an M-16" (76).

As a conclusion to the description of Rat's actions, O'Brien condenses the general reaction of the men into another gnomic aside by Jensen, who declares the brutality "amazing" and absolutely original (87). The awful humor of Jensen's song and his appreciative acknowledgement of the strange novelty of Rat's performance both undercut the causal efficacy of the sequence, which is in fact denied sequentiality by its placement within a fiction organized as an essay on writing the war story. And even while reacting with shock and sadness to the extensive catalogue of assaults on the body parts of the baby water buffalo, a reader may respond with irreverence to the exaggeration of the attenuated murder, an unwilling recognition of the kind of overstatement that signals a gag rather than a tragedy.

This subversion of narrative causality is further reinforced as O'Brien alternates accounts of action with lectures on the postmodern tests of a "true war story" that are exemplified in "How to Tell a True War Story": It cannot moralize or generalize; it will probably be obscene and most certainly embarrassing; and it will overturn convictions by muddling oppositional categories of truth and fiction, good and evil, and love and war (77, 84, 89, 90). The effect of the true war story will be to replace certainty with confusion.

As parallel scenes of descriptive violence, the deaths of Curt Lemon and the baby water buffalo are meant to suggest opposed explications of guilt and innocence. But the postmodern sabotage of the codes of reception of these scenes confronts the complexity of moral responsibility that the conventional war story may evade through the narrative attribution of cause and effect. In "The Things They Carried," Mitchell Sanders contends that the events of that story imply a "definite moral." When another soldier responds that he cannot extrapolate a meaning, Sanders counters, "There it *is,* man" (13–14). The contrasting presentations of thematic and formal violence in "How to Tell a True War Story"—evocative description set against subversive representation—substitute ethical uncertainty for the accessible "moral" of traditional storytelling, the structural equivalent to the univocal conclusion of the narrative contest defined by Scarry and Fussell.

O'Brien also gives Mitchell Sanders the last word on the slaughter of the water buffalo: "'Garden of Evil,'" he declares. In Vietnam, all sins are "original" (86). For R. W. B. Lewis the quintessential American story begins with a renovated Adam in the "Garden of Innocence" located in the geographic region he imagines is a "new" world, a mythic assumption O'Brien disputes in "Sweetheart of the Song Tra Bong." Lewis's Adam is the "hero of a new adventure: an individual emancipated from history . . . standing alone, self-reliant and self-propelling, ready to confront whatever awaited" (5). But O'Brien's protagonists' participation in the violence of Vietnam serves to annul such self-serving illusions of originality, confident self-control, as well as innocence.

For Tobey C. Herzog, in *Vietnam Stories: Innocence Lost,* the traditional theme of the initiation of a military protagonist into the depravity of war dominates central texts of literature on Vietnam, a premise O'Brien's fiction significantly complicates. The narrative of war, according to Fussell, proceeds in three mythic stages: (1) "preparation" for war, usually based on inappropriate romanticized models; (2) participation in battle, which is "characterized by disenchantment and loss of innocence"; and (3) the resultant "consideration" of the experience of war (*Great War* 130).

O'Brien's representation of the Vietnam War differs from this pattern, first, in that there is never innocence to be lost. In all three of his accounts—the memoir, his novel *Going after Cacciato* (1978), and in *The Things They Carried*—the main character cooperates with the government despite his ethical objections to the Vietnamese conflict because of an inability to face social opprobrium if he does not do so. As the narrator of "On the Rainy River" confides, "I was a coward, I went to the war" (*Things* 63). Secondly, O'Brien departs from Fussell's schema in that the dehumanizing preparation for the war in the boot camp in *If I Die* is coextensive with, not different from, the war itself; for O'Brien the war in Vietnam is the exaggeration of his nation's basic principles.

Certainly *The Things They Carried,* like the World War I literature Fussell examined, evaluates the experience of war, but O'Brien's evaluation is less decisive and more inclusive. According to Wayne Miller in *An Armed America,* stories of the Great War define the social system, not the soldier, as blameworthy: In "a world in which traditional political and social values have lost meaning . . . one seeks one's separate peace" (102). Although outraged by war, the literary doughboy emerges morally intact.

The contemplation of violence in "Sweetheart of the Song Tra Bong," however, does not allow the soldier the illusions of separation from a morally deficient culture nor abdication of personal responsibility. Postmodern in execution, this story is a compendium of references to other stories, especially those reflecting contemporary ideological assumptions about war. The setting, an encampment containing a small field hospital alongside a tent full of Special Forces soldiers, recalls two popular narratives of the Vietnam period, *M*A*S*H* and *The Green Berets,*[8] which reflect opposite strategies of assimilation of the violence of Vietnam. The first, a movie and a popular television series still rerunning, addresses the need to contain the disturbing reality of death and gore, available to stateside civilians in hitherto unknown quantities via television news. The *M*A*S*H* medics, who only sporadically treat the bodies of wounded men from the distant front lines of the Korean Conflict, spend most of their time in eccentric and playful disengagement from the expectations and red tape of the military establishment. Not only does the medical narrative repeatedly suggest that the physical damage inflicted by war can be repaired by well-intentioned Americans, it asserts through the zany antics of *M*A*S*H* characters that even participants in war, like Hemingway heroes, can maintain separate positions of moral integrity.

The second reference is to *The Green Berets,* the 1967 motion picture concocted by Hollywood and Washington in support of the ongoing war in Vietnam. In this update of John Wayne's previous roles, violence is not evaded but embraced. The American soldiers under Wayne, a Special Forces colonel, fight decisively and heroically for democracy, confident that the South Vietnamese support their intervention and that the North Vietnamese deserve technologically sophisticated extermination, certainties not universal among actual soldiers.[9] "Missing from this view," according to Herzog, "are the difficult moral issues involved with war: the moments of self-revelation on the battlefield; the confessions of fear, brutal instincts, and frustrations; and the questions of personal responsibility for violent actions" (24).

In "Sweetheart of the Song Tra Bong," O'Brien inserts an innocent American girl between these twin idylls of denial and endorsement. Scripting an apocryphal military daydream, O'Brien has one of the young medics transport his seventeen-year-old girlfriend from the States to the war. The point of the story is not just that Mary Anne Bell—a pretty blond, fresh from high school—loses her innocence, but that her loss speaks to the general ethical confusion of the war in Vietnam.[10]

According to Rat Kiley, who narrates her story, Mary Anne's transformation typifies that of any participant in the war. She begins her visit filled with dreams and goals dictated by American values. She believes that she and her boyfriend will marry, live together in a perfect home, produce three perfect children, and after a long fulfilling life, expire in one another's arms to share eternity in "the same walnut casket. That was the plan" (106). Soon, however, the young woman begins to change. Her immitigable curiosity leads her into contact with the Vietnamese countryside and the practices and procedures of both the camp's medics and its resident green berets. By the end of the second week she has begun to help treat the wounded and later begins to learn the tricks of the military trade.

As a result of her new experience, Mary Anne's appearance and her personality are transformed. She forswears cosmetics, manicures, and jewelry. She even cuts off her pretty hair to don a "green bandanna" (109). More important than the physical modification is the girl's characterological transformation. She doesn't laugh as often, her voice seems to deepen as she talks less but more forcefully, and even her face takes on a new focus and intelligence. At this point, Mary Anne no longer expresses the same expectations for the future with her lover, whom she leaves in order to participate in the *Apocalypse Now*-type military exploits of the "Greenies." Finally, she leaves them too, crossing "to the other side." To her stateside culottes and cute "pink sweater," she has added an accessory from Vietnam: "a necklace of human tongues." Assimilating the essence of Vietnam, she has redefined herself in terms of pure violence: "dangerous. She was ready for the kill" (125).

Converting the archetypal tale of a young man's initiation into the male mystery of violence to the story of a young girl on a whimsical visit opens it to fresh interpretation. The first explanation, supplied by the narrator, follows Fussell's model of the conversion of innocence to experience: She experienced what everyone did. "You come over clean and you get dirty and then afterward it's never the same" ("Sweetheart" 123). Thus, in a single stroke, O'Brien not only demolishes the masculine mystique of the violence of war as the litmus test for manhood, but also suggests deeper implications. Mary Anne's transformation is the consequence of an appeal that varies among Americans in Vietnam in intensity, but not in kind. She is presumably particularly vulnerable because her circumscribed feminine role as the archetypal American girl next door has not allowed her any access to the intoxicating excitement of masculine settings. Her previous exclusion from the operating theater or the battlefield makes the danger of Vietnam as addictive as heroin.

In place of the ideological containment of violence suggested by the M*A*S*H allusion or its sentimental celebration in the John Wayne movie, O'Brien offers an analytic depiction of its appeal that functions as a powerful criticism of normative American values. Besides the rejection of war as masculine ritual, "Sweetheart of the Song Tra Bong" posits a kind of falseness of national experience, especially feminine socialization. The existential authenticity encountered through the danger and physical extremes imposed by war is the source of its attraction. Yet, as Mary Anne's induction illustrates, the war is clearly destructive as well as empowering. That she, or any other American, can only encounter personal potential and visionary "truth" in the national practice of institutionalized death is the story's most disturbing implication. When she accuses her boyfriend of insularity, she expresses a key ethical argument of *The Things They Carried:* hidden in a "little fortress, behind wire and sandbags . . . you don't know what it's all about" (121). In "Sweetheart of the Song Tra Bong" the concept of innocence—presented as the absence of the experience of moral complexity—is rejected as a legitimate basis for morality.[11]

The stories of *The Things They Carried* represent violence in terms of opposing narrative possibilities: the unplottable experience contrasting the implicit order of "The Things They Carried"; the narrative sequence against the postmodern dislocation of "How to Tell a True War Story"; and the containing and exploiting myths invoked in "Sweetheart of the Song Tra Bong." What emerges is not another ameliorating instance of the "loss of innocence"—war imagined as something imposed on soldiers rather than enacted by them (and us)—nor even a clarification of what is right and wrong. The first story introduces the moral burden of war; the second insists on the provisional nature of the process of ethical inquiry; and the third deconstructs the categories through which such judgments are conventionally assigned: guilt and innocence, self and other, male and female. O'Brien's contradictory depictions of violence produce the thematic assertion of the moral confusion imposed by the war, and his manipulations of textual conventions violate the comfortable reception of war modeled by its traditional depiction as a test of courage, a mode of heroism, or an assertion of superiority and virtue. Instead, O'Brien's representational divergence demands the perhaps impossible ethical interrogation of the violence of Vietnam.

Like Dave Jensen, the soldier amazed by the originality of experience in Vietnam, critics have been astounded by Tim O'Brien's apparent newness. His narratives of war have been variously labeled as postmodernism; magic realism; "faction," a combination of fact and fiction; even "fictive irrealism."[12] But these metafictive labels stress his stunning epistemological effects at the expense of his troubling ethical achievement. In "The Vietnam in Me," an essay published in 1994 on the twenty-fifth anniversary of his tour of duty, Tim O'Brien emphasizes the disturbing moral legacy of the American war in Vietnam. In addition to revealing the painful symptoms of his own continuing confusion—isolation, nightmares, depression, suicidal impulses—O'Brien expresses his outrage at the massacre at My Lai by soldiers of Charlie Company on March 16, 1968, two years before he served in the same region. But he reserves his severest condemnation for the moral abdication of the United States in reaction to such incidents.

He hated everything, he reports—the dirt, "the tunnels," the landscape, even himself; and this "self-hatred" combined with "self-betrayal." He "rarely" sympathized with the Vietnamese people, because he was too frightened. And fearing his own death, after battles and the deaths of friends, he was mostly so angry he really did want to take the anguish out, like Rat Kiley, "on anything" that was available. As a result, O'Brien confides, he can understand what happened at May Lai. "I know the boil that precedes butchery." But he is quick to add that the men of the company in which he served "did not commit murder . . . did not cross that conspicuous line between rage and homicide." It is because ethical distinctions are possible, "because truth matters" even in war, that O'Brien feels "betrayed by a nation that so widely shrugs off barbarity, by a military justice system that treats murderers and common soldiers as one and the same. Apparently we're all innocent—those who exercise moral restraint and those who do not, officers who control their troops and officers who do not. In a way America has declared *itself* innocent" (53).

The necessity for moral evaluation is the central issue of *The Things They Carried*. What Scarry calls "the intolerable duality" of the narrative structure of war, which becomes the unitary moral certainty that assigns absolute righteousness to "us" and complete culpability to "them," is precisely what O'Brien's strategic sabotage of certainty is meant to forestall. For it is only through the unflinching willingness to evade the consoling simplicity built in to the formulaic war narrative that genuine responsibility can be attempted. And for O'Brien, author of the war stories in *If I Die in a Combat Zone* and *Going after Cacciato,* as well as those of *The Things They Carried,* it is the telling, the retelling, of war stories that leads to the possibility of the scrupulous analysis to which he is committed: "All you can do is tell it one more time, patiently, adding and subtracting, making up a few things to get at the real truth," (*Things* 91) which is a truth not just of texture but of accountability.

"Because Truth Matters"

Although there is no single defining plot for the American war story, there is an array of typical motifs: the noble example, the test of courage, the battle as initiation, the collective adventure of the platoon, and the disjunctive return to the civilian world. Too often, however, as Hanley argues, traditional tropes have been turned into formulas through which violence is encoded as a desirable course of action presenting war experience as male, agentless intensification—the chief social activity through which "winners" are determined. Because it supports the narrative project of war, the generic story of war is defined by its uncritical manipulation of military violence, but the literature of war I am describing is distinguished by its refusal to employ violence in the service of unexamined beliefs.

The pressure toward simplification and closure imposed by the narrative structure of war is also reflected in influential literary criticism of the Vietnam story. Sandra M. Wittman's 1989 *Writing about Vietnam: A Bibliography of the Vietnam Conflict* has over seventeen hundred entries, and they are still coming. But despite the unprecedented number of texts, which indicates that the question of Vietnam remains vitally open, some critics propose "answers" to settle the matter once and for all. Although Philip Beidler, in his 1982 *American Literature and the Experience of Vietnam,* notes the "manic contradiction" and "bizarre juxtaposition" of key works (4), he evidently distrusts the openness these devices introduce. Lamenting the inconclusiveness of American responses to Vietnam, he demands: "How, then, might one come up with some form of sensemaking for this thing—this experience already cast in the image of some insane metafiction recreating itself in actual life—and in the process find some reason to believe that the effort might be of some literary or cultural significance?" (10). In order to establish a "visionary myth" that fixes the "memory" of a "Vietnam more real than reality" (85),[13] Beidler, like Philip H. Melling and Owen W. Gilman Jr., equates fiction about the American war to Puritan and classic literature of early American imperialism. This tendency toward closure is so prevalent that Don Ringnalda describes his *Fighting and Writing in Vietnam* (1994) as "atypical" and "dissenting" largely because of his insistence "that the last thing that America needs to do with the experience in Vietnam is to make sense of it" (ix).[14]

In the literature of past wars, the simplified "sense" of the war narrative has been resisted through literary deployments of the very sensemaking apparatus used for wartime propaganda. Hemingway's concrete prose style deflated the literary pretension of political rhetoric of World War I. World War II, the first war subject to official narration by the publicity industry, was countered through the exploitation of public forms—the extended treatment of a joke, the "Catch 22" of Joseph Heller's title, and the alternative fantasy of science fiction in Kurt Vonnegut's *Slaughterhouse-Five*.[15] Both these operations are ironic in that one code of meaning contradicts another. However, because the second code in each case operates as an alternative source of a truth denied by the dominant code, irony has been inadequate to the essential confusion of the Vietnam experience. *The Things They Carried* and *The Pugilist at Rest* resist even the possibility of authenticity irony implies.

Vietnam, mediated by the TV news, as Beidler notes despairingly, was received by its combatants through the narrative formulas of television melodrama: "cartoons, commercials, cowboys, comedians and caped crusaders . . . child-world dreams of aggression and escape mixed up with moralistic fantasies" (11). This mode of reception conforms to postmodernism, the representational practice, which, according to Peter Brooker's provisional definition, "splices high with low culture," "raids and parodies past art," "questions absolutes" and "swamps reality in a culture of recycled images" (3). The spirit of popularized representation that Beidler deplores is actually the basis for the productive treatments of the Vietnam War by O'Brien and Jones.

Although Fredric Jameson decries Vietnam as the "first terrible post-modernist war [that] cannot be told in any of the traditional paradigms of the war novel or the war movie" ("Postmodernism" 176), Cornell West maintains postmodernism may serve as a source of social redefinition: "acknowledgement of the reality one cannot not know" (218). The thematic and formal innovations of Jones and O'Brien serve this goal. Their Vietnam literature juxtaposes the referential sphere of culture to the experiential sphere of the suffering and death imposed by war. What results from the gap between them is indeed "truth"—not the reflection of reality, but an invitation to engage in ethical revision.

Specifically, in *The Pugilist at Rest* "truth" proceeds from violence presented as contradiction that alienates the immature warrior from a society that does not address the perplexities introduced by his experience. In the Vietnam War, Tom does not enter the violent resolution represented by death, nor can he, having experienced the contradictions presented by the story, adopt resolution through violent identification with paternal culture. He emerges as intellectually and emotionally uncertain. In *The Things They Carried,* "the reality one cannot not know" comes from the evasion of premature thematic closure that subverts conventional stories of war in order to open the questions of responsibility. Such questions are introduced through tactics like the depiction of Vietnam as a moral landscape that challenges preconceptions. The tunnels, the allegorical hell carried over from *Going after Cacciato* and the shit field of "In the Field," "Field Trip," "Speaking of Courage," and "Notes" perform this function. The thematic concern about uncertain allocation of moral responsibility evident in "The Things They Carried" also informs the plots of "In the Field," and "Field Trip." And the difficulty of establishing an ethical perspective is expressed in stories that illustrate moral dialectics as process—"On the Rainy River" and "Sweetheart of the Song Tra Bong"—and in stories that operate as dialectical examinations of moral responsibility—"The Man I Killed," "Ambush," and "Night Life."

Both Jones and O'Brien also directly defy the premise of masculine development through violence, which is such an important feature of war adventure. By including themselves as characters in their own fiction they each deny the determinant identity supposedly secured through military violence. Although *The Pugilist at Rest* is fiction, by naming his protagonist "Tom," Thom Jones implies autobiographical overlap. About the presence of the soldier "Tim O'Brien" in *The Things They Carried,* the author told an interviewer that "All along, I knew I wanted to have a book in which my name, Tim, would appear even though that Tim would not be me" (61). Both these fictions insert the authors' names as signals of unequivalence to a historical self.

Concerned with both violence in culture and violence as culture, the deliberately indeterminate war literature of Thom Jones and Tim O'Brien confronts the false assumption that ideology and violence somehow add up to "truth." Similarly, the next two chapters decenter the murder mystery and the contemporary epic. The former considers misconstructions of "black power," while the latter deconstructs male violence as "white mythology."

6

DETECTING POWER

Ernest Gaines's A Gathering of Old Men *and*
Walter Mosley's Devil in a Blue Dress

"One should try to locate power at the extreme points of its exercise," advises Michel Foucault, "where it is always less legal in character," where it is "completely invested in its real and effective practices" ("Two Lectures" 97). Stories of detection, which investigate the extreme instances of extralegal violence, may therefore be understood as pertinent inquiries into the practical operation of power. Thus, crime fiction, contemporary critics argue, is a particularly apt medium for the negotiation of racial inequities.[1] Ernest Gaines's revision of the classical detective story in *A Gathering of Old Men* (1983) and Walter Mosley's adaptation of the hard-boiled genre in *Devil in a Blue Dress* (1990), the first volume in his Easy Rawlins mystery series, stage examinations of the new possibilities for black empowerment in the aftermath of the civil rights struggle and the Second World War, respectively.

Law and Disorder

In a recent article on Ernest Gaines's fiction, Joseph Griffin alludes dismissively to the "'whodunit' nature" of *A Gathering of Old Men* (38), but Gaines himself has noted in comments about the film version of the novel that from the first scene "it's supposed to be a mystery" (Saeta and Skinner 249). In fact, Gaines's revision of the white classic detective genre in a novel of black experience speaks to confounding racial problems: how to realize black male self-respect, value black community, and oppose discrimination dictated by white law and custom. These issues come together in a murder mystery of criminal investigation and resolution when a group of old black men "confess" to homicide. Through that assertion they unite to protect one of their number from retribution for what they believe to be his murder of a white man. The violent act by one of their own engenders a new recognition of shared exploitation and shame that is acknowledged and overcome through an act of collective responsibility, and their own violence at the climax of the novel is an assertion of recovered manhood that puts into question the social and legal system that has produced their unmanning. This change from passivity to activity, acceptance to rejection, powerlessness to power through the collective actions of the male "gathering" is structured through an amended process of detection. The classic detective genre produces a special kind of knowledge out of the consideration of violent acts. Gaines adapts this epistemological emphasis to an inquiry into the conditions of black power and modifies the detective formula to their representation.

A complete account of "the criminal act and its expiation" would include, according to Dennis Porter, attention to "the preparation for the crime, the crime itself, the investigation of the crime, the arrest of the criminal, the trial of the criminal and his punishment, which may mean his execution" (122), but the classic detective plot described by Cawelti is limited to six phases: "(a) introduction of the detective; (b) crime and clues; (c) investigation; (d) announcement of the solution; (e) explanation of the solution; (f) denouement" (*Adventure* 81–82). The formula for detective fiction significantly abridges the full process by emphasizing investigation and explanation at the expense of more complete consideration in order to deflect interest from the criminal to the detective and from the crime to its solution. This traditional formula turns the range of meanings expressed by criminal violence and communal response into a pattern of violence that constructs and reaffirms existing social authority. *A Gathering of Old Men,* however, employs the whole range of narrative features outlined by Porter. By significantly changing the style and content of the narration, rescinding the control usually reserved for the detective, and by revising the conventional conclusion, Gaines reconstructs racial power relations.

Gaines's most important alteration of the classic pattern is to include the criminal and to substitute the perpetrator's explanation of the crime—its provocation and its effects—for the classic detective's recitation of his own ratiocination. In spite of "clues" that all point to the guilt of Mathu, a highly respected eighty-year-old black man, it turns out that the "murder" was actually committed by Charlie Biggs, who returns from an attempted escape to reveal the circumstances of the crime. Having for years taken his employer's constant verbal and physical abuse despite his own extraordinary size, strength, and competence, on his fiftieth birthday Charlie reaches a turning point: "Long as I was Big Charlie, nigger boy, I took it," but, as he tells the sheriff, when a man is halfway to one hundred he should be treated with respect (189). When Beau Boutan, his Cajun boss, beat Charlie with a stalk of sugar cane, he fought back. When Boutan exchanged the cane stalk for a gun, Charlie found the courage to defend himself with Mathu's shotgun.

This story of the realization of black manhood through aggressive resistance is as old as the figure of the noble African who fights back in the slave narrative. Frederick Douglass, its best-known exemplar, recounts how after exhausting all other avenues of succor, he beat Mr. Covey, the "slave-breaker," in a two-hour battle. Having reclaimed his "manhood," Douglass "resolved that however long I might remain a slave in form, the day had passed forever when I could be a slave in fact. I did not hesitate to let it be known that the white man who succeeded in whipping me, must also succeed in killing me" (298, 299). Likewise, Charlie demands that henceforth he be addressed as "Mr. Biggs," and he returns to Mathu's cabin to deflect the blame he knows will fall on the man who has acted the part of father to him because a "nigger boy" will run away. "But a man" returns, and he is a man (187).

What makes this narrative so powerful in *A Gathering of Old Men* is that it recapitulates the stories told by many of the other "suspects" in the crime. Mat speaks of a brother who died because he was not admitted to a white hospital (38); Jacob Aguillard mourns his sister, who, as Cherry recalls, played around with both white and black men and was murdered because the whites "wanted her" for themselves (45). Billy tells of the beating that drove his son insane (80); Ding, the abuse of his niece (88); and Coot, the assault to the dignity he earned as a soldier (103–04). Yank describes the loss of his livelihood and his self-respect when he could no longer earn a living breaking horses after the Cajun farmers introduced tractors (98). Tucker describes how the Cajuns beat his brother to death after he had the temerity to win a race between his mules and Felix Boutan's tractor.

The motif of extreme abuse of black body and black spirit culminates in Gable's story of his son's execution on a trumped-up charge of rape. When the electric chair malfunctioned, the white guards shoved the dazed prisoner back into a cell until they could get someone from Baton Rouge to fix it, explaining that he wasn't dead yet, but he soon would be. And white neighbors informed the grieving parents that their son should have been grateful to die in the electric chair instead of "at the end of a rope" (101–02).[2] Besides victimization, these tales have in common the shame of the survivors for their inability to intervene. As Tucker explains, while white men battered his brother to death, he wasn't able to do anything but stand aside helplessly and "watch." His auditors share his guilt. They had all seen the degradation of brothers, sisters, fathers, and mothers and done nothing about it (97).[3]

The narratives not only recount white cruelty, they also acknowledge black powerlessness. This recitation is preparation for the acts of resistance—each of the would-be suspects claims responsibility for Beau's death, and each fights back against Klansmen bent on revenge—through which they redeem their lost agency. In addition to their common victimization, all the self-designated "criminals" share the same process of acknowledgement, resistance, and recovery. And, like Charlie, each of the old men apparently experiences this redemption through an assertion of control that is partly the result of violence. But more important, their salvation is an effect of the general dissemination of the kind of knowledge detective fiction restricts to the detective. In the classic detective story, the detective himself retains the power to interpret the situation. In *A Gathering of Old Men,* the substitution of the redemptive narratives of the "perpetrators" for the rational solution by the detective redistributes the authority of knowledge.

If the first revision is to the detective process, the second is to its central figure—the detective himself. Just as Gaines shifts the focus from the explanatory power of the traditional detective, he also displaces the detective's role in the pursuit of the enigma, initially to a diverse chorus of observers and then to an ineffectual sheriff who can neither fully comprehend the crime nor control its investigation.

Instead of depicting the authoritative detective who traditionally introduces the adventure, Gaines's book starts with an energetic black child who is supposed to be "protected" from knowledge about crime. In place of the certainty of the detective hero, Snookum reflects the uncertainty of the reader. For despite his prescribed innocence, Snookum is obviously curious about the secrets of the adult world. He has been caught by his brother "playing mama and papa in the weeds" (3) with Minnie, and it is he who provides the first glimpse of the murder at the center of the plot: Beau Boutan lying "in the weeds all bloody" (4). Those figurative "weeds" of sex and violence may also imply the unacknowledged interests motivating the detective audience's exploration of tabooed experience.[4] In the classic detective genre, the reader, protected by the detective's commitment to the morality of the dominant society, can encounter that which is forbidden, safe in the expectation that "right" will prevail. Gaines's beginning, although humorous, omits such reassurance. In A Gathering ethical attitudes are not prescribed in advance through generic formula: moral revision may occur.

A proper reaction to the crime is frequently mediated by a detective's representative, like Dr. Watson, whom Sherlock Holmes authorizes to speak in his stead. In Gaines's novel, however, there are thirteen different character perspectives from which the story is told in nineteen short chapters, and none of the actors in the central drama of the crime speaks directly. The words and actions of Mathu, Charlie, Candy, Fix and his sons, and Sheriff Mapes are reported through the limited perspectives of a veritable chorus of black and white participant observers. In the absence of the often mistaken but steady advancement of the classic detective's singular representative, there is also no formal assurance in A Gathering of Old Men of an eventual resolution of the dangerous possibilities raised by the crime itself. In place of the alternation between the reader's pursuit of false leads and the detective's interpretation of clues in the standard work, Gaines's whole novel is a "red herring." Amid the confusing welter of characters, Charlie, whose absence is merely noted, is the most unexpected of culprits. But the uncertainty produced by the form greatly exceeds its function in the production of conventional suspense to support a theme of revolutionary possibility. In effect, Gaines's novel formally rejects the classic maintenance of undeviating standards, the thematic purpose of the detective's resolution, for the disruption of a destructive pattern—the traditional Southern system of white authority and black acquiescence.

Eventually, the white sheriff does assume the role usually reserved for the detective "in charge" of the investigation, but his demotion is an important device of the novel: Sheriff Mapes, like the audience and almost all the participants, thoroughly misunderstands the crime, and he is completely unable to control its effects. Mapes, himself sixty years old and still a large and powerful man, is capable of respecting an individual like Mathu for his past displays of courage, but unable to imagine any alternative to racial domination. He expects the black old men to be craven in the face of his physical and legal authority, and he expects Beau Boutan's father, Fix, a Klan leader, to exact his revenge for the death of his son. But although the black community is still centered in the slave quarters of an old plantation, the novel is set in 1979 and change *is* possible. The old men do not crumble and Fix Boutan does not ride.

The sheriff's blindness to black capability is asserted when Johnny Paul exclaims, "you don't see what we don't see" (89). Looking at the ruins of the slave cabins, the sheriff observes only the "weeds" of deterioration. The gathered black people, on the other hand, perceive a positive heritage of survival, an ethic of hard work and sharing that produced not weeds but "flowers" (90). Johnny Paul is sustained by memories of agrarian cooperation when the black community "stuck together . . . loved and respected" one another (91–92).

Cawelti allows that it is "possible" to write a detective adventure without a detective provided someone assumes his responsibility (132). He traces the pattern of multiple narration, unusual in the detective story, from Wilkie Collins's *The Moonstone.* But this early pattern of shared narration, which proceeds to clear resolution, is contradicted by modernist practice. Despite the efforts of multiple narrators, William Faulkner's *The Sound and the Fury* is fragmentary and discontinuous to the end, Cawelti observes. The novel finally demonstrates a situation too complicated "to be understood from a single unified point of view" (*Adventure* 88).

Gaines has frequently credited Faulkner as a technical influence while denying an affinity of philosophies.[5] Whereas Faulkner uses the multiple point of view to suggest the disintegration of the old South reflected in the psyches of its citizens, who speak separately because they are incapable of unity, Gaines uses overlapping perspectives to reaffirm the shared history and values of a vital black community. Reflecting both traditional and modernist usage, the chorus of partial observations in *A Gathering of Old Men* produces both traditional and modernist effects. The many voices that share in the production of the narrative, the different visions that cooperate in the interpretation of events, combine to express both a unifying commonality of suffering and survival among blacks and to reveal a divisive political climate among whites.

In Ernest Gaines's Louisiana it was the rising poor whites of French Arcadian extraction,[6] the Cajuns with new methods of mechanized farming, who, unlike the weak descendants of the slave owners, most threatened their economic rivals, the black sharecroppers who had to rely on traditional tools and methods. But historically, the Cajuns, like the blacks, were an underclass, a "breed below" (122), as Gil Boutan reminds Candy, one of the present owners of the former plantation. Comparable prejudices against them by the white upper class may provide the incentive for the bond between Gil and a young black man with whom he plays football on a championship team at Louisiana State University. It is on the basis of this winning "Salt and Pepper" alliance that Gil rejects his father's vigilante past: In the 1970s, soon to be the 1980s, the practices of previous decades are "gone forever." (143). Without his youngest son's allegiance, Fix decides not to act against the black men who have killed his eldest. And although a remnant of die-hard Klansmen do attack the old men, they are defeated by an unexpected display of black force.

"I represent the law," Sheriff Mapes asserts (83), but it is a law sanctioned by white supremacy supported by Klan violence. And the hierarchical racial and ethnic relationships sustained by this law are in the process of transformation. The period when the Klan could "take the law into [its] hands" is over, Gil tells his father (143). The sheriff's capability to manipulate the traditional system of order through oppression fails when the old men insist, despite his physical abuse, that they are all guilty of the crime he has come to arrest Mathu for. As a result, the sheriff is deeply confused, because having employed his limited knowledge about how to deal with black people—"knocking them around"— he discovers he doesn't know what to do. When the old men unexpectedly counter his method by lining up to suffer his abuse, he merely stands "there, a big fat red hulk, looking down at the ground" (93).

To Mapes's credit, although he does not have the power to prevent it, he does wish to avoid a confrontation between the Klan and the old men. But when it comes, he is totally unable to manage it. As he explains at the trial that concludes the novel: After being shot in the first volley, "The whole fight I was sitting on my ass" (213). The effect of this devolution of the detective figure is a direct challenge to the authority and power of the institution of white law at the heart of the text.

"Wherever it appears, detective fiction always forms part of the 'discourse of the Law,'" asserts Porter (129). The classic detective novel, especially, works to contain the forces of disorder it codes as criminal. In the traditional detective story, the "solution" to the crime extends beyond the answer to the question of "whodunit" to the support of a system of justice through which both deviation and conformity are codified. In the classic version, the solution of the crime—its announcement and explanation—brings the action to a conclusion, and the story usually terminates swiftly in a scene that reasserts the ordinary and the upbeat. Even the expanded possibilities outlined by Porter emphasize the criminal's apprehension, his trial, and his punishment.

Gaines, however, deviates from both these formulas. When the group of old men meets without white supervision in Mathu's house to acknowledge the conversion to courage the day has brought about, Clatoo argues that they should be proud of their accomplishment and end the episode. They had come to "fight 'side" of Mathu and had shown themselves willing to do so. "Gentlemen," he addresses them in recognition of their newly elevated masculine status, "Let's call it a day and go back home" (179). The story could have ended there in the bloodless tradition of the classic narrative with the resumption of benign order. But the assemblage is disappointed by this reasonable suggestion, and so too, apparently, is its author.[7] It is at this point Gaines introduces Charlie's confession, which would truly exonerate Mathu, followed immediately by a four-chapter shoot-out between the old men and the Klansmen that results in the death of Charlie and Luke Will, the new leader of the Bayonne Klan.

Why does Gaines introduce the violent "showdown," a device borrowed from the Western narrative,[8] to end what has been a detective novel? One reason, certainly, is to avoid the inevitable prosecution of Charlie under white man's justice; that is, to maintain the thematic challenge by "criminal" provocation rather than endorsing the closure of the detective genre's reassertion of the status quo. A second reason is to give the aged army its opportunity to do battle. "I wanted me a fight," Mat objected to Clatoo's argument for bloodless victory, even if he "had to get killed" to have it (181).

The book concludes in the courtroom with the exoneration of the remaining suspects and with laughter shared by both blacks and whites at the sheriff's expense, a situation that may hint at the new possibility for equality under renovated law. In the final scene, Mathu chooses to ride home with his cronies, with whom he has discovered an allegiance, instead of Candy, the white owner who has previously protected him. Mathu's gesture of independence from white patronage and his acceptance of black communal ties suggest a significant change in Southern social arrangements.

Another reason for the final scenes of violence may lie in the contradictions the novel raises without being able to resolve. Does the new authority of the black man the text proposes come out of the lost experience of community under slavery or reside in the future represented by the organized struggle of the LSU football game? Both of these idealized sources operate outside the real experience of powerlessness *A Gathering of Old Men* so well depicts. Is manhood as Gaines portrays it the beginning of real social reformation or an ideology that introduces another version of constructive violence in place of political change?

With special reference to *A Gathering of Old Men,* Gaines defines "manliness" as "that moment when it is necessary to be human—it's that moment when you refuse to back down. Your conscience will not allow you to back down. . . ; dignity demands that you act" (Saeta and Skinner 242). The novel masterfully exemplifies this definition of manhood as the assertion of self-respect whatever the cost, but the plot suggests that the occasions for such assertions are rare. "This was the day," says Johnny Paul, "we was go'n get even." They would "never gather this way again," Mat declares (181). If "manliness" so defined is to be the cornerstone of racial dignity, violent contestation must be repeated, and often.

The appeal of the Western in this context is that it is structured through the narration of serial contests of male violence that establish masculine authority. The classic detective story, by contrast, formally suppresses violence by omitting a graphic description of the initial crime and rationalizing the motivations of the criminal to quash any challenge to the social standard the genre endorses. Gaines's manipulation of both these traditions finds expression in concluding scenes of a comic battle followed by a comic trial. Although he apparently endorses the masculine empowerment through violence advanced by the cowboy genre and the recovery of civil order promoted by the classic detective genre, the humorous tone of these scenes undercuts the certainty of either outcome.

Gaines's structural ambiguity is part of a continuing black narrative response to historical violence traced in Jerry H. Bryant's *Victims and Heroes: Racial Violence in the American Novel.* In contradiction to the constructive violence often perpetrated on a racial other in the white adventure tradition, according to Bryant, black writers are ambivalent about thematic violence, using it both to express white brutality and assert black manhood. Gaines's use of humor in presenting the cowboy motif questions the efficacy of violence in the struggle for racial dignity, while the mocking representation of institutionalized white justice undercuts its promise as the solution for racial injustice.

If Ernest Gaines cannot finally solve the problems of racial and ethnic inequality through thematic violence, his formal deviations from the traditional formula of the classic detective story certainly do demonstrate the redemptive value of narrative process, epitomize the cohesion of the black community, and introduce the democratization of knowledge further explored by Walter Mosley in his adaptation of the hard-boiled detective formula.

Knowledge/Power in *Devil in a Blue Dress*

Originating in the 1920s, the American hard-boiled detective story is similar to its classic British counterpart in organization, but dissimilar in content. It begins with the introduction of the detective, sets him into action in pursuit of a mystery that turns into a crime, trails him through a convoluted investigation, and concludes with the solution of the crime. The differences derive from setting—the corrupt underworld of the modern city instead of the potentially pastoral British country house or even the rural Louisiana county of Gaines's invention. In place of imposing rational discovery, the hard-boiled hero experiences bewildering initiation into the violence just under an urbane surface. Unlike the cool and remote classic detective, the hard-boiled variant is understandably human in his confusions and disappointments. For with only toughness and temerity to guide him, he is trying to fashion an ad hoc morality from the lost ethics of an impure world. The system of justice he encounters is damaged but not beyond repair. And it is his job to somehow mend it.[9]

The essence of both the classic and hard-boiled detective story is the pursuit of knowledge, and the source of that knowledge is the violence that threatens civil order. The difference between the white hard-boiled detective and Walter Mosley's black detective is the ends that such knowledge serves. Despite his cynicism, a character like Raymond Chandler's Philip Marlowe is a servant of the dominant system of law and order. But Mosley's Easy Rawlins needs to learn how the operation of that system in the post–World War II period affects the power of the black man to survive and prosper.[10] This lesson takes shape, first, through a series of mentors who teach Easy about the levels and types of violent power and, finally, through an enigmatic woman whose mystery abrogates the conventional categories of his experience. His process of detection does not result in a unitary moral code; rather, the acts of violence Easy encounters call forth a bewildering variety of ethical responses. Through the adventures and the ambivalence of the black detective, *Devil in a Blue Dress* and subsequent works in the Rawlins series enact a principle Michel Foucault would recognize: that power, like law, is not an order to be retrieved but the contingent result of specific circumstances that black men may understand through violence and adapt to their own needs for respect and freedom.

If, as the saying goes, "Knowledge is power," it makes sense that the race and class in charge has sought to curtail its access. The restriction of black knowledge is historically evident, from laws against teaching slaves to read to contemporary inequities in support for education in predominantly black neighborhoods. The violation of this restriction is certainly one of the major appeals of the black detective novel. The classic detective, like Sherlock Holmes an agent of the aristocracy, puts his highly specialized knowledge to use solving lurid crimes in a manner that protects the dominant class from the threat of or responsibility for violence. By defining criminal activity as deviation, his solutions demarcate knowledge as separate from violent power. But the later hard-boiled detective, like Philip Marlowe, seeks rather than possesses knowledge, which emerges from his informed participation in the violence that surrounds him. It is this characteristic connection between knowledge and power mediated by the narrative of detection that makes it so useful in the serious attempt to define these prerogatives for black manhood in *A Gathering of Old Men,* which diverts the privilege of knowing from the classic detective to the black community, and in

Devil in a Blue Dress, which revises the meaning and source of black knowledge.

In his seminal 1845 autobiography, Frederick Douglass recounted several key means of reclaiming the manhood denied by slavery: "You have seen how a man was made a slave; you shall see how a slave was made a man" (294). The ability to earn a free wage and the participation in a supportive fraternal community are significant elements in this reversal, but even more important are Douglass's achievement of literacy and the physical defense of his own rights in a fight with an overseer.[11]

This conjunction of knowledge and force comes to fruition for Douglass in his career as an abolitionist spokesman. In *Fighting for Life,* Walter J. Ong traces the historical roots of "the alliance between masculinity" and a combative academic style (140) in a rhetorical practice of education based on the exclusionary exercise of masculine competition: "What was taught . . . was to take a stand in favor of a thesis or to attack a thesis that someone else defended." Students "learned subjects largely by fighting over them" (122–23). Douglass, who was deeply influenced by his early discovery of the ideational confrontations structuring the debate about slavery in *The Columbian Orator,* excelled in an age when public information, like education itself, was delivered in the form of verbal combat. For him acquiring knowledge and asserting masculine force were conjoined parts of the same racial struggle.[12]

As an influential writer and speaker, Douglass demonstrated power previously restricted by literacy laws largely to whites. His violation of the racial prohibitions against knowledge and physical aggression were presented in *The Life of Frederick Douglass* as linked declarations of full humanity. Yet, paradoxically, the greater educational opportunity for blacks during ensuing decades separated these two options. In contrast to Douglass's militant assertions, Booker T. Washington connected institutional learning at Tuskegee Institute with patterns of accommodation. "The wisest among my race understand that the agitation of questions of social equality is the extremest folly," he declared (37).[13]

Influential later works from different political perspectives continued to assert the divergence of knowledge and power. Although Richard Wright, unlike Washington, presented aggression as resistance to accommodation in *Native Son* (1940), in the autobiographical *Black Boy* (1944) he proposed black literacy as an alternative to violence. In his 1964 *Autobiography,* Malcolm X portrayed the continuing schism between knowledge and power in his differing perceptions of blacks in two different Boston neighborhoods in the 1940s.

In Roxbury he envied "high-class, educated, important Negroes, living well, working in big jobs and positions. Their quiet homes sat back in their mowed yards. These Negroes walked along the sidewalks looking haughty and dignified" (48). But he was also fascinated by an alternative style: "The sharp-dressed young 'cats' who hung on the corners and in the poolrooms, bars and restaurants, and who obviously didn't work anywhere completely entranced me" (51). The most important difference between the classes of "the Hill" and the ghetto is symbolized as education in Malcolm X's account of a Roxbury teenager named Laura, who "really liked school" and planned to attend college; "keen for algebra," she intended "to major in science" (71). Although her attraction to the hip style eventually leads to Laura's degradation, initially she makes him feel "let down, thinking of how I had turned away from the books I used to like when I was back in Michigan" (72).

For Malcolm the energetic black lower-class cultural style he is so attracted to leads him into a life of frenetic violence that excludes the pursuit of education, which he associates with an enervated black middle-class. In prison, however, he pursues an ambitious program of self-education, and in his later role as a race leader is able to combine the knowledge he had previously associated with the black middle classes with the force he connected to lower-class experience in the rhetorical stance of the Black Muslim movement.

As this brief analysis indicates, the terms *knowledge* and *power*, central to the detective genre, are, within the context of black culture, historically determined, racially loaded, and gender inflected. Accordingly, the meditation on these issues in Mosley's *Devil in a Blue Dress* is from the outset historicized and politicized.[14] "I was surprised to see a white man walk into Joppy's bar," the book commences. "When he looked at me I felt a thrill of fear, but that went away quickly because I was used to white people by 1948" (1). These introductory sentences suggest that former patterns of black capitulation to white authority were in the process of change in the period just after the Second World War. Thus, before the detective conundrum is even introduced, its purpose is established: the detective's discovery of an emergent black empowerment. Easy Rawlins's qualifications for the career of detection that begins in this work include a high school education, his ability to speak "proper English" but the savvy to talk in the style of the street (10) when the occasion calls for it, and his experience as a black soldier in World War II—abilities suggesting the juncture of knowledge and power the plot unfolds.

The novel's historical situation speaks to the complex inscription of power and knowledge within a changing politics of black manhood during the postwar years, a change signified by the hero's occupational dilemma. In 1948, prior to his enlistment in the detective plot, Easy had been employed at Champion, a Santa Monica airplane factory, but he had been fired as a result of white antagonism. When faced with the choice between giving in to his boss and pride in himself during an attempt to recover his job, Easy chose the latter. Insisting that he be addressed as Mr. Rawlins, Easy asserted the boss doesn't have to rehire him, but he does have to "treat" him "with respect" (66).

Easy's situation rewrites Chester Himes's *If He Hollers* (1945), in which self-respect is not an alternative for protagonist Bob Jones, who loses his job at Atlas, a Los Angeles shipyard, in 1941. Bob's impulse to preserve his pride involves him in an inescapable cycle of personal anxiety and possible violence. Although Jones reports that he had experienced racism prior to 1941, he had not comprehended it as a terrifying, universal condition until the internment of the Japanese in California: "It was taking up a man by the roots and locking him up without a chance . . . It was thinking about if they ever did that to me, Robert Jones, Mrs. Jones' darker son, that started me to get scared" (3). To control this fear, Jones constantly imagines aggression toward its racial source. During a brawl with a redneck coworker, he reports, "I wanted to kill him so he'd know he didn't have a chance. I wanted him to feel scared and powerless and unprotected as I felt every goddamned morning I woke up" (35).

Mosley's implied citation of Himes, reiterated in his choice of the black detective genre dominated by Himes,[15] introduces the change in the status afforded by black participation in World War II. Some black soldiers, despite segregation, participated in active combat, and in 1948 President Truman integrated the armed services, affording new access to what Easy calls "the kind of freedom" that "death-dealing brings" (98). Significantly, *If He Hollers* ends with Bob's conscription, whereas *Devil in a Blue Dress* starts after Easy's military service. For Bob, violence, his own or that of a bigoted community, is a constant threat; for Easy, violence becomes a source of education.

The enigma in Mosley's work addresses not the tenuous survival of blanket exclusion, the problem for Himes, but the new options of limited inclusion, the possibility of black male "respect" and "freedom" brought about by black participation in the war. Rawlins's conventional search for a missing woman in the plot is an innovative thematic attempt to explore the conditions and constraints of new historical opportunity. It is this theme that fuels the detective's rather extraordinary pursuit of knowledge and structures the novel around his encounters with a series of black and white mentors who teach him the political implications of violent practice.

One important motive for Easy's participation in the detective adventure proposed by the white lawyer Dewitt Albright is the acquisition of knowledge,[16] as this explanation by Joppy Shag, his black sponsor in the enterprise, indicates. Although Dewitt is reputedly a "tough man," Joppy explains that Easy might earn what he needs to pay his mortgage, and he "might even *learn* sumpin' from 'im" (8) [my emphasis]. During much of the novel, Easy's dogged pursuit of such learning is developed through the detection plot—his attempt to uncover the whereabouts of Daphne Monet—but his curiosity frequently seems to exceed the riddle of the story.

For example, when he is being brutally questioned by the police, and he understands that racism makes truth irrelevant in their treatment of him, Easy still insists throughout the interview on his right to understanding. Even as he is being released, he demands to "know what's goin' on" (75). And, later, during his interview with the powerful figure behind the investigation, he presses for full disclosure. In the violent world Easy has entered, knowledge has utility as both a means of self-protection and as saleable information, yet Easy's quest for information contradicts the first option in his encounter with the police and replaces the second in his interview with his employer.

This pattern of excessive knowledge is conflated in Easy's observations before one of the climactic episodes of the novel. Approaching a small and ordinary "ranch-style" house at night, Easy is aware that he cannot see its color. Although this detail is irrelevant to his criminal investigation, it has significance as part of the overall purpose of his "detective" project. He wants to "know" the "color" of the house, just as he desires to understand how "jets" can "fly" and "how long sharks" live. "There was a lot I wanted to know before I died" (196). Easy's careful observation structures a characteristic shift from pragmatic description of the style and size of the house, which could aid him in his dangerous inspection of it, to aesthetic curiosity about its color, and on to philosophical inquiry about the nature of reality as an ultimate goal evident in his final comment: "There was a lot I wanted to know before I died."

Easy's education is, however, primarily focused on one key issue: the meaning of violence. It is, after all, the violence of war that introduced new access to power, but despite his ironic nickname, Easy knows that the connection between violence and power is a difficult concept. His instruction begins when Albright and Easy share "plain old man-talk" (22) about the experience of war. Albright differentiates between the two of them on the basis of their tolerance of slaughter. Easy was able to countenance it as an act of war, but, as Albright warns him, there are others who "can kill with no more trouble than drinking a glass of bourbon" (23).

In contrast to the amoral threat implied by Albright, his second white mentor, Mr. Carter, surprises Easy by casually revealing the weaknesses everyone else hides. This unique reaction, that opposes the "fear or contempt" most people show him, Easy concludes, is the result of an unconscious racism supported by enormous wealth. Because Carter is so rich that he doesn't need to think of Easy as human, this man could "tell" him "anything" (119).

Although in *Power and Innocence: A Search for the Sources of Violence* psychologist Rollo May restricted the category of violent aggression to the desperate means employed by those who do not have access to more effective power, Mosley's fiction epitomizes a more extensive analysis of the degrees and kinds of violence itself. As Easy learns in *Devil in a Blue Dress,* the white wealthy classes employ two types of violence. Albright's direct threat of disinterested destruction is related to May's designation of "manipulative" power as the direct control of one person by another. Mr. Carter operates through what May designates "exploitative" power, the total control over others that "presupposes" without having to reveal "violence or threat of violence" toward victims who are allowed "no choice or spontaneity" (May 104–05).

Carter's wealth underwrites power so vast that it may imply rather than invoke its underlying threat.

Weaker men may employ what May defines as "competitive" power, "the power *against* another," which is characterized by one person "going up," not so much because of what he is or does, "but because his opponent goes *down*" (107). Competitive violence is exhibited by Joppy, a former boxer, who represents raw, mindless force. His main appeal, Easy comments, is "violence" (7). Although he is ostensibly Easy's friend, Joppy is revealed as a murderer who pursues only his own self-aggrandizement. Mouse, Easy's best friend and protector, embodies a skillful violence aroused when loyalties or interests are threatened. At its most altruistic, this kind of violence is related to May's positive category, "nutrient" power, because it may use aggression *for* rather than *against* another, but Mouse's aggression is also brutally self-serving. Mouse's complicated violence represents a potential the detective, himself "a trained killer," both accepts and wishes to reject.

The types of violence practiced by Joppy and Mouse suggest the restriction of black power to defensive reaction in a white world of superior control. Easy's war experience has, however, introduced him to another kind of violence, the opportunity to demonstrate male competence through a unified struggle against a common enemy. But when Easy joined the military expecting to share in the American pride advertised in recruitment publicity, he quickly discovered the reality of a segregated army. In the black division to which he was assigned, although he was taught the mechanics of killing, no one was eager to have him "spill white blood." To this end, the white officers argued that their black troops didn't possess either the necessary "discipline" or intelligence for war, but what really scared them, Easy knew, was that that black men would achieve the "freedom . . . death-dealing" may convey (98).

Disturbed by white imputations of stupidity and cowardice during his racial restriction to a desk job at the rear, Easy eventually volunteered for the invasion of Normandy and later the Battle of the Bulge. And while there was constant racial hostility in the ranks, there was also the possibility of establishing mutual respect. He didn't mind that the white soldiers "hated" him, he explains, but if they did not "respect" him, he "was ready to fight" (98).

Like Gaines's protagonists, Easy experiences the male contest as an occasion for securing respect, but unlike Gaines's novel, which seems to endorse it, Easy's tale problematizes violence. Although during the war Easy has "killed my share" of white people (94), he tries to reject aggression. He remains deeply agitated by a murder he once witnessed by Mouse, his childhood buddy. Indeed, during the course of his investigations in this novel, Easy, although frequently beaten, does not strike back. Instead, it is Mouse who takes bloody vengeance on Easy's enemies. The opposing moral positions enacted by Easy and Mouse, his alter ego, signify the novel's deep ambivalence about the expedient of black masculine violence.

The doubling that characterizes the practice of violence is also a feature of the related theme of knowledge about violence. During times of intense danger, Easy is visited by the counsel of "the voice," a vernacular source of wisdom that seems to originate in the black communal instinct for masculine self-preservation. During his first battle, the untried soldier, threatened by a sniper, hears a voice tell him to "kill that motherfucker" because if he doesn't, and manages to live, he will be "scared" all his life (98). Sometimes, however, the voice cautions wisdom instead of violence, advising him to take his time and seize his "advantage" when he gets the chance (97). He listens to the voice, Easy explains, because it always counsels him on how to "survive . . . like a man" (99).

Unlike the "voice" in *Devil in a Blue Dress,* white hard-boiled detective fiction characteristically presents clear meanings of violence. For example, in the climactic scene of *The Big Sleep,* Carmen Sternwood lures Marlowe into a place that symbolizes the industrial destruction of an American Eden. When she begins to hiss as she tries to shoot him, violence is personified as a deceptively tempting but deeply corrupt practice Marlowe tries to avoid. On the other hand, a tough guy like Mickey Spillane's Mike Hammer uses violence crudely and often to demonstrate his virility and to advance, according to Cawelti, a "primitive right-wing" attack against democratic principles (*Adventure* 183).

But the murders in *Devil in a Blue Dress* fit into neither Chandler's characteristic pattern of condemnation nor Spillane's of approbation. After Easy has slept with his friend's girl to extract some crucial information, she is killed by Joppy. Certainly Coretta's death provides the plot with an innocent victim to motivate the detective's quest, but thematically it also repudiates Easy's irresponsible sexuality, a central attribute of Spillane's hard-boiled character, as a source of authentic male power. And Daphne Monet's offstage murder of a white purveyor of little boys to homosexual clients, although it establishes her guilt in the solution of the mystery, does not establish the corruption that Marlowe's encounter with Carmen, who deteriorates from a beautiful girl into a drooling epileptic, evinces. That she shot her victim Daphne readily admits, but she also insists he really destroyed himself (202).

Mouse's murder of Joppy serves as a central instance of moral incertitude. As Easy observes it, Mouse's violence solicits a disturbing combination of both rejection and acceptance. This execution, reminiscent of Rat Kiley's torture of the water buffalo in *The Things They Carried,* motivated by greed rather than grief, is much more horrific in effect. Turning "casually," Mouse shoots his victim "in the groin." Rocking to and fro in shock and anguish, Joppy, squealing "like a seal," tries to "grab his wound," but cannot manage it because his arms are wired to the chair. Finally, Mouse shoots him in the head. One moment Joppy had two protruding eyes, but an instant later, with a second shot Mouse turns his left eye into a gaping, gory "hole." The shot propels Joppy to the floor, making his limbs quake for several minutes. In response to this brutality, Easy says he felt "cold," but because he'd seen many men die, and because he reserves his sympathy for Coretta, Easy remains a relatively dispassionate witness to Joppy's murder (201).

Michael Kowalewski notes in analyzing *Moby-Dick* the "terrifying contrast between intimacy and brutality" that conveys both a sense of the "unexpected delicacy of life that can be so easily broken" and authorial "uneasiness" about the content of his own description (12). Similarly, in this passage the "casual" control of the killer provides an emotional contrast to the graphic brutality emphasized by the animal comparison and the harrowing physical details. Mouse's actions, meant to scare Daphne into giving him the money she has stolen, are calculatedly vicious and morally inexcusable, an implication reinforced by the revelation of his gratuitous murder of Frank Green. Yet despite his own "uneasy" ambivalence, indicated by his uncomfortable physical response to both murders, Easy comes to terms with Mouse's crimes. "It was murder and I had to swallow it," he reflects, upon learning about the second death (205).

The exaggerated intensity of the description of Joppy's murder is charged with its narrator's resistance to his own moral surrender, and the contrast between casualness and brutality in the depiction of Joppy's death emphasizes Easy's characteristic vacillation about the ethical implications of violence. One source of this uncertainty may reside in the intimate location of Joppy's first wound, which is not only shocking but symbolically significant: Violence, it appears, is a vital determinant of the loss or maintenance of manhood.

As Easy's series of mentors and doubles suggest, violence is ambiguously connected with broader issues of black manhood. In the Easy Rawlins series, Odell Jones, the most important mentor, enacts a nonviolent means to the agency and esteem necessary to black masculine identity. An employed churchgoer and homeowner, he is a source of knowledge about the black community. And when in *The Red Death,* a subsequent novel, Easy misuses this information, the older man abandons his young friend, despite the fact that in the Houston neighborhood from which they both emigrated Odell had taken the orphaned Ezekiel Rawlins into his home and cared for him as a son. It is Odell's ideal of principled security that influences Easy's deep attachment to the house he is risking his own safety in order to maintain. Easy's house, like other aspects of the novel, operates paradoxically, as at once an idyllic retreat from modern urban violence and as the motive for Easy's participation in it. He accepts the detective assignment only to pay the mortgage after losing his factory job. Mosley does not treat middle-class values with the contempt of Malcolm X; instead they represent a desire for respect and freedom that must be defended, even with violence.[17]

Criminal Discourse

Of Easy's violent recurrent nightmares about Mouse, perhaps the most telling is one in which Mouse tries to draw him away from "the largest fire fight" in history by insisting that there is no good reason to perish in a "white man's war," a charge Easy counters by declaring that he fights "for freedom" (193). Black manhood in this novel is an effect of "respect" and "freedom" worth fighting for, concepts with roots in white history as well as black experience. But although Easy's concept of respect emerges from participation in American military violence, freedom is developed through the practice of black detection.

The possibility of freedom emerges through Easy's detective experience as (1) economic independence, (2) personal autonomy, and (3) the abrogation of restrictive categories of self-definition. Half of Daphne's

132

stolen money gives Easy financial security. With the equivalent of two years' worth of wages hidden away, he announces, "I was free" (212). The actual work of detecting—which in this novel moves beyond the interpretation of situations to the manipulation of circumstances to pro- duce predictable objectives—results in a new capacity for control. At one point in his investigation Easy acknowledges a sense of "great joy" that comes from a newfound sense of autonomy, because he is operat- ing on his "own terms" for the very first time (124).

Perhaps the most important concept of freedom taught through the process of detection in *Devil in a Blue Dress* is deconstructive. Easy's experience with Daphne Monet, the enigmatic woman at the center of the plot, annuls the categories through which his world is organized. Although she presents herself as a white woman in a black world, she is finally revealed as both white and black. In the love scene between Daphne and Easy, she begins by bathing him so gently he recalls his mother, who had died when Easy was eight years old; yet Daphne talks more obscenely than the coarsest of men. Daphne functions at once as a mother and a lover, and her actions connote the stereotypically mas- culine as well as the feminine. Although she lures Easy by promising to "tell" him all that he is trying to learn, he never manages to "know [her] at all personally" (180), and when Easy tries to read her for clues to the mystery of her racial identity, he is thwarted. The truth just "isn't there." The woman was a "chameleon," Easy concludes (200). She could change herself to suit the needs of any man who needed her.

Indeed, Daphne is the very figure of enigma. Her white self, Daphne Monet, is an invented persona who imagines a father who made love to her out of an appreciation of her essential nature. However, this belief is contradicted by the incestuous violation she actually experienced as Ruby Green, a little girl of mixed blood. In this doubled character, Mosley reworks the recurrent motif of the "tragic mulatta" through the hard-boiled convention of the ambiguous woman. From nineteenth- century slave narratives through the modern novel, the white features of a black female character have guaranteed her abuse at the hands of white men and often provoked her isolation from the black community, a situation frequently resulting in insanity. She therefore traditionally elicits, according to Valerie Melissa Babb, sympathy for "lack of racial identification" (33).[18] Daphne, however, although disturbed, is clearly not a figure of pathos. Instead of testifying to the necessity of maintaining the purity of the races, she suggests the power released through violations of the various social and sexual taboos she represents. In addition to confusing racial certainties, the heterosexual relationship between Daphne and Easy is shadowed by the homosexuality inherent in her masculine characteristics and the oedipal violation suggested by her maternal behavior. What Easy searches for—and finds in Daphne— is the transgression of the status quo. His identity both as a black and as a man is open to modification. Daphne, he explains was for him a closed "door" suddenly open to him (182).

The plot reveals Daphne as a murderer, which explains Easy's rejection of her, but fails to account for the depth of his conflicting attraction. In the typical noir plot, the detective is drawn to the beautiful temptress whom he finally repudiates as the quintessence of the violent and corrupt world that has shaped her. Easy's ambivalence is, however, related to Daphne's more complex thematic function. As the register of semiotic negation, herself an unclassifiable term, she destabilizes the hierarchical oppositions that both constrain and support Easy as a black man. His love affair with her as a white woman rejects sexually imposed restriction based on white superiority. At the same time, because this episode invokes the generic convention of the tough-guy hero's sexual potency, it raises questions about the validity of masculine dominance. Daphne's anarchic potential, her personification of radical freedom, attracts Easy when it threatens white entitlement, but terrifies him when it imperils male privilege.

Unlike the traditional white hard-boiled detective who seeks to rejuvenate a transcendent system, Mosley's black detective must experience the pain and the possibility of the fundamental disorder that produces new social arrangements. This key difference is evident in a comparison between Chandler's and Mosley's treatments of the knighthood motif, which is the signature characteristic of Philip Marlowe, the "common man" as "hero," who treads "mean streets" as "a man of honor" (Haycraft 237). When Marlowe spots the "stained-glass romance" depicting a knight's inept rescue of a helpless maiden that decorates the Sternwood mansion, he wryly observes, "that if I lived in that house I would sooner or later have to climb up there and help him. He didn't seem to be really trying" (*Big Sleep* 4). Just as the king is assisted by the medieval knight, Sternwood, the failing and wealthy patriarch, relies on the loyalty and potency of the detective hero. Marlowe's detective code derives from two principles of fealty—loyalty to the client and loyalty to the law—which turn out to be the same thing: perpetuation of the decrepit paternal codes of privilege that it is the duty of the knightly hero to rehabilitate.

Porter argues that the American detective fiction developed in the 1920s merely added the conventions of literary realism and vernacular language to the static ideology of the British pattern: "in representing crime and its punishment . . . detective novels invariably project the image of a given social order and the implied value system that helps sustain it" without "any recognition that the law itself . . . is problematic" (121).

Although Easy Rawlins would like to be a conventionally moral man, his recognition of the "problematic" nature of "law" as it is applied to black citizens separates him from his white counterpart. Marlowe bases his detective code on adherence to a fixed system of justice: "Once outside the law you're all the way outside" (194). Rawlins questions its existence. He thinks murder is "wrong," and in a better world a murderer would face "justice," but he doesn't believe justice exists "for Negroes" (121).

In the final paragraphs of the novel, Easy submits his own evolving ethics to the wisdom of Odell, his moral mentor. Is it "wrong," he wants to know, not to report a guilty man because he is your friend? Odell advises that friendship is paramount. But, Easy continues, what if you decide to implicate somebody else, even though he is less guilty than the first man? Odell explains that you have to assume that the person implicated was just unlucky (215). Thus it is that the most important father-mentor in the novel rejects the premise of "law" for the practice of loyalty that adjusts to changing circumstances.

In *Black Betty* (1994), when Easy Rawlins notices that the "suits of armor designed for tiny little men" lining the hallway of a wealthy home contrast "two larger metal figures; maybe six feet each," he is informed that after the plague killed off much of the population of medieval Europe, those remaining could enjoy a better diet. As a result they grew bigger, "and some of the biggest put on armor" (307). In contrast to Chandler's use of this motif, the imagery of knighthood here is not a signal of preeminent principles that must be reconstituted. Instead, its artifacts suggest contingent episodes in a history of shifting power relations.

Such a perspective, according to Foucault, alters the source of knowledge. Traditional power relations, he theorizes, descend from a system of social authority invested in a sovereign ruler to Enlightenment principles of rights enforced through a structure of laws. But during the eighteenth and nineteenth centuries another complex of power relations evolved based on the diverse negotiations of everyday life. To discover this kind of power without political center—most apparent where it "surmounts the rules of right" and is sometimes expressed in "violent forms" ("Two Lectures" 96)—is a good definition of the practice of the black detection of Easy Rawlins. For much is learned in *Devil in a Blue Dress* at institutional locations of the black community that are pointedly extralegal. The cultural hub, for example, is "John's Place," a speakeasy during prohibition and an illegal, unlicensed nightclub afterward.

In *Devil in a Blue Dress,* Mouse worries about Easy's penchant for the pursuit of knowledge, fearing that learning will make Easy think "like a white man," but Mouse is wrong.[19] Easy's practice of detection is in fact a study of modern power where it is most available, in its diverse forms of violent intervention that subvert the white sovereign system. The new form of power defined by Foucault is polymorphously productive: It circulates within the body politic to construct, define, destroy, and alter its own effects. Although the contemplation of local instances of power is the modus operandi of all hard-boiled detectives, the Foucauldian result of Easy's study is the freedom to define, reject, or alter the conditions violence discloses. Like the classic detective novel, *Devil in a Blue Dress* includes a recitation of the solution, but Easy's public explanation completely redefines actual events to signify a contingent relationship with all established truths. The possibility of such freedom is supported by the novel's other manipulations of detective discourse: the variety of definitions of power supplied by Easy's series of mentors, the implication of alternatives in the characterological doubling of Daphne and between Easy and Mouse, the deconstructive solution of the central enigma, and the moral ambivalence of the detective hero.

In *Discipline and Punish,* Foucault traces the transition from the spectacle of criminality represented by the scaffold to the interiorization of social control in the classic detective novel: "The great murders had become the quiet game of the well-behaved" (69). But the energetic revisions of detective genres by Gaines and Mosley shake things up. By reintroducing a focus on criminal violence as a source of knowledge, they effectively frame potent questions about the meaning of power relations affecting African American communities at historical points of possible change. In addition, they reconnect the black themes of power and knowledge in renovated forms that depart significantly from classic and hard-boiled detective stories and several other ideological narratives, including the anti-detective novel, the folk tradition of the bad black man, the adventure convention of constructive violence, and the contemporary epic.

The anti-detective novels of writers like Vladimir Nabokov and Thomas Pynchon studied by Stefano Tani substitute for the conservative politics of the mystery genre "the decentering and chaotic admission of . . . non-solution" (40). In place of irresolution, however, the detective works of Gaines and Mosley seek alternative conclusions. And in contradiction to avant garde futility, they acknowledge the potency of what Fox Butterfield calls "the black bad man" hero (63). Not "romanticized as noble outlaws," brutal folk characters like Stagolee and Railroad Bill mirrored the turn-of-the-century frustration of African Americans caught in a system of "disenfranchisement, Jim Crow laws, and lynching" as expressions of anger without hope of social redemption (*God's Children* 64). Butterfield argues that this popular figure has inspired the use of aggression to acquire a specious "respect" in place of genuine power, particularly in black urban communities influenced by the heritage of a Southern "code of honor" operating through violence.

In stories that acknowledge its influence, Gaines and Mosley both invoke and demote this mythic and social pattern. The predicament of the old men, Mathu, and Charley in Gaines's novel is certainly addressed through force, and Mouse's practice of violence is definitely portrayed in Mosley's works as an important aspect of black masculine identity. But the redistribution of detective authority in *A Gathering of Old Men* and *Devil in a Blue Dress* argues that knowledge is not only possible, it is a more reliable means to power than violence. In both works knowledge consists of understanding the conditions of power in order to recognize opportunities for authority within the dominant system and to discover sources of potency within the black community. As David Glover and Cora Kaplan define it, the purpose of detection is the recognition of such conditions: "What's at stake in both the old and new hard-boiled is who the people are and what their relation to the public spaces of speech and action may be" (215).

Just as the treatment of violence in *A Gathering of Old Men* and *Devil in a Blue Dress* does not endorse the black ideology of futile "respect," it also rejects the white ideology of constructive violence. By decentering dominant systems of law and order, these novels refuse the alliances between men and society negotiated by constructive violence in such works as Richard Harding Davis's *Soldiers of Fortune*. One of the most important carryovers from the Western formula theorized by Slotkin to the urban frontier of detective fiction is the construction of the white male through the destruction of the racial other. According to Bethany Ogdon, standard hard-boiled fiction presents the "urban, multiracial" environment through "demeaning descriptions of other people," "their perverted psychologies," their "diseased physiognomies," and their "destroyed bodies" as "a series of negations" that "construct a mirror against which a hyper-masculine identity appears" (76). This conventional structure—the white detective's specious masculine identity contrasted to the degraded racial other as a source of fantasized male power—points up the departure the Easy Rawlins series represents.

Mosley's choice of the so-called noir genre is not without irony. The violence Rawlins encounters does not create a racialized other; instead his unstable identity is negotiated through violent knowledge in pursuit of contingent power that develops out of economic opportunity and discursive authority. Critic Robert Crooks credits Mosley's challenge to the American frontier mythology reinscribed in hard-boiled fiction, yet faults him for failing to represent a leftist solution. But solution of neither the crimes of the narrative nor the problems of society is the real objective in Mosley's crime fiction. Easy's special accomplishment is to articulate power relations through white and black violence. Like Gaines in this respect, Mosley represents rather than resolves complicated historical issues of the multiracial society "Easy" so uncomfortably inhabits.

Concern with the special problems and prerogatives of black knowledge and power makes the contemporary black detective narratives of Ernest Gaines and Walter Mosley distinct from the "white" epic forms analyzed in the next chapter. The supportive communal relations fostered by father figures in *A Gathering of Old Men* is antithetical to the abject failure of paternal mentoring in Russell Banks's *Continental Drift*, and the productive communal relations in *Devil in a Blue Dress* contrast the absolute insufficiency of community in Don DeLillo's *Libra*.

7

WHITE EPICS

Russell Banks's Continental Drift *and*
Don DeLillo's Libra

Unlike the boy's life narrative, the Western, the war story, and the mystery of previous chapters—for which the conventional adventure genres were formalized within the last century—the epic, the long narrative poem recounting the legendary accomplishments of a national hero, originates in the oral tradition, the mythic prehistory of all forms of written literature. Although Northrop Frye, as well as Robert Scholes and Robert Kellogg, traces the dominant influence of features of that form in the novel, it would be fruitless to posit a direct correspondence of the classical epic to current texts.[1] Instead, as Wallace Martin suggests, "society and literature" may "change in a cyclic rather than a linear pattern; if so the imaginative strains of recent fiction may auger a return (with a difference) to myth" (32). The definitive "difference" argued here is that Russell Banks and Don DeLillo do indeed directly or indirectly invoke aspects of the traditional epic in order to dramatize the effects of its impossibility in the context of contemporary society.

The epic, according to Michael Bernstein, tells "the tale of the tribe" in the "voice of the community's heritage 'telling itself'" (14). Georg Lukács's designation of "the epic individual, the hero of the novel" (66) forecasts the direction of my argument. For Lukacs, the "hero" is "problematic" (43), because although he is traditionally coextensive with his community, the modern "epic individual" is also "the product of an estrangement from the outside world" (66).[2] Similarly, Russell Banks's and Don DeLillo's postmodern epic figures recall the inherited epic tradition of a hero connected "by indissoluble threads to a community whose fate is crystallized in his own" (Lukacs 67) even as they paradoxically embody the failure of communal integrity.

The rejection of royalty has played havoc with the American imagination. Within a monarchical system it was still possible to believe that a single man could consolidate all the virtues ascribed to the state. As Ralph Waldo Emerson asserted, however, within democracy such aspirations were distributed over the body politic such that "The state of society is one in which the members have suffered amputation from the trunk, and strut about so many walking monsters,—a good finger, a neck, a stomach, an elbow, but never a man" (64). The singular underlying postulate of epic form, for Jeremy M. Downes, is the recovery of integrative authority: "epics focus . . . on the *recursion* to the traditional script, on the quite deliberate . . . assumption of the forms of epic power, voice, and story" (23). It is precisely the dream of securing access to authority—the public power that seems to elude them—that motivates the protagonists of *Continental Drift* (1986) and *Libra* (1989).

Even in the absence of any possibility of its attainment, the contemporary epic records the continued longing for the whole and representative man, the man whose developmental trajectory stands not for the achievement of the individual ego but for the integration of the state. What *Continental Drift* and *Libra* represent is the epic in its decay. Although their scope extends beyond the narratives of persons to explore the meaning of national events, these novels record public failure rather than epical victories. Monsters rather than kings, Banks's and DeLillo's protagonists, aware of their own troubling disintegration, seek to embody the characteristics of the public man, to become the ideal American, but the violence that distinguishes their projects does not result in the realization of their ambitions. *Continental Drift* and *Libra,* cast in the long shadow of the epic hero, reveal instead the impossible dream of the representative man, the failure of the American vision of manhood.

The contemporary epic hero has in fact descended from a representative ideal into an antihero: "Not simply a failed hero but a social misfit, graceless, weak, often comic, the embodiment of ineptitude and bad luck in a world apparently made for others" (Frye, Baker, and Perkins 39). As Ihab Hassan explains, the "Hero, who once figured as Initiate, ends up as Rebel or Victim" (9). Despite his contraction of heroic status, however, the present-day epic antihero still incarnates a historical complex. Robert Raymond DuBois of Banks's *Continental Drift* (1985) casts himself as victim, and Lee Harvey Oswald of DeLillo's *Libra* (1988) is a self-deluded rebel, but each represents an encyclopedic compilation of the ideological illusions and economic limits of contemporary

America. The antihero's personal defects emblematize a nation's shared deficiencies. For both of these contemporary epic protagonists, the struggle to define a workable sense of self involves the destruction of others, yet their violence leads not to identity but to death and to notoriety, which, according to *Libra,* institutes the public labeling of the depersonalized individual. After committing notorious violence, the perpetrator becomes a "chapter" in the nation's imagined story, through misadventure becoming "historic" (198).[3]

The central generic axiom of the epic—that the adventure of the male hero exemplifies the civil achievement of a particular historical group— extends to contemporary novels in which a representative man tests the rectitude of the social system that has shaped him. Unlike the present-day cowboy and the boy, whose narratives dispute the possibility of mature social organization, the epic protagonist participates in the fully formulated system of culture and language that Lacan designates as the Symbolic order. But like the black detective of the preceding chapter, in *Continental Drift* and *Libra* he bears witness to a "law of the Father" that is inadequate to his needs. Nevertheless, unlike the black detective, whose inquiry defines modifications and alternatives, the protagonist of the "white epics" developed by Russell Banks and Don DeLillo embodies his system through a failed struggle to make it adequate. The heroes of Banks's and DeLillo's novels experience lack of communal meaning and social order as a problem of power and try to reestablish the terms of masculine selfhood that is supposed to support it. *Continental Drift* exposes the destructive psychic and social manipulation of racial others through which a representative white male tries to establish his own identity, while *Libra* exemplifies the delusive cultural strategy designated by Jacques Derrida as "white mythology."

Of the epic themes specified by Northrop Frye, *Continental Drift* is an innovative revision of the Odyssean "epic of return": "a romance of a hero escaping from incredible perils and arriving in the nick of time to claim his bride and baffle the villains." Our reaction to this outcome, Frye explains, is a "prudent sense, rooted in all our acceptance of nature, society, and law, of the proper master of the house to reclaim his own" (*Anatomy* 319). Thus the traditional quest-return of the epic hero naturalizes the validity of general attitudes. Yet the violence through which the warrior-quester affirms his rightful position in the classical text is precisely the motif that defines the inadequacy of the representative American in Banks's ironic epic. In *Continental Drift* Bob DuBois's failed quest annuls an array of stereotypical masculine roles: the artisan, the self-made man, the family man, the athlete, the movie hero, and the good man. A similar nullification through violence is evident in *Libra*'s postmodern adaptation of the epic trope of katabasis. DeLillo's version of the traditional figure of descent to the underworld does not introduce the expected heroic transcendence. Instead, it displays the communal violence that reveals an absence of authenticating power at the heart of the state.

The Voyages of Bob DuBois

One of Odysseus's greatest triumphs is unifying two divergent epic patterns—the masculine journey of adventure and the return to domestic security—into a single identity by the conclusion of his story. In *The Odyssey* he successfully uses violence for diverse purposes: to acquire a reputation for prowess in battle, to secure the safety of his companions and himself against external threats, to reestablish a bond with his son, Telemachus, and to affirm his position as husband to Penelope and ruler of Ithaca. One effect of these achievements is that violence provides a bridge between the masculine voyage and the feminine home.

Although Banks alludes to the epic tradition in his "Invocation" to *Continental Drift,* he also forecasts deviations from type. Because the novel tells a tale of twentieth-century America, it does not require the services of a "muse." Its purpose is to account rather than recount, to present not represent (1–2). Rather than the chronicle of stable social achievement reflected by Greek epic, Banks conceives the narrative of Bob DuBois as a disruptive intervention into conditions out of which contemporary history is being made: "memory" is not what is needed. Instead one must come to terms with the "pity" and "anger" of white Christian America's masculine fixation on sexuality and race and assume an appropriate "middle-class" remorse (1).

Instead of connecting the ideologies of men's and women's lives as does the constructive violence of the classical epic, violence in *Continental Drift* signals an endemic condition of boundaries—personal, racial, national, and international—that the protagonist cannot breach. And the split between gendered expectations assigned to American men and women is complicated in the novel by the interweaving of Bob's story of seeking identity and status with that of a Haitian woman, her infant, and her nephew—the tale of an immigrant family's struggle to reach America.

Bob DuBois's personal odyssey takes him from an unsatisfactory existence as a New England mechanic to the failure of his new life as a Florida charter-boat skipper. Metaphors of journey express his competing, inadequate cultural formulations of masculine identity as well as his failed relations with women and children. The Odyssean motif of the outward voyage defines Bob Dubois's quest for male power. His experience of sexual and economic impotence in New Hampshire motivates his move to Florida to satisfy his yearnings for a better life, while the masculine personas he adopts in that project are organized through the trope of heroic travel.

All his life he has associated deep-sea fishing with the satisfaction of a confused requirement for "competence" (71). During his youth Bob had helped his friend Avery Boone restore a fishing boat, and his own excursions in the waters around New England provided the measure of his deepest contentment. The happiness that the boat gave him, he confides to Avery, was a result of the sense that he "owned" himself whenever he was on board (199–200). When as an adult he becomes captain of Avery's boat, sometimes his work also affords him a satisfying sense of self-sufficiency. Standing alone on the bridge, guiding the *Belinda Blue* out into the quiet water of the bay, Bob feels peaceful. Enjoying at that moment a sense of authority, he can believe himself a "rock of a man" (256).

But it is another boat, his brother Eddie's spanking new 150-horsepower speedboat, that provokes Bob's greatest fears of inadequacy. When he first saw the craft, all glass, chrome, and sparkling deck, Bob felt resentment, envy, and humiliation. Perhaps Bob's greatest failure is not financial, as he fears, or moral, as he comes to believe, but rather it is the inability to understand the difference that these two vessels represent—a Marxian distinction between the gratification of labor symbolized by the fishing boat and dissatisfaction with the surplus value of an ostentatious plaything signified by the speedboat. This confusion is rooted in a key episode that Bob recounts to his wife. Once, when they were both young, Avery Boone had shown Bob a magazine advertisement that featured a good-looking man carrying a case of whiskey through the tropical surf, a "forty-foot catamaran" floating on the bay behind him. "'That's me,'" Avery exclaimed, a reaction Bob had shared (29).[4]

Ideology, according to Louis Althusser, enlists individuals into a system of values through *interpellation,* a process like hailing someone in the street. In response to the call, "Hey, you there!" an individual recognizes himself as its subject (174). For Althusser, this instance of recognition is hypothetical, because everyone already knows by virtue of living in a culture the definition of being that he recognizes in the instance of the call. Bob's example of his response to the hailing of the whiskey ad is a formal instance of his assent to capitalistic values that are already a part of him. And yet, Bob's self-recognition in this inter-pellation is ambiguous. In the ad, the success represented by the case of expensive Haig & Haig is deliberately confused with the skill sug-gested by the catamaran and the freedom from restraint signaled by the desert island. Bob's difficulty in untangling these discrepant contem-porary signals is complicated by an American history of contradictory attitudes about masculine identity.

In *Manhood in America,* sociologist Michael Kimmel defines the con-flicting typologies of masculinity that developed along with the nation. From the first, there existed the European yeoman type Kimmel des-ignates "the Heroic Artisan," who is characterized by devotion to in-dependence, virtue, hard work, and skill at a craft or profession (16). Although Bob's working-class background promotes the quest for com-petence through labor he associates with the *Belinda Blue,* his father's factory job has apparently not confirmed the possibility of artisanal val-uation, and his own work repairing furnaces in New Hampshire affords him only a minimal sense of independent accomplishment.

The solid virtues of the republican Heroic Artisan are not easily con-flated with the meretricious objectives of the industrial "Self-Made Man," but this is what the contrasting connotations of boats in the novel suggest that Bob is trying to do. The values of the Self-Made Man as Kimmel defines him, like his fortune, are "uncomfortably linked to the volatile marketplace." "Mobile, competitive, aggressive in business, the Self-Made Man [is] also temperamentally restless, chronically insecure, and desperate to achieve a solid grounding for masculine identity" (17). The uncertain achievement of these values, projected onto the acquisi-tion of flashy consumer goods like the speedboat, is embodied by Bob's brother, who explains his personal credo as the "religion" of buying and selling. Although Bob might have "sold" his skills when he was fixing furnaces, Eddie insists that in the "real world" defined by money, skills don't matter because they simply do not possess the commodity value of "things" (*Continental* 76–77).

The opposition between these two definitions of masculine integrity through "skills" or "things," unresolved by the nautical trope of *Continental Drift,* is further complicated by Bob's participation in the modern ideology of a third type, the "domestic man," who attempts to define the essentials of his character outside the conflicted economic arena through close relations with a family (Kimmel, *Manhood* 159–60). Although Bob believes he deeply values his wife and his children, this commitment is difficult for him to honor. When he is troubled by the violent events that threaten his shaky sense of masculine worth—such as when Eddie kills himself after his business ventures fail, or when Bob himself kills a black man robbing Eddie's liquor store—Bob characteristically pledges to abandon his extramarital affairs and increase his domestic devotion. Yet in spite of his good intentions, the DuBois family's unmet financial needs constantly challenge Bob's core aspirations for success, competence, and freedom.

The genuine tenor of Bob's domestic return is manifested in metaphors of destructive travel by land, which contrast the heroic sea-voyage motif that expresses his deeper yearnings. For example, the emotional constriction of Bob's life in New Hampshire is experienced as a ride in a prison cart across Siberia. In this daydream he pictures himself helplessly bound in the back of a rough wagon, drawn across a frozen landscape by an ancient and infirm nag (*Continental* 23). After he shoots the robber, Bob imagines himself as a mindless vagrant, unsure of how he came to acquire the wounds that denote an unacknowledgeable history of strife (151). And upon discovering he cannot save his brother, although Bob longs to take off in his car and never stop, he doesn't believe there are any more new places (318). So the very metaphor—male travel—through which Bob seeks to claim an epic identity also discloses the contradictions in the contemporary American version of this quest.

Although violence reveals Bob's ultimate failure to unify the disparities in the ideologies of manhood, this outcome is veiled in the unfolding of the plot. Bob's appeal as a protagonist is his emerging awareness of the contradictory nature of his quest and his attempts to cope with self-division. These efforts take epic forms: Bob struggles to become the noble hero of his own narrative and he experiences "otherness" the way Odysseus explores alien people and places. It was "possible" during the late 1970s, confides the narrator of *Continental Drift,* to come of age in the United States without knowing any black people "well enough" to learn their names. Bob's obsession with Marguerite, a black woman, seems to be based on his Odyssean desire to move beyond cognitive limits. Despite his curiosity, however, this reach beyond the self is ineffective, because Bob doesn't possess the imagination to comprehend that to be a "woman" is not like "being a man" and to be "black" is not at all like "being white" (100–01).

Whereas Bob's troubled relations with women may be attempts to expand his self-concept, his even more troubled relations with men are efforts to retain the integrity of self that he experiences as constantly threatened, a pattern originating in Bob's relationship with an inadequate father. The effects of paternal failure are expressed in the novel through the masculine metaphor of sports. Successful youthful athletes, Bob and his elder brother, Eddie, enjoyed local reputations as high school hockey champions known as the "Granite Skates," but the boys' father habitually withheld recognition for this achievement. For example, when Bob's hometown paper ran a complimentary headline announcing he had won a state championship, his father ignored the news, leaving the son unsettled and humiliated (272–73).

Sports continue to function throughout Bob's life as a paradoxical index of both desire for paternal approval and its devastating absence. He recalls the important occasion of a single trip with his father to see Ted Williams play baseball, and his extreme discouragement when the player—whom he considered a "God"—did not take the field (279). Bob's awkward adult encounter with Williams in a sports store in Florida reveals his continuing confusion. Interrupting Williams's transaction, Bob spews out his adolescent admiration, becoming disturbingly aware of his intense feelings, especially regarding his father (277).

In an essay on the connection between athletics and male identity, Michael Messner theorizes a basis for Bob's profound emotional response. "With no clear cultural rite of passage into adult manhood— indeed with no clear cultural *definition* of masculinity," sports can be a "powerful force in shaping [an athlete's] self-image." The significance of public admiration is important proportionally to the young man's lack of determinate identity, but the identity conveyed by sports is itself unstable, dependent on the fluctuation between winning and losing and the variable admiration of an audience. "The young man must continually prove, achieve and *re*-prove, and *re*-achieve his status. As a result, many young athletes learn to seek and *need* the appreciation of the crowd to feel that they are worthy human beings," according to Messner (57). Shaped by athletics, a boy's ability to attain confidence may be very precarious. In Bob's case, his father's active ambivalence further exaggerates this difficulty.

Because he does not attain the symbols of conspicuous consumption prized by the Self-Made Man, Bob does not, in his own estimation, secure the public approbation his sports-based process of externalized identification would require, so he seeks an alternative structure of valuation in the project of moral improvement. Messner quotes a middle-aged athlete, former Olympic contender Russ Ellis, regarding a similar transition: "Somehow we all think that we're going to wind up on the cover of *Time,* or something. . . . That some day, somewhere, you're gonna be *great,* and everyone will know and recognize it? Now, I'd rather be great because I'm *good*—and maybe that'll turn into something that's acknowledged, but not at the headline level" (65). Ellis remains uncertain about a project of valuation based on virtue; "somehow" he hopes, being morally "good" will come to replace the publicity and recognizable achievement that he previously sought as a source of self-identification. Yet he does appear to be shifting toward an internal ethical standard, a shift that also marks the typical developmental trajectory of the male hero of American cinema.[5]

And, in fact, Bob's wavering efforts to achieve a vague goodness follow a pattern comparable to that of movie adventure. For Kimmel, the movie *Casablanca* (1942) concludes with a resolution similar to that attempted by Ellis—and by Bob. Bogart, he notes, frequently played "a self-interested and selfish man, who during the course of the film, finds himself putting aside his self-centeredness, and taking a moral stand for good." By forfeiting his own longings through relinquishing Ingrid Bergman at the end of *Casablanca,* Bogey "repudiates the Self-Made Man's dogged egoism" to achieve the "self-transcendence that is required of a hero" (*Manhood* 233).

As Bob's quest for masculine identity becomes increasingly uncertain, he too becomes more concerned with goodness. Although Bob admits he has problems knowing "right from wrong" (*Continental* 69) and is therefore probably neither (104), he hopes to use "guilt" as an instructive guide (173) in his impossible attempt to achieve "redemption" (416) at the end of the novel. While this ambition may imply that Bob is capable of transforming himself by trading the dream of success for the pursuit of ethics, its similarity to the Hollywood ending implies that the project of moral improvement probably serves another purpose. In fact, during his depressed period in New Hampshire, Bob had relied on the narrative structure of film in order to cope with his unrewarding life. His own actions, he imagined, were like the slow scenes in movie previews, useful as lead-ins to more important coming attractions. But after his move to Florida, things change; he feels the "scenes" he is living have become "cinematic high points" containing all the "violence" typical of "action" movies (301).

The first of such scenes is the familiar gunfight between the "good guy" and the "bad guy." After his first date with Marguerite, Bob returns to the small liquor store he manages for his brother to phone for help because his car will not start. Inside, he faces an armed intruder—the black villain of Eddie's racist warnings—who, pointing a shotgun at Bob's head, demands the day's take. Because Bob had already deposited the contents of the register at the bank when he closed for the night, he cannot satisfy the agitated gunman, who is being urged by his craven accomplice to blow Bob away. Although he is frightened, Bob foils his opponent with a ruse. Pretending to retrieve the deposit bag, Bob grabs the loaded pistol Eddie had insisted he keep on hand to frighten off the "dark-skinned crazies" (67) and shoots the man in the arm. At this point, Bob's righteous status is not in doubt. But his subsequent actions are more questionable. As the wounded man tries to escape, Bob, adopting the manner of a television hero, takes careful aim and deliberately shoots him. The intruder falls, grunting and gurgling, dead of a shot straight through the mouth.

Although abhorring the violence of his actions, when he later spots the escaped second intruder in Marguerite's car, Bob indulges in an elaborate movie chase motivated by mixed emotions: worry about her "safety," fury at what he takes as her "betrayal," desire for his brother's "approval," "rage" at the kid who had urged his own execution, and an oddly abstract need for a "clarifying act of revenge" (175). Unlike the similar robbery-murder of Richard Bausch's *Violence,* in which the plot of constructive violence fails and initiates the protagonist's genuine examination of his own condition, Bob's accession to the same ideology as the robbers—belief in the myth of violence as self-construction—negates the possibility of the self-realization he thinks he is seeking.

The next significant violent episode occurs when the two strands of the novel—Bob's story and the account of Vanise and her nephew, Claude—merge as Bob agrees to smuggle a group of Haitians into Florida. During the voyage, Bob shows affection to the forthright boy by inviting him to the bridge to steer the boat, addressing him as "son," and even placing his own captain's hat on Claude's head (359). However, when the coast guard attempts to board the *Belinda Blue,* Bob stands by distractedly, allowing his mate to force the Haitians at riflepoint overboard to their deaths rather than face the criminal consequences of his illegal business. Young Claude, who has become the leader of the group, is the first to jump. In this climactic scene, Bogart would have sacrificed his freedom to save the boy. But despite his grief, Bob does not do so, thereby relinquishing his penultimate chance to become a moral hero.

Based on Bob's shocking immorality in the drowning of his Haitian passengers, it is possible to read *Continental Drift* as a personal ethical project that fails. Unable to construct a "good" identity, Bob, then, deserves his violent death during his last try for heroism, the mismanaged attempt to return to Vanise, the only survivor, the money he had received for the safe passage of the immigrants. According to this interpretation, the character, not the system, seems to be at fault.[6] But to attribute Bob's moral insufficiency to his own inadequacy fails to address the society that produced him. Although the hypothesis of Bob's personal failure could support the comforting illusion that an integrity mediated through the ideologies of American manhood is indeed possible, Bob's story, the countertext of the Haitian journey, and the narrative point of view of *Continental Drift* undercut this assumption.

Those scenes in which Bob is responsible for deadly violence against blacks rescind his dubious effort to relate to Marguerite, negate his vague gestures toward ethical transformation, and indicate the destructive narcissism of the masculine identity he is seeking. For psychologist Erich Fromm, *narcissism* is the destructive characterological state "in which only the person himself, *his* body, *his* needs, *his* feelings, *his* thoughts, *his* property are experienced as fully real" (227).[7] The lack of capacity for genuine imaginative engagement with any life beside one's own is the fatal flaw of American manhood as *Continental Drift* presents it. Instead of forging a connection to Marguerite, their lovemaking, as Bob fantasizes it, is a cultural discourse of exploitative stereotypes. He visualizes himself as a "white boat" and her as the tawny sand of a "beach" near a beckoning jungle (111). Never aware of his own racism, Bob fires the unnecessary second shot that kills the first black intruder and indulges in a homicidal rage against the second.

Even his touching interaction with Claude is conducted from the unallayed perspective of American white superiority. Bob's affectionate paternal gesture toward the boy, placing the cap—which the novel figures as the emblem of his masculine authority—is a sign of self-replication. His horrifying acquiescence to the murder of the Haitians certifies the predominance of his own desires over the unrecognized needs of others. Bob's voyage out, then, conducted through vicious relations with racial "others," does not move beyond his own need to discover a positive masculine identity and the cultural impossibility of that quest. The epic story of the construction of the American male self in *Continental Drift* is a structure of narcissism so dominant that it is finally impossible for Bob to imagine significance in terms other than the conflicted ideologies of American masculinity in which he participates.

Ideological Journeys

"In the history of patriarchal civilization—and as yet there are no other kinds—," explains Eric J. Leed in *The Mind of the Traveler,* "humanity has worn the mask of masculinity, and travel has been the performance of that persona. . . . Man's search for eminence, for recognition, for a consummation and certainty of self has long been channeled through the agency of travel" (220).[8] But in *Continental Drift* the quest motif, Odysseus's legacy to the American male hero, is transgressively shadowed by its opposing articulation through the narrative journey of a young woman and a boy.

Instead of the attainment of self-possessed identification promised by the masculine traditions shaping Bob's adventures, the Haitian journey is a story of accident, insecurity, passivity, and victimization. Vanise and Claude both suffer the natural disaster of a hurricane and the human misfortune of extraordinary exploitation and brutal rape. They move from boat to boat, never certain of where they are going or whether they can survive the process of getting there. They exist in a kind of permanent state of "middle passage" (215) that culminates on the *Belinda Blue* with Claude's death and Vanise's insanity.

Bob is both attracted and repelled by the Haitians' extremes of inertness and willfulness (350), which he does not want to acknowledge in his parallel journey toward the promise that America represents—fantastic hopes, shaped by ads featuring manufactured images of masculine desire—"red sports cars" and beautiful women. It is this manipulative fantasy, he surmises, that had caused him, like the men in the ads, to trade "everything for nothing" (357). But if Bob is vaguely aware of the similarity of his own situation to that of the Haitians, he completely fails to recognize the crucial difference—economic power—between himself and his passengers. He does not see that the deprivation of the Haitians shapes what he assumes is "wisdom," and because of his own confusions about personal financial deficiencies, he does not see reflected in the abject powerlessness of the boat people the terrible power he indeed possesses by virtue of his position and his nationality. His moral failing derives from not realizing in himself what he has identified in others: The problem with the wealthy, as Bob sees it, is that they refuse to recognize the actual "power" they have over the lives of others (352).

The extraordinary omnipotence of the novel's narrative perspective addresses this problem of the recognition of power. Not merely a conventional platform from which to observe the actions and thoughts of the characters, the godlike point of view is capable of conflating geological and political action. Early on, the narrator describes a scene in which it appears "as if" the entire population of the earth, "millions" of "human creatures . . . traveling" form a "subsystem inside the larger system of currents and tides, of winds and weather, of drifting continents and shifting, uplifting, grinding, cracking land masses" (39).

This viewpoint—derived, I suspect, from the photographic technology of American space exploration—is capable of abstracting exorbitant human suffering into impersonal natural pattern. "Seen from above," 150 million Somalians—men, women and children fleeing the deadly drought- and war-induced poverty of their region—"would resemble" nothing so much as the natural ocean currents engendered yearly by the Southwest Monsoon. From this elevated perspective, the desperate migration of the starving Africans would "seem natural, unalterable." Viewed like weather, their experience would seem "tragic," perhaps, but "fault" or even corrective action would appear irrelevant; "ideology" would seem a form of vanity" (40).

Maintained for the first ten pages of the second chapter, matching Olympian outlook with magisterial style, this tour de force passage descends from a carefully placed "as if." The insistent hypothetical beginning rescinds the suppositions the passage propounds—that distance can literally naturalize and aestheticize human suffering and that "ideology" really doesn't matter. In fact, the stylization of the passage critiques the narrative misconstruction of political and human realities. Its massive falsification of war, drought, and forced migration corresponds to the distortions that Bob's story dramatizes on an intimate scale. The manipulation at both these levels results from an ability to step far enough away from an action to be able to misconstrue its human effects.

For ideology does matter, and the style and plot of *Continental Drift* are an elaboration of its consequences. Since motivation for ideological falsification is the universal human yearning for the minimal control afforded by simplified explanation, Bob's destructive beliefs about American manhood are comparable to Vanise's reliance on *les Invisibles,* the devouring "loas" of the voodoo religion, which provide a narrative structure for the regulation of Haitian destiny (231). But the reassuring beliefs of neither Bob nor Vanise give them power over the death and deprivation that is their lot. Thus, the galactic deceptions of the imaginary "continental drift" passage are discounted by the personal sufferings of Bob, Vanise, and Claude, which are the true focus of the text.

Although novels are products of culture and therefore a form of ideology, according to Althusser, art can intervene in the automatisms that govern the ideological process by "revealing its traces and effects." By devising an "intaglio" that "'depicts' a *determinate* absence . . . very precisely inscribed in . . . pertinent *differences,*" art can expose ideology through "the fact that a painted object does not conform to its essence, is compared with an object other than itself; in the fact that normal connexions . . . are inverted" ("Cremonini" 237). *Continental Drift* can be understood as just such an intaglio—in which the design is laid beneath the surface of the story of the experience of Bob DuBois. What he takes to be its essence—the epic adventure of the discovery of "self"— is reversed by his inscription through "pertinent differences" from competing ideals. Thus Bob's story is revealing precisely because it fails to conform to dominant ideological patterns of individual importance and masculine power, and its failure makes the "normal connexions" underlying Bob's assumptions available to scrutiny and rejection. The "determinate absence" of male social identity is the epic subject of *Continental Drift,* a theme manifested through the failures of Bob's pursuit of a heroic self.

The juxtaposition of Bob's American journeys with those of the Haitian family indicates a similar inadequacy of real relations that they can neither understand nor control. Similarly, the competing ideals of masculinity—proletarian competence, bourgeois success, and domestic affection, which Bob's serial adventures cannot integrate—inscribe American manhood as an impossible achievement. Finally, the ineffective recourse to the practice of violence in many episodes of Bob's experience implies the absence of access to available sources of power. Bob's tantrum, in which he wrecks the pitiful belongings in his family's Florida trailer in response to his own sense of lack of control and deprivation, is a signal instance. In like manner, the rapes of the Haitian characters by the ignorant sailors and others are best understood as the desperate devices of impotency. Certainly this is the literal situation in Vanise's victimization by Jimmy Grabow, who must beat her in order to attain sexual arousal. This intertextuality of the Haitian and American stories of powerlessness suggests a connection between individual experience of masculine frustration and international patterns of irresponsibility.

Like the interweaving systems of natural force—wind, weather, air, and water currents in Banks's elaborate analogy—power is not an isolable object but a broad interdependence of resources and culture—wealth, influence, knowledge, capital, energy, raw materials, prestige, and so forth. Unlike in *The Odyssey,* where the quester's voyage out is complemented by domestic connection and the warrior's violence serves the goal of personal and social integration, Bob's attempt to differentiate a determinate self out of larger forces of which he is unaware takes the form of a violence marked by futility. The emphatic separation between black and white, male and female, American and Haitian enacted by Bob's violent acts exposes the epic narcissism of the American male dream of self-reflexive potency that is destructive to individuals and wider community. Bob DuBois's violence inscribes America's general failure to address determinant issues of power. The last sentences of the *Envoi* to *Continental Drift* articulate the purpose of the novel as the "sabotage" and "subversion" of an unproductive system: "Go, my book, and help destroy the world as it is" (421).

Epic Katabasis in *Libra*

The first paragraph of *Libra* introduces the boy who grows up to become Lee Harvey Oswald engaged in an emblematic pursuit: riding the New York subway system to the far reaches of the city. With his hands pressed against the glass window at the front of the first car, he feels the train smash through darkness at the "edge of no-control" and savors the brutal intensity: sound so much like pain he felt it as a "personal test," the "iron" of the track so "potent" he "almost" tasted it, like something he had placed in "his mouth" when he was a child. Roaring past them on the train, he knows that he is different from the static people waiting outside in the semidark, and during a year of "riding" for the sheer thrill of it, he never doubts that there is anything so "compelling" in the "famous city above" not available within the "tunnels" running below (3–4).

This passage epitomizes the boy's sense of "inner force" and "secret power" that, despite his quest to recover precisely these attributes in the Marine Corps, his defection to the Soviet Union, and his attempt on the life of President Kennedy, the man would "never again" experience (13). The covert animation of the subway journey is achieved as a result of figuratively tasting "iron"; that is, incorporating a technological order that serves to differentiate Oswald from all the other anonymous waiters in the dark. Its agency is activated through violent sensation in an alternative underground universe that is the obverse of unsatisfactory actuality. The quest for identification, the desire for power, the alienated secrecy, and the violent masculine "test" are elements central to the projects of Oswald and the coconspirators DeLillo invents for him, but the artificial underworlds occupied by these characters derive from established literary precedent.

In the traditional epic plot, the hero completes a cycle that takes him from surface reality to a mythic lower world and back to daily life. The achievement of this cycle in *The Odyssey* allows Odysseus to review the past achievements of an assemblage of Greek warriors and precedes his return to his homeland. In *The Aeneid* it provides a vision of a glorious Roman future that inspires the founding of the nation-state. In the later

epics of Milton and Dante, the vertical trope fully supplants other traditional horizontal movements of masculine adventure. Both of these
Christian poets define the collective beliefs of a religious community,
literally to hell and back, through the figure of descent followed by
ascent. In later works, however, *katabasis*—that is, movement downward without compensatory upward motion—may indicate less a stage
of development shared by a political or religious group than a setting
symbolic of personal turmoil that sets the protagonist apart from his
world. Omitting the representation of epic return, Romantic images of
the underground setting signal extremes of individual predicament.

In Edgar Allan Poe's oeuvre, for example, the characteristic cellars
and crypts may be read as the negative reflections of untenable worldly
projects.[9] Freud's adoption of the spatial metaphor of a subterranean
"unconscious" at the end of the nineteenth century codified an imaginable space of antimeaning in which socially unrealizable goals could
nevertheless still convey power.[10] The discovery of the alternative force
of the "lower world" of impulsive drives and uncanny experience is
an extension of the Romantic project to contrive outside the limits of
social and economic circumscription the imagined power of an uncon-
tained "other" region and incorporate it through literary representation
into the experience of the self.

Don DeLillo details and explodes this ineffective strategy, which is
represented in *Libra* as the central psychic structure of contemporary
America. Certainly Oswald's story is the defining instance of this "underground" ideology, but his signature settings and psychological projects are replicated by all the other characters. The netherworlds of Milton's hell and Dante's inferno, epic sites of grandeur and organization,
are reduced in *Libra* to the impoverished spaces occupied by Oswald,
of which the prison cell to which he is confined at the marine base in
Atsugi, Japan, is the most revealing example. Although he attempted to
"feel history" in his "cell," it turned out to be an Orwellian chronicle of
"no-choice" (100). Instead of the revolutionary possibility of historical
engagement that Oswald seeks in the homonymic communist "cell"
(37) he dreams of joining, his actual experience is of radical confinement and abridged freedom. Imprisonment, he understands, is the predictable outcome of his social situation, the place he'd been heading for
since birth, another of the "stunted rooms" in which he had always
lived (100).

Like Oswald, the CIA-financed conspirators, despite economic privilege, also occupy confined spaces, sometimes literally below ground,
always symbolically "underground" in the sense of existing in a criminal realm beneath the surface of ordinary existence. Win Everett, who
initiates the plot, having been eased out of active service after the deba-
cle of the Bay of Pigs, works out of a basement office in a Texas women's
college and forges false documents in his own cellar. T-Jay Mackey, who
recruits and trains gunmen for the operation, recalls the disturbing atmosphere of the "small" and "strange rooms" he has occupied (68).
David Ferrie, the "bag man" and the "spiritual adviser" who indoctri-
nates Oswald, is first glimpsed in the "small room" behind another oper-
ative's office (29). Oswald has initially encountered him in a dark, rank
room crowded with old food containers and a cage full of white mice,
a room seemingly suspended in its own time (42). Larry Parmenter,
another agent, occupies a Washington home notable for a "tininess" and
"unnoticeability" (123) that provides his wife with the necessary illusion of safety. Finally, Nicholas Branch, who, after the fact, is charged
with the task of compiling a secret authoritative history of the assassination for the CIA, lives like a captive in the hermetic study the agency
has built for this purpose, a constricting space overflowing with contradictory documentation, a room of "theories and dreams" (14), the
"room of growing old" (59). His genuine topic, he decides, is neither
"politics" nor violent crime, but "small rooms" and the men who occupy them (181). This predominant setting, connoting confinement, de-
basement, isolation, powerlessness, and unreality, contradicts (even as
it recalls) the deviant power, illicit passion, and esoteric knowledge of
the epic-inspired "undergrounds" of traditional literature and revolutionary politics. It is notable in this regard that DeLillo titles a recent
novel *Underground* (1997).

The shared metaphor of restrictive setting, of which Oswald provides the primary example, casts him as the representative man of a
degenerate underworld. And, like the epic protagonist, he has a heroic
mission: to break "out of the room of self" (DeCurtis 48). But that is impossible. As early as the Atsugi brig experience, he realizes that the
restricted places of "basic Oswald memory" (35) represent a fundamental situation: "prison," a life-long condition contradicting all "politics and lies." More affecting than religion it was a "truth" nobody
could counter (101). None of the characters, however, makes use of this

"counterforce" (101) as a grounding existential certainty. In the face of isolated constriction they all develop sustaining illusions.[11] The conspirators participate in the collective fantasy of violent escape that results in the assassination of the president. Instead of isolation, inertia, disorganization, and weakness, the projected execution provides a sense of engagement in a mutual goal, a simulated source of energy and order, an illusory access to the power Kennedy is believed to represent.

White Mythologies

The complex mechanism of this putative conversion of frailty to power through violence is usefully addressed by reading the conspiracy plot in *Libra* through Jacques Derrida's discussion of metaphoric process in "White Mythology: Metaphor in the Text of Philosophy." In this important essay Derrida theorizes the operation of supplementarity by rejecting the assumption that the process of metaphor authenticates a term by reconnecting it to an originary concept. Rather, he argues that metaphor is a vehicle of unpredictable exchange because the assertion of resemblance through which metaphor functions is also an admission of difference: to define what something is like is, in the same gesture, to admit what something is not and to thereby open its meaning to unanticipated alternatives. But traditional accounts of metaphor do not generally acknowledge this second operation—"a displacement with breaks . . . reinscriptions in a heterogeneous system, mutations, separations without origin" (215)

Libra is, of course, DeLillo's imaginary account of the assassination of President Kennedy, but it is also an examination of violence as agency in contemporary society. The murder of the president is plotted as a transfer of value, a metaphoric project that Oswald and the conspirators construe as the appropriation of the kind of metaphysical authorization Derrida deconstructs. Instead of the authority the conspirators hope to establish through violent assertion of similarity, the novel discloses the supplementation inherent in the metaphoric differentiation Derrida emphasizes.

Derrida's principle of supplementarity begins with "a profound nostalgia" for a "lost" and imaginary "presence" (Adamson 637). In *Libra* this condition is evident in the shared desire of the male conspirators for the recovery of a power they have never actually possessed. Like Oswald in his boyhood subway journeys, each has in the past imagined

himself in terms of a system—the CIA for some, the Cuban Revolution
for others—that he interpreted as providing access to authority. But the
projected similarities have proved inadequate. In the novel, the underlying absence of the longed-for Derridean "presence" is manifested by
the utter failure of the assassination to produce power for Oswald or
anyone else. In both theory and novel what is generated instead is the
"chain of vicarious substitutions" Derrida calls the *supplement,* a term
that while seeming to suggest completion is possible, actually denotes
the cumulative differentiation that infinitely postpones it. It is the nature of the supplement, as Derrida defines this effect, to both "add itself" as "surplus" meaning and to intervene *"in-the-place-of"* meaning
(*Grammatology* 144–45). In *Libra,* this substitutive "chain" takes the
form of linked acts of unsatisfactory violence—the abortive invasion of
the Bay of Pigs, the failures of the CIA and Cuban conspirators, Oswald's
muddled enlistment in the assassination, and Jack Ruby's copycat execution of the wrong man. For Derrida, supplementation signals the
unavailability of whatever is sought as authentic by producing instead
"an infinite chain" that proliferates as "a mirage of the thing itself"
(*Grammatology* 157). A Derridean reading of *Libra* reveals violence as
a compensatory "mirage" rather than a means to power.

"White mythology," the phrase Derrida adapts from Anatole France
for the title of his essay, specifies the mirage effect at work throughout
male European tradition:

Metaphysics—the white mythology which reassembles and reflects
the culture of the West: the white man takes his own mythology,
Indo-European mythology, his own *logos,* that is the *mythos* of his
idiom, for the universal form of that he must still wish to call
Reason. . . .
White mythology—metaphysics has erased within itself the fabulous scene that has produced it, the scene that nevertheless
remains active and stirring, inscribed in white ink, an invisible
design covered over in the palimpsest. (213)[12]

Joseph Adamson emphasizes that Derridean supplementation per-
forms as both "compensatory substitution" and "violent usurpation"
(647). In the designation of "white mythology" just quoted, Derrida emphasizes the predominance of the first rhetorical effect, the reiterative
vision of plenitude of white European male imagination. It is left to

Libra and narratives like it to literalize the second. While the conspirators in the novel participate in the universalized system of supplemental error Derrida calls *white mythology,* DeLillo's exposition also
fully renders the implications of "the fabulous scene" of metaphoric
inversion that white male myth obscures: the reiterated and unproductive violence upon which mythic constructions of male identity
depend.

Derrida begins his discussion of metaphoric process with the Aristotelian assertion of similarity between terms: "Metaphor consists in
giving the thing a name that belongs to something else, the transference
taking any of several forms, including analogy" ("White" 231). As Aristotle defines this form, "when there are two terms, two by two, analogy
consists in stating the fourth instead of the second and the second
instead of the fourth." "Analogy," Derrida observes "is metaphor *par
excellence*" ("White" 242). This formal definition of analogy introduces
the metaphorical objective of Oswald's attempt to shoot Kennedy in
Libra. Oswald, fully aware of his limitations, wishes to substitute Kennedy's supposed power for his own impotence, and in order to do so he
must establish a relationship of similarity between himself and the president so substantial that it can alter their differing degrees of power.
But the proper analogical relation between them is, according to the
Aristotelian definition, that Oswald is to Kennedy as powerlessness is
to power (Oswald : Kennedy :: powerlessness : power), which inscribes
the equivalent relation of the second and fourth terms, Kennedy = power,
leaving Oswald's condition of powerlessness unchanged.

However, as Derrida argues, the process of metaphor seems to open
possibilities beyond propriety. Because the admission of difference in
the relations introduced by the assertion of similarity allows for disparate meaning, Derrida considers metaphor a kind of catachresis,
which "in general consists in a sign already affected with a first idea
also being affected with a new idea, which itself had no sign at all, or
no longer properly has any in language" ("White" 255).[13] Metaphoric
transference understood as a catachretic process is the "violent, forced,
abusive inscription of a sign upon a meaning which did not have its
own sign in language. So much so that there is no substitution here, no
transport of proper signs, but rather the irruptive substitution of a sign
to an idea, a meaning, deprived of their signifier" ("White" 255). This
description allows us to understand Oswald's violent project in *Libra*

as a catachretic proposition that attempts the reversal of relations of power by forcing a connection consisting of empty terms and illicit meanings. The "proper" analogy—Oswald : powerlessness :: Kennedy : power—would be "forced" into a catachresis—Oswald : power :: Kennedy : powerlessness.

It is not so much that by killing Kennedy Oswald could steal Kennedy's actual power, derived from political authority, wealth, and family status. But the assassination, from Oswald's mythic perspective, would violently shift the values of terms, substituting the plenitude of Kennedy's imagined power for the negative sign of Oswald's powerlessness to effect the reversal of signification—Kennedy in the place of Oswald. Through this spurious exchange, Kennedy would be reduced to the impotence of death, whereas Oswald would be suffused with power. *Libra* textualizes this ideological substitution as two operations: the imposition of similarity through "coincidence" and the institution of difference through violence.

Oswald imagines an identification with John F. Kennedy on the basis of a few accidental and insignificant similarities. For example, he found it meaningful that his wife, Marina, and the First Lady were both pregnant at the same time. Further, having read that the president liked James Bond novels, the writings of Mao Tse-tung, and a book called *The White Nile*, Oswald made it a point to acquire some of the 007 novels and Mao's biography. He even tried to get *The White Nile* from the library, but when it was unavailable he borrowed *The Blue Nile* in its place. Finally, Oswald noted that, like himself, Kennedy was weak at spelling and had poor "handwriting" (311–12).

These inconsequential resemblances can be codified into the empowering ideology of "coincidence" articulated by David Ferrie. There is a "pattern" in occurrences, he explains: "Something in us has an effect on independent events." What we can consciously observe is only a part of the story, and because we "extend in time," we are able to "make things happen" (330). This specious philosophy of empowering coincidence is the rationale that Ferrie, Oswald's handler, advances for assassination. "Think of two parallel lines," he commands. "One is the life of Lee H. Oswald. One is a conspiracy to kill the President." There is, he tells the potential killer, a "third line" born of "dreams, visions, intuitions, prayers, out of the deepest levels of the self" that can "bridge" the first two lines. Not "generated by cause and effect" like the first two, the third line, lacking any "history we can understand" cuts through time and across causality to force a "connection," putting "man on the path of his destiny" (339).

Thus the vital underworld of epic power, degraded to psychologism in Romantic terror, reemerges as spurious motivation in DeLillo's contemporary adaptation of katabasis. Within this arational narrative, murder provides an extreme means of forced "connection." At the instant of execution, the murderer and his victim would share an ultimate experience at the same moment—a literalized instance of co-incidence.

If the ideological system at work in *Libra* advances "coincidence" as the instrument of psychological substitution, it promotes violence as the agency of political change. The conspiratorial narrative of political violence at the heart of the assassination plot is rooted in the concept of revolutionary insurrection. T-Jay Mackey explains that "plots, conspiracies, secrets of revolution" were once distinct from the power of government. But in the world of the novel, all the "secrets that matter," like nuclear weaponry, are controlled by the White House (68). Revolutionary theory locates the source of authentic change, in contrast to dangerous coercion, outside existing structures of power, in an underground relation to existing authority. Revolutionary violence is therefore deemed a necessary corrective to the failure of the state, which for DeLillo's conspirators is fully manifested in President Kennedy's inadequate support for the Bay of Pigs invasion to depose Castro.[14]

In *Libra,* however, violence does not bring about political transformation, and instead of change it institutes a *différantial* sequence of Derridean supplementation. To read the assassination of Kennedy in terms of Derrida's theory of metaphor as a species of cultural production is to recognize an event resulting from the dream of power rather than the forces of history, in spite of Oswald's flirtation with political "struggle."[15] Aside from its situation in the circumstances of Oswald's biography and Kennedy's office, beyond the anomie of the conspirators there is surprisingly little political content in *Libra.* According to De-Lillo, Oswald's fascination with Marxist revolutionaries grew out of his identification with their confinement rather than their policies: "I think he had a strong identification with people like Trotsky and Castro, who spent long periods in prison. I think he felt that with enough perseverance and enough determination these men could survive their incarcerations and eventually be swept by history right out of the [small] room" (DeCurtis 52). For all of the male characters, the primary value of conspiratorial projects is the provision of an ahistorical source of illusory potency: "Secrets are an exalted state, almost a dream state." Secrets are a "vitalizing" means of "stopping the world so we can see ourselves" within it, explains Win Everett (*Libra* 26). Oswald, especially, embodies the need for this illusion. He needs to discover a "structure" that "includes him, a definition" that can determine where he fits in. But as a "zero in the system," he cannot (357). And although the need for a renovated "structure" is clearly evident in the novel, the political ideals of its intended nature are not presented.

If the assassination in *Libra* falters as political action, it certainly fails as psychological reorganization. In DeLillo's novelization of the event, Oswald does not fire the fatal bullets, he does not experience his own empowerment, and his confinement to jail afterward is merely a replication of his basic condition. What Oswald's violence does produce is supplemental versions of itself. Jack Ruby's powerlessness, muddled thinking, alienation, desire for approval, and manipulation by others is a close parallel to Oswald's situation, and Ruby's murder of Oswald reiterates Oswald's attempt on Kennedy. Empty repetition, rather than the achievement of meaning, is the tropological pattern of the novel: "Secrets" generate "their own networks" (22).

For Derrida, the inevitable failure to recover a nonexistent originary plenitude through metaphor produces the endless chain of related terms he designates as *supplements*. Although the conspirators are seeking male power, what is produced by the assassination is supplementary violence that "fills a void." Effecting "no relief," such violence is revealed as the symbol of a dream and "the mark of an emptiness" (*Grammatology* 145). The supplemental structure of *Libra*, by anatomizing the occultation of male power as the cultural practice of "white mythology," demonstrates that constructive violence is a mythological process. In the novel, the anti-Castro gunman whom DeLillo casts as the actual killer of Kennedy gives voice to this theme when he reminisces about Castro's appeal. Fidel, he explains, had the "magical . . .force" of "myth" (184).

According to Roland Barthes, the impact of the "force" of "myth," like that which the conspirators of the novel assign to political leaders, derives from the narrative appropriation of history in the service of ideology. Through this process, a meaning derived from concrete social relations is drained of specific content and turned into the formal emblem of a social belief; thus "meaning loses its value but keeps its life" (118). No doubt, in the course of history there have been men whose deeds of war were equivalent to the values and aspirations of their group and tales were told to mark this congruence, but the contemporary epic of Don DeLillo is not among them. *Libra* deliberately denudes the actual event of Kennedy's assassination to show the evolution of Barthean myth. By substituting a false history, the novel undercuts the ideology of violent construction.

The "best weapon against myth," Barthes posits, "may be to mythify it in its turn, and to produce an *artificial* myth. . . . All that is needed is to use it as the departure point for a third ideological chain, to take its signification as the departure point of a second myth" (135). This in fact is DeLillo's strategy. If we understand the lost history of male heroism as a first chain of signification and the ideological formula of constructive violence as the second, *Libra* creates a countermythic third "myth" out of the assassination of the president. An ironic counterpart to Ferrie's three-strand theory, the novel plots the "third line" as a satiric annulment of his katabatic ideology of "coincidence."[16] The assassination plot, a catachretic experiment that results only in supplementary expansion, uncovers the failure of a special instance of "white mythology" that endorses violence as a means to the dream of lost power.

Both Bob DuBois and Lee Harvey Oswald, despite their adoption of the violence certified by public myths, die powerless. But the central problem revealed by both *Libra* and *Continental Drift* is not the failure of violence to produce power; it is the failure of society to provide any accessible definition of power based on its genuine production and function within the social body. Instead of economic analysis, as suggested by Marxist thinkers, or discursive function, as posited by Foucault, the contemporary West endlessly disseminates through the genres of masculine adventure an ideology of a male power divorced from social organization that may be regulated through individual recourse to violence. The revisions of epic by Russell Banks and Don DeLillo thematically and formally challenge this mythic formulation by highlighting the inadequate but necessary correlation between national ideals and individual lives and dismissing violence as the productive connection between the citizen and power.

CONCLUSION

Textual Violence, Actual Violence

Setting aside some of the common arguments against fictive violence—
that children may imitate its cruelty, for example, or that the audience
for violence may become acclimated to increasing brutality—*Violent
Adventure* has argued that textual violence does significant cultural
work: On the one hand, it organizes the expectation that aggression
creates male power; on the other, it disputes this ideology. Perhaps
even more important, contemporary adventure fiction by American men
points to the inadequacy of socialization in communities that rely on
violence as a primary means to masculine identity. Certainly one implication of this contention is that as a society we would benefit from a
clearer comprehension of the actual structures of power that a belief in
constructive violence obscures. Another, the subject of this final chapter, is that we all need a better understanding of how violence in texts
affects brutality in the world—in America, where young men in increasing numbers have made bombs or secured guns in order to murder their
classmates, and in the larger world, where young men and women are
making themselves into bombs to destroy their enemies. The real stories
of such unimaginable acts have made it increasingly imperative to consider the connection between vicious fact and violent texts.

My collegiate edition of *Webster's* dictionary defines *violence* as a
"physical force used so as to injure or damage," and it is just this primary insistence on the infliction of harm that marks the difference
between actual violence, which is essentially destructive, and textual
violence, which represents rather than directly inflicts damage. This
clear distinction between action and representation is not maintained
in practice, however. Psychiatrist John Gunn argues that although violence is destructive in occurrence, it may be constitutive in conse-

quence by influencing hierarchical order within and among communities (14–18). In fact, the evident injurious effect of violence is frequently recoded by social groups to establish values and practices. René Girard claims in *Violence and the Sacred* that the blood feuds of traditional society prompted scapegoat sacrifice, and this ritual containment of violence in one propitiatory act provided the basis for formal religion and concomitant civilization. And in *Preposterous Violence,* James B. Twitchell contends that throughout history violent spectacles, from bear baiting to popular fiction,[1] have provided "socializing rituals" (13) that help young men to make the transition from competitive "individual sexuality" to "pairing and reproductive sexuality" (15).[2]

The Fight

The specialized narrative functions of actual violence evident in these instances are greatly augmented by the prevalent uses of violence in narrative forms ranging from personal conversation to public performance and formal literature. Three examples of the narrative figure of *the fight,* the competitive conflict central to all forms of adventure—an oral anecdote, an autobiographical incident, and a modern short story—allow us to consider the complicated intersection of story and reality in a range of situations and literary types.

In his research for *Language in the Inner City,* William Labov was particularly successful in generating oral narratives by asking young men to respond to the question "Were you ever in a fight with a guy bigger than you?" (354). One respondent, Larry, reported a violent altercation he had with a classmate who asked for a cigarette after Larry insisted, "I won't give my las' one to nobody." As Larry describes the conclusion of the incident, "After I got through stompin' him in the face, man, you know, all of a sudden I jus' went crazy. An' I just wouldn't stop hittin' the motherfucker. Dig it, I couldn't stop hittin' 'im, till the teacher pull me off o' him. An' guess what? After all that I gave the dude the cigarette. Ain't that a bitch?" (375).

For my purposes, what is remarkable about this account is Larry's half-conscious realization that the fight is not about the cigarette, which he willingly cedes to his opponent. Instead, it is a symbolic attempt to establish the terms and limits of personal force—what he will and will not do, and by extension, who and what he is and is not—as the basis for a limited sense of personal control. Interrupted by the genuine authority, the teacher, the effort is evidently unsuccessful. So instead of the expected resolution of the issues of power and identity through violence, the narrative ends with the protagonist's bemusement about the unexpected termination of the episode. Nevertheless, although a full understanding of the fight's motivation is beyond him, it exists as a prior condition to the altercation, or Larry would not have interpreted his friend's request as a challenge that warrants an aggressive response (a situation repeatedly encountered, he confides).

Larry's story and its interrogative coda show that the issues and values negotiated by violent confrontation are socially scripted, however personally undefined. That is, *the fight,* even in this personal account, is a narrative trope, a public sign, that structures personal experience. Although violent altercation is commonly assumed to be the loss of control, an aberrant departure from civilized order by a private individual, as Larry describes it fighting is not a deviation from the rules of society; it is, in fact, a product of their realization.

Some of the social expectations embedded in those rules are apparent in Luis J. Rodriguez's story of a prizefight. In *Always Running* (1993), a memoir of his "Gang Days in LA," Rodriguez recounts his participation in a community outreach boxing club. Like the center's educational facility that Luis helped to construct and the nutritional outreach program he devoted many hours to, boxing is understood as a positive means to community identity. The club's patron, Kid Maravilla, a neighborhood hero, embodies the public acclaim and the monetary reward that boxing promises. The Kid's beautiful girlfriend, who first talks to Luis on the occasion of his big fight, and his manager's encouraging attribution of *jaspia,* or hunger, to the young pugilist, further specify the terms of successful masculine identity boxing can institute: money, admiration, and sex. Excited about a match that could ultimately lead to Junior Olympic competition, Luis invites his estranged family to witness it. During the bout, it is their faces that are, initially, the register of his accomplishment and, finally, the reflection of his defeat:

> My sisters whooped and hollered. My brother flashed a grin. I felt great. I must win; so many people depended on it. (153)

> My eyes crossed over several rows of faces to the direction of my family. They were all on their feet. My sisters had their hands up to

their mouths. Joe looked awkward, like he didn't know whether to congratulate me for trying or to give his condolences. And Mama— I could see Mama had been crying. (155)

By representing the family as the image of the rewards and risks, Rodriguez emphasizes the collective nature of the personal expectations about male violence formally encoded in boxing. And, indeed, public approval makes prizefighting the conduit for limited actual power in the form of the purse and the accompanying approbation. But Rodriguez's dependence on his family's response also suggests that, for him, genuine sources of masculine identity reside in relations that cannot be negotiated by fighting, even prizefighting.

If the social investment apparent in oral and written accounts of *the fight* is, as I am suggesting, a representative condensation of the pervasive ideology of constructive violence, the idealization of that concept is epitomized by the prizefight, which novelist Joyce Carol Oates examines in her essay *On Boxing* (1986). An individual boxer frequently fights out of anger against oppression by poverty and racism and in hope of wresting the kind of limited rewards Luis Rodriguez sketches in his autobiography. It "is reasonable," Oates asserts, "to assume that boxers fight one another because the legitimate objects of their anger are not available to them. . . . You fight what's nearest, what's available, and what's ready to fight you. And if you can you do it for money" (63). But there is more to it. Two men hitting one another, no matter how strong or accomplished, are only fighting. In order to qualify as boxing, the same activity requires a referee and spectators. The presence of rules and an audience demonstrates that the activity in the ring is socially regulated, but it may also suggest that the rewards structured by boxing are of a general significance far greater than titles or purses.

As Oates sees it, the referee exists to absolve the crowd: "He is our moral conscience extracted from us as spectators so that, for the duration of the fight, 'conscience' need not be a factor in our experience" (47). Thus, it is not sadism, an appetite for violence itself, that fuels the enthusiasm of onlookers, or such absolution for the suffering inflicted through conflict would not be necessary. And even imaginative identification with the status of a hero is not sufficient motivation. Instead, for Oates, boxing as a public institution is grounded on the universal fear of powerlessness—the kind of "pain, humiliation, loss, chaos" (26) symbolized by the knockout punch.[3]

As she notes, there is inevitably a turning point in a match when the male spectators will begin to favor the victor, no matter whom they had rooted for at the start. Through this shift, the "ritual" purpose "of fighting is always honored. The high worth of combat is always affirmed" (73). The purpose the crowd chooses even over the fighters is ceremonial perpetuation of the illusion that actual limitations can be transcended (77), that a fighter can fend off powerlessness. This ideal expectation is advanced through "a story without words" (11) plotted around the staged conflict of two dangerous men. Boxing is the performative assertion "of a world model in which we are humanly responsible not only for our own acts but those that are performed against us," Oates explains (13).

Winning, the very essence of the illusion of power this drama promotes, is about successfully managing everything that endangers the self—all that is threatening projected onto the actions of the opponent. But as Oates stresses, it is only within the metaphoric space of the ring that such perfect power can be imagined as the effect of violence. Perhaps because of its focus on the threat of impotence (a word that makes the concept of male sexual prowess a type for any other conceivable form of capacity), boxing is, according to Oates, "for men, and is about men, and *is* men. A celebration of the lost religion of masculinity all the more trenchant for its being lost" (72).

Ernest Hemingway's well-known short story "The Battler" (1925) concentrates on the social meanings of the masculine losses incurred through fighting and boxing. After a railroad employee forcibly ejects the adolescent Nick Adams from a boxcar, he wanders into the camp of two hobos who turn out to be a punch-drunk white boxer, a former champion, and his black caretaker. These encounters structure three different presentations of the nodal plot of *the fight*. The first violent confrontation has occurred just before Nick picks himself up and dusts himself off at the beginning of the story. A "son of a crutting brakeman" had lured him into position and shoved him off the moving freight train (97). Humiliated by his own credulity, Nick is still mulling over this event when he meets Ad Francis, the ex-prizefighter. Ad helps him to interpret the incident by reporting that the brakeman had looked proud and happy strutting across "the top of the cars" afterward. "It must have made him feel good to bust you," he comments. And in support of Nick's expression of a desire to strike back, he advises, "Get him with a rock sometime when he's going through" (98).

The second confrontation, narrowly averted, occurs after Ad and his traveling companion, Bugs, have shared their dinner of ham and eggs with Nick. The self-styled "crazy" boxer, who had previously welcomed Nick, then begins to try to provoke him into a fight: "You're a snotty bastard. You come in here where nobody asks you and eat a man's food. . . . Hit me. . . . Try and hit me" (101). Bugs prevents the threatened "beating" by striking Ad on the base of his skull with a well-worn black-jack. Ushering Nick out of the camp before Ad comes to, Bugs explains Ad's hostility, a regular occurrence, by confiding details about the prize-fighter's background—the "too many" blows that made him "simple," the failed marriage that damaged him further, and the destructive prison experience during which he had met Bugs.

According to Philip Young, Bugs, also described as "crazy" in the story, exhibits a "very discomforting and oily courtesy" toward "Mister Francis" and "Mister Adams," whom he never addresses in a less deco-rous style. This formality by a black character toward whites denotes for Young an "obsequious and ironic servility" (207). To condemn Bugs's speech as disturbing, even manipulative, implies that he is trying to subvert the racial relations inscribed in the text—and implies the critic's fear that he may be able to do so. But the rest of the diction in "The Battler" refutes this possibility.

The seven-page story identifies Bugs in terms of race no fewer than twenty-five times. Whereas Ad Francis is occasionally labeled as "the ex-prizefighter," Bugs is constantly tagged as "the negro." As he ap-proaches the campfire where Ad and Nick have met, still shrouded by the obscurity of evening, Bugs appears an uninflected "man." But Nick's emphatic, amended response to the figure calling a friendly greeting as he moves out of the darkness is racial classification: "It was a negro's voice. Nick knew from the way he moved that he was a negro" ("Bat-tler" 100), and once so designated, Bugs is thereafter the exemplar of a subjugated race. The third-person narrative assigns the epithet *nigger* four times, one of which is Nick's own ascription. Therefore, however he may feel about the situation, Bugs's submissive style accords with, rather than threatens, the system of racial privilege assigned by the story.

To read Bugs as Young does, as a challenge to the status quo, is to intimate that the "change" (102) Bugs effects by striking Ad at the base of the skull really disturbs the power relationships of the story. But the preponderant evidence of racially inflected labels throughout suggests that no violence by Bugs can transform his situation. Despite repeated application of the well-worn blackjack, Bugs remains a black man in a world under the control of whites—even a damaged ex-fighter and a callow stranger. And in Ad's case, the blow that fells him merely interrupts his aggression, which Bugs believes will resume as soon as Ad recovers from its immediate effects. Obviously, Bugs's violence cannot provide access to what the former fighter continues to require: some evidence of the power that he feels he has lost.

Despite a setting external to community, social codes and standards shape all the confrontations in the story. Like race relations, economic conditions influence the outcome of aggression throughout. Nick's desire to gain experience of the world through travel—a "natural" right of male passage, it would seem, in the context of Hemingway's oeuvre—is thwarted by the devious brakeman, an agent of the railroad company's financial regulation of the means of access. In effect, Nick's personal manhood, the story hints, is held hostage to economic authority in the public domain. And given this condition, violence can only secure the illusion of power. The swaggering brakeman, like his victim, is ultimately governed by railroad policy, and does not gain any actual control over the conditions of his existence by manhandling the vulnerable boy. Likewise, neither would Nick secure any real empowerment by sniping at the bully with a rock hurled from the rail bed.

The threatened altercation between Ad and Nick also underscores the illusory nature of power in the story. Although Nick has eaten Ad's food, at Bugs's warning the boy had refused to lend his grotesque host the knife he asked to borrow. Not withstanding this failed exchange, Nick could not have provided what Ad is actually trying to secure. Ad's counsel of anonymous vengeance on the brakeman implies that the ex-fighter, like the boy, can only manage the symbolic substitution of aggression for the authority he lacks. Like Nick's yearning for ineffectual revenge, Ad's threats of violence are not a genuine means to the potency his request for Nick's knife intimates he wishes to recover.

The most significant financial relationship is between Ad Francis and Bugs. Although the pair are living a tramp's existence, they are not strictly bums, who in the period of the story were usually homeless because of indigence, nor hobos, who rode the rails in search of employment. In fact, Ad, who got rich as a prizefighter, receives a monthly check for his maintenance from his former wife, and Bugs is probably compensated for his care of the ex-boxer. Both, then, enjoy at least limited actual power, but Ad is emphatically an *ex*-boxer. A recognizable "loser," he no longer possesses the ability to sustain or project the belief that life can be mastered. And as Oates makes clear, it is not the prize he wins but the illusion he serves that secures a boxer's value. Failing this function, as the setting emphasizes, Ad is isolated from society, the real source of power and manhood. This exclusion from community, combined with his monstrous appearance—an outward sign of the deviance that also afflicts his mind—indicates that male aggression, even elevated to the status of boxing, has failed to secure the social connections the story of his marriage implies he needed.

On the basis of these three brief examples of fighting as constructive violence in narrative operation, we may conclude (1) that, as in Larry's narrative, whatever power—that is, the ability to control or effect circumstances favorable to development—an individual has may be threatened by the needs of others; (2) that in these circumstances, the fight, or any aggressive struggle, is more likely to be a reminder of powerlessness than a means of control, a general condition witnessed by Rodriguez's memoir; (3) and that, as "The Battler" stresses, dependence on aggression precludes anything but limited participation in the communal systems and discourses that actually empower.

The trope of the fight implies the constant reiteration of two destructive lessons: the assertion of masculine powerlessness and the recommendation of a largely inexpedient method of addressing that condition. This self-defeating cycle, sanctioned by the community, inevitably produces anger and only rarely (such as within the special conditions of the prizefight) secures limited access to power. In addition, it deflects attention from the discursive or material sources of genuine power within society. But "The Battler," which began with young Nick's naive desire for brutal revenge, instructs the male initiate in the futility of violence as a means to effective power, and, so understood, demonstrates to its readers that constructive violence *can* be challenged through narrative interrogation and critical analysis.

Violence in Narrative Structure

The characterizations and themes we have just examined do not exhaust the many formal uses of literary violence. Acting with extraordinary flexibility, representations of violence commonly inform many narrative features, which also influence social values and practice. Narrative, like drama, is not real action but an imitation of an action, organized by Aristotle's specification of completeness—having a beginning, a middle, and an end—and violent incident plays a prominent role in all of these definitive stages. Violence frequently signals the Proppian condition of social divergence or *lack* that usually initiates a story, which commences, according to Tzvetan Todorov, when "a stable situation" is "disturbed," an event frequently plotted as an act of violence, a pattern clearly evident in Ernest Gaines's *A Gathering of Old Men* when an unknown assailant murders the white boss of a Louisiana plantation. As a consequence of the initial deviation from expected order, "there results a state of disequilibrium; by the action of a force directed in the opposite direction" a similar but nonidentical state of equilibrium is reestablished (Todorov, *Poetics* 111). That opposition is also often represented as a violent act, the contest of bodies, wills, or ideas that produces first the conflict and finally the resolution of the story by eliminating the agonistic struggle that structures the action throughout. In Gaines's novel the racial struggle defines the conflict, the repercussions of the murder organize the structure, and the climactic shootout between the black elders and the Klan secures the resolution.

In the important middle phase of "disequilibrium," which generally comprises most of the fully developed narrative, violence is prominent as an agent that complicates or facilitates the movement of the plot; as an intensifier of characters, themes, settings, or episodes; and as a method of orientation toward actions and characters. For example, the violent incidents involving the protagonist of *Continental Drift*—the robbery, the brother's suicide, and the deaths of the Haitian passengers—order the plot in Russell Banks's novel; the young men of Tobias Wolff's autobiography and short stories experience violence as central aspects of characterological development; the violence of actions and characters in Pinckney Benedict's *Town Smokes* infuse ordinary boys' lives with dramatic meaning; and the assassination plot in Don DeLillo's *Libra* orients the conscious and unconscious philosophies expounded by the multiple participants in the shared project of murdering John F. Kennedy. And not only does violence arrange and intensify narrative content, but it also assigns social significance.

Certainly the shock value of violence as incident or description alters perceptions of the importance of the characters, ideas, or attributes of narrative. The incident of the robbery in Richard Bausch's *Violence,* for instance, changes everyday meanings to imbue everything—the scruffy robbers and the mundane protagonist himself—with a temporary sense of extraordinary significance. This intensification of value through the deviation from familiar norms can affect all of the meaning codes of place, person, and reference to which violence is attached.[4] And the inclusion of violence also affects its perception. *Focalization,* or the presentation of narrative through the "mediation of some 'prism', 'perspective', 'angle of vision'" (Rimmon-Kenan 71) is negotiated by violence as an activity already coded with received values that the text invokes. The metaphoric representation of the Gulf War in terms of a football game or a "surgical strike" did much to shape its popular reception as a positive political act; in the same manner, the presentation of a football game or political campaign as an act of war colors its reception dramatically. In *The Things They Carried,* Tim O'Brien's representation of Lemon's death in Vietnam as the violation of a boy at play exploits this effect to raise disturbing questions about guilt and innocence.

Although actual unscripted action is unpredictable and open to diverse results, the imitated action of generic narrative always imputes significance and imposes predictable outcomes. The murderous acts of school killers may derive from a fundamental confusion about this key difference. Their destructive actions may be paradoxical attempts to secure the order that textual violence creates within adventure fiction. The heroic selfhood modeled by Richard Harding Davis's fiction, for example, is the kind of end result that could easily appeal to a confused teenaged boy. Although the inevitable "resolution" supplied by traditional fiction is the antithesis of real chaos and destruction, such error may be a predictable consequence of narrative process.

In *S/Z* Roland Barthes postulates the extraordinary ability of story to generate expectations from the interaction of five narrative codes. The *proairetic code* predicates predictable actions, such as the opening of a door being followed by the entrance of a character. "Such sequences," according to Barthes, "imply a logic in human behavior" (18). The *her-*

meneutic code introduces an enigma that the reader is teased into trying to solve in the course of the reading. Through that participation, the hermeneutic elements operate to construct the action of the text as logical within the apparent experience of the reader. The repetition of violent acts in formal sequences converts them to proairetic and hermeneutic formulas of expected results and cause and effect relations. In this way, generic adventure fiction redefines the destruction inherent in actual violence as a stage in a constructive order. But actions are not only converted into recognizable causal chains by narrative patterns, they are also charged with social valuation.

Barthes's *semantic, symbolic,* and *social codes* schematize systems of descriptive reference that place the plotted action within a recognizable context of preexistent meanings already inscribed in language, literature, social relations, and common knowledge within a given society. For example, Davis plots imperial war in *Soldiers of Fortune* as a developmental expedient in the familiar cultural narrative of a young American's progress toward success. Through this assignment of social reference, violence as narrative formula is encoded as a seemingly natural and socially productive means to masculine development in the genres of male adventure. In fiction, the relation of characters to the violent activities of the initial and central stages of narrative aligns them with predictable social codes of meaning, while the violent resolution typical of the adventure formula establishes the predominance of one side of a binary contest in the same way that the narrative component of war imposes unitary definition upon complex experience. Thus, although violence does not produce power, its inscription in fiction certainly encourages the presumption that it does.

Violence permeates narrative structure because, as even this brief analysis confirms, it is so successful in influencing beliefs. Particularly in adventure genres, violent action, this study argues, formulates expectations about agency, authority, and emergent masculine identity. Indeed, this process is so effective it promotes the widespread expectation that real violence can script the same significances as fictive acts. Michael Kaufman argues that male violence addresses many issues of power and identity in contemporary masculine experience:

The act of violence is many things at once. At the same instant it is the individual man acting out relations of sexual power; it is the violence of society—a hierarchical, authoritarian, sexist, class-divided, militarist, racist, impersonal, crazy society. . . . In the psyche of the individual man it might be his denial of social power-lessness through an act of aggression. In total these acts of violence are like a ritualized acting out of our social relations of power. (1)

Another contemporary gender theorist, R. W. Connell, asserts that violence is prominent in political relations among men. Military fighting, murder, and assault, he points out, are almost exclusively male "transactions." Violence is used to assert "boundaries" and "exclusions," as in gay bashing; to claim dominance in group struggles, as in gang violence; and to impose "a reactionary gender politics," as in the terrorist bombing of abortion clinics (83). These disparate impositions of violent regulation are united in that they are all employed in an effort to secure assumed privilege through genuine brutality.

Deviation, Intensification, and Alignment

As Connell's examples suggest, the consequences of basing real experience on textual expectations may be deleterious. This is especially true of the expectations about masculine maturation structured by traditional adventure fiction, as the following two stories illustrate. In the first, the maturing boy gets bigger, stronger, smarter, and more skillful in the arts and industries practiced within his community. As his competencies emerge from his experience, he gradually begins to participate in the sexual, social, and economic networks that organize his society. His adult identity is a feature of the many roles that he practices, and the agency and status that comprise his power are an effect of the degree and prowess of his participation within the authorizing activities of his group. Within such a system, his masculine "self," an effect of varying active negotiations, is necessarily multivalent and essentially unstable. Something like this process characterizes (or should characterize) the actual lives of men, I believe. But our understanding of the complex social system shaping such mastery is obscured through reliance on the second story of magical maturation.

In this story the undefined boy is supposed to become an empowered man through constructive violence. After this event, his adult identity, his male "self," is understood as constant, integrated, individual essence. Tobias Wolff's autobiographical *This Boy's Life* provides a telling example of this model in operation. Young Toby, who imagines that he can turn from an uncertain boy into a Western hero through the possession of a rifle, manages to secure a .22-caliber rifle as a gift from one of his mother's suitors. He "needed" the gun, he explains, "for the way it completed me when I held it" (23). But Toby quickly realizes that mere possession does not ensure identification. At first content to clean the rifle, strike brave poses with it in front of the mirror, and pretend to shoot, eventually he loads the gun and kills a squirrel instead of the "two old people" he had been aiming at from his apartment window. Distressed by his own brutality, he knows that despite his efforts to resist the temptation, he will be drawn to aim and fire again. From the perspective of adulthood, Wolff observes: "All my images of myself as I wished to be were images of myself armed" (27).

Although he fails, Toby employs violence to try to depart from his position of powerless boy. And in spite of his distaste for actual destruction, in the absence of any genuine understanding of power and any real means to its acquisition, constructive violence seems to be his only option. The trajectory of this coveted conversion follows what I propose as the typical pattern laid down by the ideology of constructive violence: *deviation* from ordinary experience through *intensification* of circumstance and character in the service of *alignment* with a new system of valuation. But although Toby does experience the intensity of deviation from his ordinary experience, his action does not secure his alignment with his image of "Western" man, the false ideal of masculine empowerment through armed aggression he cherishes.

It is impossible to review Wolff's prescient account without noting its correspondence to the expanding series of schoolyard assassinations by teen and preteen boys: three dead in Moses Lake, Washington; two in Bethel, Alaska; four in Pearl, Mississippi, including the mother of the assailant; three in West Paducah, Kentucky; five in Jonesboro, Arkansas; four, including the mother and father, in Springfield, Oregon; fifteen, including the assailants, in the massacre at Littleton, Colorado, and so forth. Writing in the *New York Times,* Timothy Egan reports the similarities among the first six cases, conditions that also apply to the Columbine High School slayings and the 2001 assaults in San Diego County, as well as to Toby's narrative: Each of the adolescents felt isolated and abused, each had easy access to guns, each was influenced by cultural images of male killers, and several recorded their intentions in written form.

Although much attention has been paid to the availability of firearms, and experts have testified to the sense of powerlessness affecting these young men, despite frequent condemnations of media we have not really begun to understand the relation of textual to actual violence in these cases. Yet it is a fact that Barry Loukaitis, the fourteen-year-old from Moses Lake who opened fire on his algebra class, wrote a violent poem for ninth-grade English;[5] Kip Kinkel, the fifteen-year-old from Springfield, Oregon, who killed his parents in addition to two others at Thurston High School, read aloud a journal entry in his English class about murdering fellow students; Luke Woodham of Pearl, Mississippi, heard to say in televised portions of his confession that he expected to become "famous," left explanatory journal entries and authored a detailed last will and testament; and, in the words of a *New York Times* special report, Eric Harris and Dylan Klebold had plotted "their lethal assault in a journal of hatred for about a year" and had read "frightening essays" to their Columbine classmates (Belluck and Wilgoren A1).

Political liberals discover the cause of the carnage in the accessibility of arms and call for stricter gun control legislation, while conservatives condemn the infectious violence of popular culture (Hunt). Both of these interpretations find support in the facts of the cases cited—guns were obviously too readily available to these unhappy young men, who were, by their own reports, deeply attracted to violent masculine images promoted by cinema, music, and video games. But these assessments are incomplete. In addition to practicing destruction, the school killers were, I believe on the evidence of their own production, attempting to secure male empowerment through inscription—the very deviation, intensification, and masculine realignment promoted by constructive violence. Like the youthful version of himself in Wolff's autobiography, these boys were trying to write in blood the violent scripts they believed could turn them into men.

But to restrict the problem of male narrative violence to the aberrant reactions of a few confused boys, no matter how awful their acts, is to ignore broader significances addressed by contemporary male authors. As literary scholar Judith Fetterly charges, all of America is suffering "from a national narrative that valorizes violence, that defines masculinity as the production of violence" (888). The schoolhouse murderers of our recent history, like the characters of the narratives in *Violent Adventure*, apparently experience the crippling inaccessibility of developmental patterns modeling genuine relations of power. As a group, these texts ascribe the failure of masculine maturation to the inadequacy of cultural institutions that regulate power—the family, the legal, economic, and military establishments—in addition to the cheat of a reliance on the ideological promise of violent masculine conversion. In the light of this vision of public failure, we can begin to comprehend private enactments of the textual magic of constructive violence, and we need such understanding in order to challenge the cultural fantasy that informs the violent act.

All of the postmodern works studied mount such challenge by interrupting the sequence of deviation, intensification, and alignment. Key modern short stories of *The Virile Anthology* introduce the paradoxical necessity of violent intervention at the same time they narrate its failure to secure the survival of its practitioners. In contemporary stories, Pinckney Benedict's and Richard Ford's young male protagonists experience the violence of adult males as inevitable signals of inadequacy rather than as paths to power. Thom Jones and Cormac McCarthy use surreal episodes to convey the grotesque ineffectuality of violence. Tim O'Brien, Russell Banks, and Don DeLillo deconstruct public myths of constructive violence to reveal the ethical inadequacy of contemporary society. Throughout this study, this deflection exposes the impossibility of masculine development and the unavailability of a social structure that could support it. Boys do not achieve power or mature identity in contemporary adventure texts, and the social institutions regulating familial, legal, political, military, and economic relations, dominated by destructive plots of constructive violence, are inadequate to the central task of socialization.

Any proposal that violent representation should be censored is obviously not the answer to the problem of violence in society. If anything, this study implies that we should be encouraging the insights violent texts invite. In life, violence is one of many forms of the imposition of force; in literature, violence is a privileged figure through which the workings of abstract "power" are articulated in individual life stories and particularized social contexts. To analyze narratives of violence is therefore to investigate the ways in which violent acts are conceived in

179

the personal and political lives of men and the ways in which men conceive of their own lives through the narrative trope of violence. The elements of narrative, unlike those of experience, are easily manipulated; hence, through literature the consolidation of masculine identity and violence may be challenged and the social power it organizes may be questioned.

The texts of this study, by a variety of American men writing in assorted styles across a range of political positions, indicate that constructive violence is a detrimental code that should and can be broken. Their choice of the adventure narrative shows that contemporary male writers are not rejecting the project of masculine identity, nor refuting the need for masculine power, nor even, in most cases, revoking the notion of masculine privilege. What their revisions to violent adventure do demonstrate is that the structures through which acts of violence are represented may operate in a complex system of possibilities to contest the literary, social, and psychological power relations that code texts of violence and that texts of violence code.

NOTES

Introduction

1. Because rape is notoriously underreported, some experts suggested that the figure might be closer to one out of every three (Mithers 190).

2. On December 20, 1996, Clifford Krauss reported an unprecedented 16 percent drop in the New York City crime rate. Noting that some other major cities, like San Francisco and Las Vegas, have also decreased rates of major felonies, he observed that some cities, like Newark and Hartford, show increases (A1, B4). The good news continued when a study of statistics on homicide and cocaine use from six cities from 1987 to 1993 revealed a decline from the heights of the mid-1980s (Butterfield, "Drop"), and the Associated Press reported that homicide rates in major cities continued to drop in 1997. New Orleans had 25 percent fewer homicides. New York City and Los Angeles saw a 21 percent and 20 percent reduction, respectively. However, the same study showed dramatic increases in some smaller cities; for example, Camden, New Jersey, and Denver, Colorado ("L.A., New York Homicides Fall" 20). On April 14, 1997, the AP summarized the downward trend with the headline "American Violent Crime Down 12.4 Percent," a report based on the comparison of Bureau of Justice Statistics comparing 1995 to 1994 ("American Violent Crime" 2). Yet Kenneth Lovett, in November 1997, reported that despite FBI statistics showing a drop of 13.4 in Manhattan crime statistics, "twenty-two, mostly upstate [New York] counties in 1996 saw increases in violent crimes such as murder, rape, assault, and burglary" ("Smaller Cities").

James Garbarino emphasizes that the escalating problem of violence among young men may be obscured in the national statistics that fail to take into account the increased incarceration of potential killers arrested in crackdowns on juvenile crime, which has been rising. Citing FBI statistics that juvenile arrests for violent or potentially violent crime (possession of weapons, aggravated assault, theft, and murder have risen 50 percent between 1987 and 1996, as well as the "seven-fold increase in serious assault by juveniles since World War II," he contends "that no longer can any of us believe that we and our children are immune to lethal youth violence" (8). All of these tendencies—the high base rate of violence, slight statistical drops in some violent crime, and the increase in some areas and activities—continue to characterize the present period.

3. If a Martian were to observe the unreasonable and repeated resort to warfare on this planet, Konrad Lorenz argued, the inevitable conclusion would be that "human behavior, and particularly human social behavior, far from being determined by reason and cultural tradition alone, is still subject to the laws prevailing in all phylogenetically adaptive behavior" (229).

4. In an overview published in 1999, W. James Potter reports that according to reviews published in 1994 and 1998 the number of studies on media violence range from 3,000 to 3,500 (2)—a volume reflecting a high degree of public concern. In 1994, for an extensive and continuing study of television violence by the Center for Communication Policy at the University of California at Los Angeles, commissioned by ABC, CBS, NBC, and Fox at the urging of Senator Paul Simon, scholars from various universities engaged in extensive analysis of programming and found many reasons for apprehension. For example, in 1997 Dale Kurkel of the University of California noted a predominance of "attractive" violence in children's cartoons. Violent portrayals in this genre "present perpetrators as attractive," brutal acts go "unpunished," there seem to be "minimal consequences to victims," and they "appear realistic" to a substantial audience under seven years of age. This "sanitized" and "glamorized" violence, he concluded, poses "high risk" for naive viewers ("Conference on Television"). Although noting a general decline in overall network violence, in 1998 the same commission report reported a disturbing increase in "shockumentaries" that simulate "real" violence in shows devoted to animal and police activities (Mifflin). Again, a major issue seems to be the audience's ability to make realistic assessments of the violent portrayals. These two findings on different kinds of televised violence suggest to me the broader need for the kind of analysis of the uses and context of violent representation that *Violent Adventure* applies to literature.

5. In *Mayhem* (1998), Sissela Bok cites a *New York Times* editorial published on Jan. 26, 1995, as the source of this statistic (159, n. 6).

6. Bok cites Edward Donnerstein, "Mass Media Review: Thoughts on the Debate," *Hofstra Law Review* 22 (1994), p. 14, n. 93. Citing the American Psychological Association, Garbarino puts the influence of television on youth violence as "accounting for 10 to 15 percent of the variation in violent behavior" (108). While media imagery is evidently detrimental, it is by no means the only or most important cause of violence in contemporary society.

7. In condemning simplistic attributions of social violence to instinct or media, I am not dismissing the importance of these fields to a necessarily multifaceted understanding of a complex problem. Helpful nonreductive reviews of current theories about biology and media in the study of violence can be found in Debra Niehoff's *The Biology of Violence* and W. James Potter's *On Media Violence,* both published in 1999.

8. Martin Green argues that the adventure story developed as the historical complement of colonization: The "adventure narrative" is the "generic counterpart in literature to empire in politics" (37).

9. According to Alastair Fowler, the dynamic form of genre is elaborated into sub-genres by adding particularized subjects or motifs (111–12).

10. Ralph Cohen argues in "Do Postmodern Genres Exist?" that contemporary study of genre is valuable precisely because it contributes to an understanding of the social conditions in which genre plays a part.

11. Because, as Fredric Jameson explains in *The Political Unconscious,* "a genre is essentially a socio-symbolic message" that is "immanently and intrinsically an ideology in its own right" (141), "generic discontinuities" operate as disjunctive "protopolitical acts" (149). See also Rosalie Littell Colie's *The Resources of Kind* (1973) and Alastair Fowler's *Kinds of Literature: An Introduction to the Theory of Genres and Modes* (1982) for useful references for contemporary studies of genre.

12. As Tzvetan Todorov declares in *Genres in Discourse* (1990), "Like any other institution, genres bring to light the constitutive features of the society to which they belong" (19).

13. See also Linda Kintz's 1996 article "Conservative Cowboy Stories: Adventures of the Chosen Sons" on right-wing adaptations of the Western myth to current political objectives.

14. In *Masculinities,* gender theorist R. W. Connell contends that hegemonic constructs of gender, which reflect dominant social arrangements supported by both cultural ideals and "institutional power" (77), can be challenged to allow the expression of alternatives. The contemporary writers of this study are engaged, I am arguing, in just such a challenge.

1. The Hero of the Hour

1. See Richard Slotkin's thorough discussion of the frontier archetype in *Regeneration through Violence: The Mythology of the American Frontier, 1600–1860.* See Martin Green's *Dreams of Adventure, Deeds of Empire* for an extensive definition of heroic attributes of the literary expression of British imperialism, especially chapter 7, "Popular Literature and Children's Literature." See also Gail Bederman's *Manliness and Civilization: A Cultural History of Gender and Race in the United States, 1880–1917* for a historical account of the influence of Theodore Roosevelt, whose values greatly affected the constructive violence portrayed by Davis.

2. Davis comments that his titular reference is to MacIver's autobiography, *Under Fourteen Flags,* which since its publication would need a more inclusive title to cover further adventures.

3. Green credits the nonfiction of Samuel Smiles, born in 1812, with the promotion of "the cult of machinery" initiated in Defoe's *Robinson Crusoe.* Through such works as the *Lives of Engineers,* "Smiles complained that history had been monopolized by kings and warriors, and claimed attention for engineers, the heroes of peace" (Green 205).

4. Fairfax Downey cites Davis's collection of despatches from the Boer War, *With Both Armies in South Africa,* published in 1900 for the reporter's descriptions of the war.

5. Downey cites Davis's *With the Allies* (1914) for this description.

6. See also the first chapter of John McClure's *Late Imperial Romance* (1994) for an account of the fissures and contradictions in British literature of imperialism during the same period.

7. In "Violence and Sacrifice in Modern War Narratives," a 1994 study, Evelyn Cobley notes, "Leaving little room for the soldier to display the aggressive personality required of war heroes, mechanized warfare results in a new perception of the soldier" (78).

2. The Paradox of Virility

1. This story is titled "Turnabout" in *The Collected Stories of William Faulkner.*

2. See Levinson, et al., *The Seasons of a Man's Life,* 97–101, for a discussion of the importance of the mentoring relationship.

3. Boys' Lives

1. *The Making of Masculinities: The New Men's Studies,* edited by Harry Brod, and *Changing Men: New Directions in Research on Men and Masculinity,* edited by Michael S. Kimmel, both published in 1987, provide representative essays.

2. See the *New York Times Book Review* articles on *Town Smokes* and *This Boy's Life.* Of Benedict's collection, Diane McWhorter observes that the book begins by invoking "'a coming of age' strategy," (13) puts "in for" a "piece of the Huck Finn legacy" (14), but "screech[es] off the pastoral path" through fiction that reveals "the fraudulence of mythology" in a culture where "the preferred form of communication is murder" (13). In his review of *This Boy's Life,* Joel Conorroe notes that Wolff's book is a *Bildungsroman* comparable to modern novels of artistic development (28).

3. Kimmel cites E. Anthony Rotundo, *American Manhood.*

4. Patricia Meyer Spacks cites Erikson's *Young Man Luther,* 113.

5. Timothy Beneke argues that the need to appear tough is the key ingredient of a range of destructive practices meant to demonstrate masculine identity: "Men engaging in a gang bang, committing political torture, bashing a gay man; white men deriding blacks and boys torturing a bug, are all in danger of being regarded as less manly by other men if they empathize or try to help" (41).

6. Of course, there are alternative forms of this plot, as Propp's analysis of typical functions structuring the Russian folktale suggests. Endings may include any or all of the following structural moves: the resolution of the hero's task, the recognition of the hero, the transfiguration of the hero, the punishment of the hero's opponent, the marriage of the hero, his ascension to the throne (62–64). My point is that the formal development of the story stresses the successful development of the hero figure, especially his acquisition of whatever signals status and power in his society.

7. See also Joseph Campbell's *The Hero with a Thousand Faces,* which posits the quest motif as the archetypal plot of traditional narrative.

8. Erich Fromm's *The Anatomy of Human Destructiveness* outlines the psychology of such reaction in his theory of malignant aggression.

9. A good theoretical discussion applicable to this futile gesture is to be found in

Jeffrey T. Nealon's analysis of resentment in the chapter on "White Male Anger" in *Alterity Politics*. Employed to "protect" the self rather than change the world, Nealon explains, resentment inevitably reveals "failure, absence, or lack" (144).

4. Lacanian Westerns

1. See comparable studies of adaptations of the Western genre in Jane Tompkins's *West of Everything*; Paul Smith's "Eastwood Bound"; and chapter 5, "Westerns," in Roger Horrocks's *Male Myths and Icons*.

2. See Lacan, "The Meaning of the Phallus,"(*Feminine* 76, 83) as to the child's initial expectation that the mother will possess the phallus. What is at issue in this scene is the boy's desire to retain this illusion. The "discovery of the castration of the mother" and the consequent loss of the illusion of integrity she authorizes in the mirror stage inaugurates the Symbolic definition of self in the binary divisions of language. See Lacan, *Écrits,* 282.

3. Wolves, a primary motif throughout *Blood Meridian,* also appear as an important symbol in *The Crossing* (1994). The central male character, also a Western boy, is introduced through his almost otherworldly experience of a wolf pack and the plot develops as an attempt to rescue a wolf.

4. See Slotkin and Drinnon for historical analysis of the violence in Western texts.

5. McCarthy told Richard B. Woodward in a 1992 interview that "there's no such thing as a life without bloodshed" and that the expectation of some kind of improvement "is a really dangerous idea" (36).

6. Horrocks reads the violence in the conventional Western as the ethical justification of imperialism (58, 77), an ideological premise that *Blood Meridian* exposes and exploits.

7. John Emil Sepich cites Ralph A. Smith's "The 'King of New Mexico' and the Doniphan Expedition" for these horrifying statistics on the outlay of one frightened Mexican town that paid a large bounty on Comanche scalps:

> Pay as a private in the United States army at [the time of the novel] averaged about fifteen dollars a month, when bonuses were included. A group of Indian hunters averaging about fifty men and paid two hundred dollars a scalp would have to bring only four scalps into Chihuahua City in order to exceed the army's rate of pay. . . . [James] Kirker's group was known to have killed as many as two hundred Indians on a single trip, bringing in one hundred and eighty-two scalps. Taking the averages, this is sixty times more than the men would have earned in other employment. At one point Chihuahua owed James Kirker about $30,000. (124)

8. See Steven Shaviro on the importance of ritual in the novel.

9. See also Thomas Pughe's "Revision and Vision: Cormac McCarthy's *Blood Meridian*," in which he interprets the figure of the judge in McCarthy's anti-Western as the "link between the barbarization of the gang and the European civilization that Lukacs associates with 'progress'" (378).

10. See also Brian Evenson's "McCarthy's Wanderers: Nomadology, Violence, and Open Country," in which he links the judge's homelessness to the practice of extreme exploitation (47).

11. See also Nell Sullivan's "Cormac McCarthy and the Text of Jouissance," which in closing suggests the centrality of a Lacanian representation of "unassuageable lack" in McCarthy's novels (122).

12. Julia Kristeva explains this Lacanian figure as the "father in individual prehistory," a "Third Party" whom the boy's Imaginary mother desires (23, 251).

13. Lacan provides this description of the normative mirror stage:

This jubilant assumption of his specular image by the child at the *infans* stage, still sunk in his motor incapacity and nurturing dependence, would seem to exhibit in an exemplary situation the symbolic matrix in which the *I* is precipitated in a primordial form, before it is objectified in the dialectic of identification with the other, and before language restores to it, in the universal, its function as subject.

This form would have to be called the Ideal-I, if we wished to incorporate it into our usual register . . . But the important point is that this form situates the agency of the ego, before its social determination, in a fictional direction. (*Écrits* 2)

14. Rick Wallach's observation of both the emphatic immaturity, "the pediatric symbolism" (127) of feature in the representation of the judge and the "troubling complementarity" of the kid and the judge (128) supports a reading of the suspension of progress and the nondifferentiation of self and other of the Imaginary stage.

15. This destructive denouement may be understood as one outcome of the condition Julia Kristeva calls "abjection." As Stephen Frosh glosses it: "The fragility of [the] early subject/object boundary is extreme, making the first motion of the subject-to-be one that can be overwhelmed, producing a state of genuine abjection, of being devoured . . . Without mediation, this is precisely what happens in the relationship between the desiring mother and the despairing child" (135).

16. See also Shaviro 145–46 on the relation of *Blood Meridian* to Deleuze and Guattari.

17. Dana Phillips also notes the repetition of this phrase: "The most often repeated sentence in *Blood Meridian*," she observes, "is 'They rode on'" (443).

18. Tompkins interprets the typical Western setting as a dramatization of psychological impulse: "The monolithic, awe-inspiring character of the landscape seems to reflect a desire for self-transcendence, an urge to join the self to something greater" (76).

19. Dee Brown's *Bury My Heart at Wounded Knee* and Michael Lesy's *Wisconsin Death Trip* employ comparable repetition of horrific pattern to the study of Western history.

20. See also Joseph Tabbi's *Postmodern Sublime: Technology and American Writing from Mailer to Cyberpunk* (1995), which theorizes the sublime in contemporary fiction as an expression of "nonverbal technological" realism (xi), and Barbara Claire

Freeman's *The Feminine Sublime: Gender and Excess in Women's Fiction* (1995), which reads sublimity of theme and style as liberating "encounters with excess" (3). In "Sublimity and Skepticism in Montaigne" (1998), David L. Sedley helpfully summarizes the current debate about the concept of sublimity as an effect, suggesting transcendence of epistemological limits or as the figuration of skepticism about that capacity. McCarthy's use of the figure suggests the latter position. Of the collection of articles on this issue in *Of the Sublime: Presence in Question* (1993), edited by Jean François Courtine and others, Jacob Rogozinski's discussion of violence and Kantian indeterminacy in "The Gift of the World" is most relevant to my position.

21. Ironically, it is the psychotic effusions of another defective judge, Judge Schreber, whom Freud studied, that led Lacan to his theory of psychosis. See *Écrits: A Selection*, "On a question preliminary to any possible treatment of psychosis" 179–225.

22. See Phillips's "History and the Ugly Facts of Cormac McCarthy's *Blood Meridian*" for an analysis that articulates, as does this essay, the novel's refusal of conventional narrative pattern but insists that the predominant violence portrayed cannot be read as any kind of "sign or symbol" (435) and that *Blood Meridian* cannot be understood politically (449), a conclusion disputed here.

23. The revisionary forms of the Western that Cawelti examined in his 1976 *Adventure, Mystery, and Romance* depart from the formula of benign aggression enough to present "a sense of human depravity and corruption that almost seems to take a delight in the destructiveness of violence by accepting it as an inevitable expression of man's nature." However, even this type of Western continued to present violence as "the product of morally purposeful individual action in defense of the good group" (259). Ford and McCarthy rescind this principle.

5. Young Goodmen at War

1. Cohan and Shires are quoting Roland Barthes's *Image, Music, Text* here.

2. Ted Solotaroff's observation on the ambiguity produced by the conflict between "a licensed id and a fragile ego" (256) makes a parallel point.

3. Rebecca Norris reports in *American Health* that Jones himself suffered grand mal epileptic seizures as the result of a boxing match during his service as a U.S. Marine, and his symptoms were initially misdiagnosed as schizophrenia (96).

4. O'Brien's novel *Going after Cacciato* was winner of the National Book Award. His story sequence *The Things They Carried* was a *New York Times Book Review* "Editor's Choice 1990." Thom Jones's short story "The Pugilist at Rest" was the recipient of a 1993 O'Henry Award.

5. In *Dreams of Adventure, Deeds of Empire*, Green posits that the representation of the feudal British warrior class was modernized in the imperial eras of expansion dominated by merchant classes as the expression of gentlemanly bearing, an ideological middle ground that combined the noble status of inherited privilege with the aspirations of the bourgeoisie at the same time as it obscured military force as the basis of economic colonization.

6. The quotation Hanley cites comes from Doris Lessing's *Prisons We Choose to Live Inside,* in which Lessing argues for the open acknowledgement of the pleasurable excitement with which many people respond to the activities of war.

7. Paul Fussell notes the constant trope of the game in World War I literature. Not only did writers compare battles to football, regiments were encouraged into battle by leaders who supplied balls to kick into enemy territory. "Modern mass wars," he explains, "require in their early stages a definitive work of popular literature demonstrating how much wholesome fun is to be had at the training camp" (18). O'Brien's invocation of this war-as-the-play-of-boys metaphor reverses the assumptions that war, like games, is bound by rules, that winning is of paramount importance, and that the uncomplicated companionship of young males is an important result of military experience.

8. Both of these popular films were adapted from fiction: Robin Moore's bestselling *The Green Berets* (1966) and Richard Hooker's *MASH* (1970).

9. John Wayne's iconic significance in the promotion of male military adventure is widely noted. See, for example, Myriam Miedzian's *Boys Will Be Boys: Breaking the Link between Masculinity and Violence* and Mark Gerzon's *A Choice of Heroes: The Changing Faces of American Manhood.*

10. Tobey C. Herzog argues that the moral ambiguity of the American experience of Vietnam resulted from the special circumstances of the war (51–59). The isolation of individual soldiers created by the practice of separate assignments to military units, limited tours of duty, and rapid transitions from military to civilian life caused many problems. The every-man-for-himself arrivals and departures to and from field units made difficult adjustments the problem of separate individuals rather than obstacles shared with a supportive group, and the limited tours may have encouraged an emphasis on individual survival at the expense of other goals. Widespread American opposition to the war also contributed to a sense of ethical uncertainty, and the dispersion of the enemy throughout the whole country made observable geographical progress impossible. Similarly, since it was frequently difficult to distinguish between friend and foe in field maneuvers, it was often hard to define what was procedurally correct in many circumstances. The measurement of success in body counts, fired by media coverage and political pressures on commanders, was particularly pernicious. An emphasis on scoreboard numbers, Herzog argues, "led to inflated claims and, at times, American soldiers' callous disregard for civilian lives" (53). The media image of the crazed and bloodthirsty American soldier may have contributed to its occasional reality, as did the general availability of drugs and alcohol.

11. See Rollo May's *Power and Innocence* for an exposition of the kind of "pseudo-innocence" that O'Brien dramatizes here (49–50).

12. Slabey 205–10, Calloway 213, L. Smith 96. Don Ringnalda provides a comprehensive discussion of O'Brien's metafictional practice in chapter 5 of *Fighting and Writing the Vietnam War.*

13. In *Vietnam in American Literature,* Philip H. Melling argues that the "key" to

understanding Vietnam is pursuing historical continuity in order to "avoid the dead end of absurdity and the postmodern faith of a surrender to fragments" (xiii, 16). Owen W. Gilman, in "Vietnam and John Winthrop's Vision of Community," urges Americans to discover in the experience of Vietnam something like the affirming "ideal" that "vitalized" the Puritans (139).

14. Similarly, Kai Tal rebukes four traditional critics for their attempted "total reduction of the war to a metaphor" (223), comforting in its conformity to previous mythic and historical ideology.

15. Citing *Catch-22*, Fussell comments that irony is the "one dominating form of modern understanding" (*Great* 34–35). In *Wartime: Understanding and Behavior in the Second World War*, Fussell describes these two texts as primary examples of a literature dependent on a thematics of "blunders" (31), the ironic exploitation of the distance between right and wrong.

6. Detecting Power

1. See Thomas Michael Stein's "The Ethnic Vision in Walter Mosley's Crime Fiction," Peter Freese's *The Ethnic Detective*, Theodore O. Mason Jr.'s "Walter Mosley's Easy Rawlins: The Detective and Afro-American Fiction," and Robert Crooks's "From the Far Side of the Urban Frontier: The Detective Fiction of Chester Himes and Walter Mosley."

2. This communal recitation is a good example of the trope Karla F. C. Holloway identifies as *African American mourning stories*, "narratives scripted out of the ways of our remaking, our remembering our bodies and the conditions of dying" (34). This predominant motif is a performative ritual meant to both acknowledge violence and transgress the boundaries that it reveals.

3. In a 1983 interview with Mary Ellen Doyle, Gaines explains that he "had stories for twice as many men." The stories he included were composite rather than actual events, but some of those he chose not to include recounted actual events:

> I had heard of a fight between a Black and a white sharecropper racing to the derrick with their sugar cane. I had heard of a sixteen-year-old young man electrocuted for supposedly killing a white man; he was partially insane. A man told me that the electric chair didn't work and they garrotted him, choked him to death. . . . I had heard these stories not from Blacks but from whites. Another woman told me of going to town with her little girl, a fair-skinned child; an insane white woman tried to take the child because "she was too beautiful to be a nigger." In the book, one of the mulatto men tells this, how they fought and fought until the white woman got the child and slammed its head on the ground and killed it. That killing did not occur, in fact, though the fight did. I cut that story out. The point of all these stories is that these things happen. (167)

4. Cawelti notes that Freudian interpretations of the detective story are commonplace, but he argues that "where the detective's solution always projects the guilt back onto an external character, the Freudian method exposes the conflicting motives in

our own minds" (95). Gaines's reversal here, I am arguing, has something of the same effect. The form of this novel, with its multiple narration and participatory emphasis implicates the reader.

5. In an interview with Fred Beauford in 1972, Gaines exclaimed, "Mechanical things. Yes! Yes! Of course. Faulkner showed me a lot about things like that and I have no interest in his philosophy. I could no more agree with his philosophy than I could agree with [Governor] Wallace's" (19).

6. Gaines created a fictive Louisiana county "to catch some of the things that are important in my own America, the narrow little space my people were allowed to move in and out of" (Blake 144).

7. See also Suzanne W. Jones's discussion of Gaines's imposition of the double ending in "Reconstructing Manhood: Race, Masculinity, and Narrative Closure in Ernest Gaines's *A Gathering of Old Men* and *A Lesson Before Dying*," in which she argues that "the two endings support contradictory themes about violence and masculinity." The shoot-out implies that "fighting is the only satisfying and manly way to resolve an argument," while the trial proves that "talking can produce results" (54–55). However, by associating the first ending with black needs and the second with the white accomplishment of the rejection of violence enacted through the Gil plot, her fine article leaves me with the unfortunate impression that violent resolution is an especially African American priority.

8. See Cawelti's *The Six-Gun Mystique* and *Adventure, Mystery, and Romance: Formula Stories as Art and Popular Culture,* chapter 8, for a full exposition of the Western formula.

9. See Cawelti, *Adventure, Mystery, and Romance,* chapters 6 and 7.

10. The books in the Easy Rawlins series are generally set in the various decades of the detective's life and incidentally introduce issues of black relations to changing historical contexts. For example, *The Red Death* places Easy in the 1950s in the context of the FBI's pursuit of communists. *A Little Yellow Dog,* set in the 1960s, introduces the escalating violence in criminal communities because of more prevalent drug traffic. The series includes *Devil in a Blue Dress* (1990), *A Red Death* (1991), *White Butterfly* (1992), *Black Betty* (1994), *A Little Yellow Dog* (1996), and *Gone Fishin'* (1997), which provides the early background to the otherwise chronological series.

11. See Ronald T. Takaki's *Violence in the Black Imagination* (17–35) for a discussion of Douglass's special relation to issues of violence.

12. I am arguing that Douglass's assumption of the role of educated speaker utilizes one of the modes of power of his historical period. For an alternative reading that sees this fashioning of role as acquiescence to patterns of white masculine identity, see Richard Yarborough's "Race, Violence, and Manhood: The Masculine Ideal in Frederick Douglass's 'The Heroic Slave.'"

13. "It is at the bottom of life we must begin, and not at the top. Nor should we permit our grievances to overshadow our opportunities," he preached in his Atlanta Exposition Address in 1895 (36).

14. As Mosley stated in an interview, one of the most important objectives in the

Easy Rawlins mystery series is historical and political recuperation: "the books are really about Black life in Los Angeles" and recreate "historical events which Black people have been edited out of" ("On the Other Side," 11).

15. Chester Himes's Harlem Crime Stories series, begun in 1965 with *Cotton Comes to Harlem*, also includes *The Heat's On, Run Man Run, All Shot Up, The Big Gold Dream, The Crazy Kill, The Real Cool Killers, A Rage in Harlem*, and *Blind Man with a Pistol*. The humorous cynicism of Himes's detective figures, Grave Digger Jones and Coffin Ed Johnson, contrasts Easy Rawlins's more naive pursuit of knowledge.

16. This theme of black male pursuit of knowledge is noted by the author as a characteristic preoccupation: "I especially love black men and the way we deal with life in America, the way that we understand, the way that we pass through things" (Sherman 35).

17. See also Mason's discussion of the house as a symbol of the "extreme fluidity" of Easy's complex negotiations of racialized codes (178–79). Joppy, too, as the proprietor of the butcher's bar where the action begins, is connected to the motif of ownership.

18. Valerie Melissa Babb identifies the tragic mulatto as a figure of "cross-racial interaction" in works by both black and white authors: William Wells Brown's *Clotel; or, The President's Daughter*, Charles W. Chestnutt's *The Wife of His Youth and Other Stories* and *The Marrow of Tradition*, James Weldon Johnson's *Autobiography of an Ex-Colored Man*, Harriet Beecher Stowe's *Uncle Tom's Cabin*, and Mark Twain's *Pudd'nhead Wilson* (142, n. 13).

19. Although Thomas Michael Stein interprets Mouse as representative of a black segregationist position in contrast to Easy who stand for integration (202), it is, in fact, Mouse who is essentially allied with the white world. His murders of Joppy and Frank remind Easy of the manipulative violence represented by Dewitt Albright.

7. White Epics

1. A claim for a contemporary version of the epic might be founded, however, on the contention by John P. McWilliams Jr. in *The American Epic* that the "essence of the *epos* is heroic narrative" in any narrative form that has "power over its audience" (6).

2. An influential alternative view is Mikhail Bakhtin's argument for the expiration of epic form in the modern world in *The Dialogic Imagination*.

3. This passage effectively parodies Paul Zweig's contention that identification is a central quest of *The Odyssey:* "Only through risk and trouble will the adventurer finally gain his identity. But after he has proved himself . . . his name bursts from him, through arrogance perhaps, but also through a sort of natural overflow" (24–25).

4. Banks's observation to Pinckney Benedict in an interview published in 1995 can serve as a gloss on this passage: "We have to understand our weaknesses and fears and the degrees to which we are manipulated by corporate culture" ("Russell Banks" 28).

5. Film theorist Laura Mulvey argues that classic films deeply engage issues of masculine identification by promoting "visual pleasure" through representing the

female body as the object of visual consumption. From the Freudian perspective of much contemporary film criticism, this preoccupation is disturbing because it produces masculine castration anxiety by unconsciously reactivating the threat to the achievement of masculine identity that the woman's lack of a penis signifies in the oedipal process. As a consequence of this effect, the popular film frequently attempts to resolve ideological contradictions concerning manhood.

6. To blame him as an individual relates Bob's failure in *Continental Drift* to that of other protagonists of American Realism from whom he descends. In Theodore Dreiser's *An American Tragedy* and Sinclair Lewis's *Babbitt,* for example, the detailed descriptions of consumer goods do more than establish verisimilitude. The extraordinary emphasis on setting in these novels, despite their ironies, seem to invest the social context of consumption with an apparent solidity that contrasts the moral uncertainty of both protagonists, so that the moral flaws appear to be a result of character rather than context.

7. Erich Fromm defines the basis of moral development in terms of response to the "contradictions" a man must struggle to resolve: "He is forced to overcome the horror of separateness, of powerlessness, and of lostness, and find new forms of relating himself to the world to enable himself to feel at home." The result of this constant endeavor, "character," is the "relatively permanent structure" of "strivings" through which he attempts to meet these needs (255). Bob's narcissism is a failure of the project of character formation as Fromm defines it.

8. According to Eric J. Leed, stories of travel traditionally provide foundational accounts of "lineages, states, civilities, reputations as a product of male potencies" (223).

9. Thus in "The Black Cat" the murderous attack on a domestic pet is an inversion of the narrator's failing marital relation; significantly, the figure of the violated cat appears in bas relief on the blasted wall of his incinerated domicile (65). The mysterious apparition of Poe's cat intimates a psychologized habitation for a literature in which personal isolation from social relation replaces the hero's epic achievement of community, and destruction replaces creation as narratable meaning.

10. If we assume that massive industrialization during the period erected barriers to individual control, then psychoanalysis, as Lionel Trilling claims, can be understood as one of the "culminations of Romantic literature" (34).

11. There is, however, a gender difference in response to this restriction. The women, the wives of Everett and Parmenter, take refuge in compulsive frumpiness and strained "irony" (*Libra* 17, 123), respectively. Marina Oswald, Lee's wife, believes in "fate" (201). Marguerite Oswald, Lee's mother, defends her own flailing domesticity. Protesting that she always managed, despite privation, to make a supportive home for her son, she also claims to be the menacing mother of boys' nightmares (48–49). The protective tactics of the women suggest a retreat into the retractive conditioning imposed by the "small rooms" of their experiences.

12. I also intend the term *white mythology* to resonate with Robert Young's arguments in *White Mythologies*. Like Young, who argues that Western thought has traditionally defined "History" as appropriative totalization, both Banks and DeLillo

found their novels on historical events that reveal the Western tendencies of exploitation and incorporation of that which is perceived as other. Banks narrativizes the consequences of the general condition Young calls "the egotism of the preoccupation of being with itself" (14), while DeLillo parodies what Young designates as the "process of a continuous, unfinalizable supplementation" (xii).

13. Derrida is quoting from Fontanier, *The Supplement to a Theory of Tropes.*

14. The psychology of revolution in *Libra* is probably best understood in terms of *ressentiment,* a concept Friedrich Nietzsche defined in *The Genealogy of Manners* as "The slave uprising in ethics [which] begins when *ressentiment* becomes creative and brings forth its own values: the ressentiment of those to whom the only authentic way of reaction—that of deeds—is unavailable, and who preserve themselves from harm through the exercise of imaginary violence." Fredric Jameson notes, however, that as it appears in literature *ressentiment* is more ambivalently presented. In George Gissing's novels, for example, the theme of *ressentiment* tends to "embarrass and to compromise even those on whose behalf it seems to testify" (*Political Unconscious* 201, 203). DeLillo apparently believes in the validity of Oswald's resentment. "I see contemporary violence," he told Anthony DeCurtis, "as a kind of sardonic response to the promise of consumer fulfillment in contemporary America" (57). But his representation of Oswald's failed appropriation of power also indicates the impossibility of corrective connection between the individual and the state on the basis of this concept. Instead of being incorporated into the privileged warfare of a functional society, as is the case of Achilles's rage in the *Iliad,* Oswald's *ressentiment* becomes the complex around which the degraded dream of originary authority is organized.

15. From the epigraph to *Libra,* which is quoted from a letter by Oswald to his brother, Robert.

16. The effect of his own example, the novel *Bouvard and Pecuchet,* Barthes explains, is a result of Flaubert's provision of a "semiological solution" that avoids "the major sin in literary matters, which is to confuse ideological with semiological reality" (136). I am arguing that the effect of *Libra* is comparable.

Conclusion

1. James B. Twitchell's broad analysis includes many forms of popular spectacle: cave painting and Renaissance frescoes, as well as comic books, movies, and television.

2. To "propagate efficiently," Twitchell explains, men "must be competitive to a point just short of violent." To be noncompetitive is "to risk not having a genetic future." Yet the violence of masculine competition involves the same risk (36). This dilemma is resolved through violent spectacle, "the cultural dream protecting us from the biological nightmare" (285), in which the display of male aggression as "willingness to fight" deflects actual combat (38).

3. Joyce Carol Oates uses these particular terms to define what writers have in common with prizefighters.

4. Elaine Scarry's theory of the discursive relation of meaning and anguish in *The Body in Pain: The Making and Unmaking of the World* provides the structure of

transference effected by violence. In war and political torture, pain is real but its effects may be discursive. In both of these causal transactions the immitigable actuality of physical suffering and death is used to authorize the ideologies of the social groups that are successful in administering force. During torture this effect occurs in three steps: (1) the infliction of pain, (2) the objectification of the subjective attributes of pain, and (3) the translation of the objectified attributes of pain into the insignia of power (51). Scarry defines this process as the predictable reversals of the organizing oppositions of body and voice, tortured and torturer, private and public. The vehicle of symbolic exchanges of meaning, violence not only inflicts suffering to assert dominance, it can be used to shift perceptions of authority. It is to this semiotic effect that violence owes its thematic prominence in narrative. Violence, then, is more than action—or the Aristotelian "imitation of an action" that defines the "drama" of pain, in Scarry's suggestive term—it is a privileged action that transacts complex, predictable transversals of value. In life as well as literature, violence is a privileged theme because it adapts a fundamental experience, extreme physical pain, to the narrative manipulation of social power.

5. I look at his body on the floor,
   Killing a bastard that deserves to die,
   Ain't nothing like it in the world
   But he sure did bleed a lot. (Egan A22)

WORKS CITED

Adamson, Joseph. "Supplementarity." *Encyclopedia of Contemporary Literary Theory: Approaches, Scholars, Terms*. Ed. Irena R. Makaryk. Toronto: U of Toronto P, 1993. 637–38.

Althusser, Louis. "Cremonini, Painter of the Abstract." *Lenin and Philosophy, and Other Essays*. Tr. Ben Brewster. New York: Monthly Review Press, 1971.

——. "Ideology and Ideological State Apparatuses." *Lenin and Philosophy and Other Essays*. Tr. Ben Brewster. New York: Monthly Review Press, 1971.

"American Violent Crime Down 12.4 Percent." (AP) *Daily Star* [Oneonta, NY] 14 Apr. 1997: 2.

Arendt, Hannah. *On Violence.* New York: Harcourt, 1970.

Babb, Valerie Melissa. *Ernest Gaines.* Boston: Twayne, 1991.

Bakhtin, Mikhail. *The Dialogic Imagination: Four Essays.* Ed. Michael Holquist. Tr. Caryl Emerson and Michael Holquist. Austin: U of Texas P, 1981.

Banks, Russell. *Continental Drift.* New York: Ballantine, 1986.

Barthes, Roland. *Mythologies.* Tr. Annette Lavers. New York: Hill and Wang, 1972.

Bausch, Richard. *Violence.* New York: Vintage, 1993.

Beauford, Fred. "A Conversation with Ernest J. Gaines." *Conversations with Ernest Gaines.* Ed. John Lowe. Jackson: UP of Mississippi, 1995.

Bederman, Gail. *Manliness and Civilization: A Cultural History of Gender and Race in the United States, 1880–1917.* Chicago: U of Chicago P, 1995.

Beidler, Philip D. *American Literature and the Experience of Vietnam.* Athens: U of Georgia P, 1982.

Belluck, Pam, and Jodi Wilgoren. "Shattered Lives—A Special Report; Caring Parents, No Answers, In Columbine Killers' Pasts." *New York Times* 29 June 1999: A1, A14.

Benedict, Pinckney. *Town Smokes: Stories.* Princeton, NJ: Ontario Review Press, 1987.

——. "Russell Banks." Interview with Russell Banks. *Bomb* 52 (summer 1995): 24–29.

——. *The Wrecking Yard: Stories.* New York: Doubleday, 1993.

Beneke, Timothy. *Proving Manhood: Reflections on Men and Sexism.* Los Angeles: U of California P, 1997.

Berger, Maurice, Brian Wallis, and Simon Watson, eds. *Constructing Masculinity.* New York: Routledge, 1995.

Bernstein, Michael André. *The Tale of the Tribe: Ezra Pound and the Modern Verse Epic.* Princeton, NJ: Princeton UP, 1980.

Bersani, Leo. "Realism and the Fear of Desire," chapter 2 of *A Future for Astyanax: Character and Desire in Literature* (1976). Rpr. in *Realism.* Ed. Lilian R. Furst. New York: Longman, 1992.

Bibby, Michael. *Hearts and Minds: Bodies, Poetry, and Resistance in the Vietnam Era.* New Brunswick, NJ: Rutgers UP, 1996.

Blake, Jeanie. Interview with Ernest Gaines (1982). *Conversations with Ernest Gaines.* Ed. John Lowe. Jackson: UP of Mississippi, 1995.

Blankenhorn, David. *Fatherless America: Confronting Our Most Urgent Social Problem.* New York: Basic Books, 1995.

Bok, Sissela. *Mayhem: Violence as Public Entertainment.* Reading, MA: Addison Wesley, 1998.

Bold, Christine. "Popular Forms I." *The Columbia History of the American Novel.* Ed. Emory Elliott. New York: Columbia UP, 1991.

Brod, Harry, ed. *The Making of Masculinities: The New Men's Studies.* Boston: Allen & Unwin, 1987.

Brooker, Peter. Introduction: "Reconstructions." *Modernism/Postmodernism.* Ed. Peter Brooker. New York: Longman, 1992.

Brooks, Peter. *Reading for the Plot: Design and Intention in Narrative.* Cambridge: Harvard UP, 1992.

Brooks, Van Wyck, and Otto L. Bettmann. *Our Literary Heritage: A Pictorial History of the Writer in America.* New York: Dutton, 1956.

Brown, Bill. "Popular Forms II." *The Columbia History of the American Novel.* Ed. Emory Elliot, et al. New York: Columbia UP, 1991.

Brown, Dee Alexander. *Bury My Heart at Wounded Knee: An Indian History of the American West.* New York: Holt, Rinehart & Winston, 1970.

Bryant, Jerry H. *Victims and Heroes: Racial Violence in the African American Novel.* Amherst: U of Massachusetts P, 1997.

Burgess, Anthony. *A Clockwork Orange.* New York: Norton, 1986.

Burke, Kenneth. "Literature as Equipment for Living." *The Philosophy of Literary Form: Studies in Symbolic Action.* New York: Vintage, 1957.

———. *The Rhetoric of Religion: Studies in Logology.* Berkeley: U of California P, 1970.

Butler, Judith. *Gender Trouble: Feminism and the Subversion of Identity.* New York: Routledge, 1990.

———."Melancholy Gender/Refused Identification." *Constructing Masculinity.* Ed. Maurice Berger, et al. New York: Routledge, 1995.

Butterfield, Fox. *All God's Children: The Bosket Family and the American Tradition of Violence.* New York: Knopf, 1995.

WORKS CITED

——. "Drop in Homicide Rate Linked to Crack's Decline." *New York Times* 27 Oct. 1997: A12.

Calloway, Catherine. "Pluralities of Vision: *Going after Cacciato* and Tim O'Brien's Short Fiction." *America Rediscovered: Critical Essays on Literature and Film of the Vietnam War.* Ed. Owen W. Gilman and Lorrie Smith. New York: Garland, 1990.

Campbell, Joseph. *The Hero with a Thousand Faces.* New York: Meridian, 1956.

Carmichael, Thomas. "Lee Harvey Oswald and the Postmodern Subject: History and Intertextuality in Don DeLillo's *Libra, The Names,* and *Mao II.*" *Contemporary Literature* 34.2 (1993): 204–18.

Cawelti, John G. *Adventure, Mystery, and Romance: Formula Stories as Art and Popular Culture.* Chicago: U of Chicago P, 1976.

——. *The Six-Gun Mystique.* Bowling Green, OH: Bowling Green State University Popular Press, 1984.

Center for Communication and Social Policy, University of California, Santa Barbara. *National Television Violence Study 2.* Thousand Oaks, CA: Sage Publications, 1998.

Chandler, Raymond. *The Big Sleep.* 1939. New York: Vintage, 1992.

Chodorow, Nancy. *The Reproduction of Mothering: Psychoanalysis and the Sociology of Gender.* Berkeley: U of California P, 1978.

Cobley, Evelyn. "Violence and Sacrifice in Modern War Narratives." *Sub-stance* 75.3. (1994): 75–99.

Cohan, Steven, and Linda M. Shires. *Telling Stories: A Theoretical Analysis of Narrative Fiction.* New York: Routledge, 1988.

Cohen, Ralph. "Do Postmodern Genres Exist?" *Postmodern Genres.* Ed. Marjorie Perloff. Norman: U of Oklahoma P, 1989.

Colie, Rosalie Littell. *The Resources of Kind: Genre-Theory in the Renaissance.* Ed. Barbara K. Lewalski. Berkeley: U of California P, 1973.

"Conference on Television Violence." By the Center for Communications Policy. C-Span. 27 Mar. 1997.

Connell, R. W. *Masculinities.* Berkeley: U of California P, 1995.

Conorroe, Joel. "Fugitive Childhoods." Rev. of *This Boy's Life* by Tobias Wolff. *New York Times Book Review* 15 Jan. 1989: 3, 28.

Courtine, Jean François, et al. *Of the Sublime: Presence in Question.* Tr. Jeffrey S. Librett. Albany: State U of New York P, 1993.

Crane, Stephen. *The Red Badge of Courage, and Selected Prose and Poetry.* Ed. William M. Gibson. New York: Holt, Rinehart & Winston, 1968.

Crooks, Robert. "From the Far Side of the Frontier: The Detective Fiction of Chester Himes and Walter Mosley." *College Literature* 22.3 (Oct. 1994): 68–89.

Davis, Charles Belmont, ed. *Adventures and Letters of Richard Harding Davis.* New York: Charles Scribner's Sons, 1917.

Davis, Richard Harding. *The Bar Sinister.* 1916. New York: Charles Scribner's Sons, 1917.

——. *Captain Macklin: His Memoirs.* New York: Charles Scribner's Sons, 1902.

WORKS CITED

——. *Soldiers of Fortune.* 1897. New York: Charles Scribner's Sons, 1909.

——. *Real Soldiers of Fortune.* New York: Charles Scribner's Sons, 1906.

DeCurtis, Anthony. "'An Outsider in This Society': An Interview with Don DeLillo." *Introducing Don DeLillo.* Ed. Frank Lentricchia. Durham, NC: Duke UP, 1991.

Deleuze, Gilles, and Felix Guattari. *Anti-Oedipus: Capitalism and Schizophrenia.* Tr. Robert Hurley, Mark Seem, and Helen R. Lane. New York: Viking, 1977.

DeLillo, Don. *Libra.* New York: Penguin, 1989.

Derrida, Jacques. *Margins of Philosophy.* Tr. Alan Bass. Chicago: U of Chicago P, 1982.

——. *Of Grammatology.* Tr. Gayatri Chakravorty Spivak. Baltimore: Johns Hopkins UP, 1976.

Douglass, Frederick. 1845. *The Autobiography of Frederick Douglass. The Classic Slave Narratives.* Ed. Henry Louis Gates Jr. New York: New American Library, 1987.

Downes, Jeremy M. *Recursive Desire: Rereading Epic Tradition.* Tuscaloosa: U of Alabama P, 1997.

Downey, Fairfax. *Richard Harding Davis: His Day.* New York: Charles Scribner's Sons, 1933.

Doyle, Mary Ellen. "A MELUS Interview: Ernest J. Gaines—Other Things to Write About." *Conversations with Ernest Gaines.* Ed. John Lowe. Jackson: UP of Mississippi, 1995.

Dreiser, Theodore. *An American Tragedy.* New York: New American Library, 1981.

Drinnon, Richard. *Facing West: The Metaphysics of Indian-Hating and Empire-Building.* Norman: U of Oklahoma P, 1997.

Eagleton, Terry. *Ideology: An Introduction.* London: Verso, 1991.

Egan, Timothy. "Where Rampages Begin: A Special Report; From Adolescent Angst to Shooting Up Schools." *New York Times* 14 June 1998: A1, 22.

Emerson, Ralph Waldo. "The American Scholar." *Selections from Ralph Waldo Emerson.* Ed. Stephen E. Whicher. New York: Houghton Mifflin, 1960. 63–80.

Erikson, Erik H. *Childhood and Society.* New York: Norton, 1963.

Evenson, Brian. "McCarthy's Wanderers: Nomadology, Violence, and Open Country." *Sacred Violence: A Reader's Companion to Cormac McCarthy.* Ed. Wade Hall and Rick Wallach. El Paso: U of Texas at El Paso, 1995.

Faulkner, William. *The Collected Stories of William Faulkner.* New York: Random House, 1948.

Fetterly, Judith. "'Not in the least American': Nineteenth-century Literary Regionalism." *College English* 56.8 (Dec. 1994): 877–91.

Fiedler, Leslie A. *Love and Death in the American Novel.* New York: Criterion Books, 1960.

Fiske, John. *Television Culture.* New York: Methuen, 1987.

Fitzgerald, F. Scott. *The Great Gatsby.* New York: Collier Books, 1980.

Ford, Richard. *Rock Springs: Stories.* New York: Vintage, 1987.

Foucault, Michel. *Discipline and Punish: The Birth of the Prison.* Tr. Alan Sheridan. New York: Vintage, 1979.

WORKS CITED

———. "On the Genealogy of Ethics: An Overview of Work in Progress." *The Foucault Reader*. Ed. Paul Rabinow. New York: Pantheon, 1984.

———. "The Subject and Power." Afterword to *Michel Foucault: Beyond Stuctural-ism and Hermeneutics,* Second Edition with an afterword by and an interview with Michel Foucault. Eds. Hubert L. Dreyfus and Paul Rabinow. Chicago: U of Chicago P, 1983.

———. "Truth and Power." *The Foucault Reader.* Ed. Paul Rabinow. New York: Pantheon, 1984.

———. "Two Lectures." *Power/Knowledge: Selected Interviews and Other Writings, 1972–1977.* Ed. Colin Gordon. Tr. Colin Gordon, et al. New York: Pantheon, 1980.

Fowler, Alastair. *Kinds of Literature: An Introduction to the Theory of Genres and Modes.* Cambridge, MA: Harvard UP, 1982.

Freeman, Barbara Claire. *The Feminine Sublime: Gender and Excess in Women's Fiction.* Berkeley: U of California P, 1995.

Freese, Peter. *The Ethnic Detective: Chester Himes, Harry Kemelman, Tony Hiller-man.* Essen: Verlag Die Blaue Eule, 1992.

Freud, Sigmund. "Creative Writers and Daydreaming," *The Standard Edition of the Complete Psychological Works of Sigmund Freud.* Vol. 9. Ed. and trans. James Strachey. London: Hogarth Press, 1961.

———. "The Dissolution of the Oedipus Complex," *The Standard Edition of the Complete Psychological Works of Sigmund Freud.* Vol. 19. Ed. and trans. James Strachey. London: Hogarth Press, 1961.

Frohack, Wilbur Merrill. *The Novel of Violence in America.* 1946. Dallas: Southern Methodist UP, 1957.

Fromm, Erich. *The Anatomy of Human Destructiveness.* New York: Holt, Rinehart & Winston, 1973.

Frosh, Stephen. *Sexual Difference: Masculinity and Psychoanalysis.* New York: Routledge, 1994.

Frye, Northrop. *Anatomy of Criticism: Four Essays.* Princeton, NJ: Princeton UP, 1957.

Frye, Northrop, Sheridan Baker, and George Perkins. *The Harper Handbook to Literature.* New York: Harper & Row, 1985.

Furfey, Paul Hanly. *The Gang Age: A Study of the Preadolescent Boy and His Recreational Needs.* New York: Macmillan, 1926.

Fussell, Paul. *The Great War and Modern Memory.* New York: Oxford UP, 1975.

———. *Wartime: Understanding and Behavior in the Second World War.* New York: Oxford UP, 1989.

Gaines, Ernest J. *A Gathering of Old Men.* New York: Vintage, 1983.

Gallop, Jane. *Reading Lacan.* Ithaca: Cornell UP, 1985.

Garbarino, James. *Lost Boys: Why Our Sons Turn Violent and How We Can Save Them.* New York: Free Press, 1999.

———. "Young Murderers." *American Educator* (summer 1999): 4–9, 46–48.

Gerzon, Mark. *A Choice of Heroes: The Changing Faces of American Manhood.* Boston: Houghton Mifflin, 1992.

WORKS CITED

Gilman, Owen W., Jr. "Vietnam and John Winthrop's Vision of Community." *Fourteen Landing Zones: Approaches to Vietnam War Literature*. Ed. Philip K. Jason. Iowa City: U of Iowa P, 1991.

Girard, René. *Violence and the Sacred*. Tr. Patrick Gregory. Baltimore: Johns Hopkins UP, 1977.

Glover, Douglas. Review of *The Wrecking Yard*. "The Elemental Element of Pinkney Benedict's Peculiarly American Myths of Character." *Chicago Tribune* 26 Jan. 1992: 7+.

Glover, David, and Cora Kaplan. "Guns in the House of Culture? Crime Fiction and the Politics of the Popular." *Cultural Studies*. Ed., and with an introduction, by Lawrence Grossberg, Cary Nelson, Paula A. Treichler, with Linda Baughman and assistance from John Macgregor Wise. New York: Routledge, 1992.

Gordon, Colin. Afterword. *Power/Knowledge: Selected Interviews and Other Writings, 1972–1977*. Ed. Colin Gordon. Tr. Colin Gordon, et al. New York: Pantheon, 1980.

Grayson, Charles. *Stories for Men: A Virile Anthology*. Garden City, NY: Garden City Publishing Co., 1944.

Green, Martin. *Dreams of Adventure, Deeds of Empire*. New York: Basic Books, 1979.

Griffin, Joseph. "Creole and Singaleese: Disruptive Caste in *Catherine Carmier* and *A Gathering of Old Men*." *Critical Reflections on the Fiction of Ernest J. Gaines*. Ed. David C. Estes. Athens: U of Georgia P, 1994.

Gunn, John. *Violence*. New York: Praeger, 1973.

Gusdorf, Georges. "Conditions and Limits of Autobiography." *Autobiography: Essays Theoretical and Critical*. Ed. James Olney. Princeton, NJ: Princeton UP, 1980.

Hall, Michael. "Desperately Seeking Cormac." *Texas Monthly* 26.7 (Jul. 1998): 76–79+.

Hall, Stephen S. "The Bully in the Mirror." *New York Times Magazine* (22 Aug. 1999): 31–35+.

Hanke, Robert. "Theorizing Masculinity With/In the Media." *Communication Theory* 8.2 (May 1998): 183–203.

Hanley, Lynne. *Writing War: Fiction, Gender, and Memory*. Amherst: U of Massachusetts P, 1991.

Hansen, J. T. "Vocabularies of Experience." *America Rediscovered: Critical Essays on Literature and Film of the Vietnam War*. Ed. Owen W. Gilman and Lorrie Smith. New York: Garland, 1990.

Harper, Philip Brian. *Are We Not Men?: Masculine Anxiety and the Problem of African-American Identity*. New York: Oxford UP, 1996.

Hassan, Ihab Habib. *Radical Innocence: Studies in the Contemporary American Novel*. Princeton, NJ: Princeton UP, 1971.

Hawthorne, Nathaniel. "Young Goodman Brown." *Hawthorne: Selected Tales and Sketches*. Ed. Hyatt H. Waggoner. New York: Holt, Rinehart & Winston, 1970.

Haycraft, Howard, ed. *The Art of the Mystery Story: A Collection of Critical Essays*. New York: Grosset and Dunlap, 1946.

Hemingway, Ernest. "The Battler." *The Complete Short Stories of Ernest Hemingway.* Ed. Finca Vigía. New York: Charles Scribner's Sons, 1987. 95–104.

———. "The Snows of Kilimanjaro." *The Complete Short Stories of Ernest Hemingway.* Ed. Finca Vigía. New York: Charles Scribner's Sons, 1987. 39–56.

Hernadi, Paul. *Beyond Genre: New Directions in Literary Classification.* Ithaca: Cornell UP, 1972.

Herzog, Tobey C. *Vietnam War Stories: Innocence Lost.* New York: Routledge, 1992.

Himes, Chester. *If He Hollers Let Him Go: A Novel.* 1945. New York: Thunder's Mouth Press, 1986.

Hogben, Matthew. "Factors Moderating the Effect of Televised Aggression on Viewer Behavior." *Communication Research* 25.2 (Apr. 1998): 220–47.

Holloway, Karla F. C. "Cultural Narratives Passed On: African American Mourning Stories." *College English* 59.1 (Jan. 1997): 32–40.

Holman, C. Hugh, and William Harmon. *A Handbook to Literature.* 5th edition. New York: Macmillan, 1986.

Horrocks, Roger. *Male Myths and Icons: Masculinity in Popular Culture.* New York: St. Martin's, 1995.

Howland, Bette. "Innocence Meets Violence in American Literary Tradition." Review of James Fenimore Cooper's *The Leatherstocking Tales* and Cormac McCarthy's *Blood Meridian. Chicago Tribune* 25 May 1986: 33+.

Hunt, Albert. "Lessons of Teen Violence." *Daily Star* [Oneonta, NY] 13 June 1998: 4.

Jameson, Fredric. "Generic Discontinuities in Science Fiction: Brian Aldiss' Starship," *Science Fiction Studies #2* (173), 57–68.

———. "Modernism and Imperialism." *Nationalism, Colonialism, and Literature.* Terry Eagleton, Fredric Jameson, and Edward Said. Minneapolis: U of Minnesota P, 1990.

———. *The Political Unconscious: Narrative as a Socially Symbolic Act.* Ithaca: Cornell UP, 1981.

———. "Postmodernism and Consumer Society." *Modernism/Postmodernism.* Ed. Peter Brooker. New York: Longman, 1992.

Jewett, Robert, and John Shelton Lawrence. *The American Monomyth.* Garden City: Anchor Press, 1977.

Johnston, John. "Superlinear Fiction or Historical Diagram? Don DeLillo's *Libra.*" *Modern Fiction Studies.* 40.2 (summer 1994): 319–42.

Jones, Suzanne W. "Reconstructing Manhood: Race, Masculinity, and Narrative Closure in Ernest Gaines's *A Gathering of Old Men* and *A Lesson Before Dying.*" *Masculinities* 3.2 (summer 1995): 43–66.

Jones, Thom. *The Pugilist at Rest: Stories.* New York: Little, Brown, 1993.

Kaplan, E. Ann. *Rocking Around the Clock: Music Television, Postmodernism, and Consumer Culture.* New York: Routledge, 1987.

Kaufman, Michael. "The Construction of Masculinity and the Triad of Men's Violence." *Beyond Patriarchy: Essays by Men on Pleasure, Power, and Change.* Ed. Michael Kaufman. New York: Oxford UP, 1987.

Kimmel, Michael S. *Changing Men: New Directions in Research on Men and Masculinity.* Newbury Park, CA: Sage, 1987.

———. *Manhood in America: A Cultural History.* New York: Free Press, 1996.

Kindlon, Dan, and Michael Thompson. *Raising Cain: Protecting the Emotional Life of Boys.* New York: Ballantine, 1999.

Kintz, Linda. "Conservative Cowboy Stories: Adventures of the Chosen Sons." *Boys: Masculinities in Contemporary Culture.* Ed. Paul Smith. Boulder, CO: Westview Press, 1996.

Kowalewski, Michael. *Deadly Musings: Violence and Verbal Form in American Fiction.* Princeton, NJ: Princeton UP, 1993.

Krauss, Clifford. "New York Crime Rate Plummets to Levels Not Seen in 30 Years." *New York Times* 20 Dec. 1996: A1, B4.

Kristeva, Julia. *Powers of Horror: An Essay on Abjection.* Tr. Leon S. Roudiez. New York: Columbia UP, 1982.

Kronick, Joseph. "*Libra* and the Assassination of JFK: A Textbook Operation." *Arizona Quarterly* 50.1 (spring 1994): 109–32.

Labov, William. *Language in the Inner City: Studies in the Black English Vernacular.* Philadelphia: U of Pennsylvania P, 1972.

Lacan, Jacques. *Écrits: A Selection.* Tr. Alan Sheridan. New York: Norton, 1977.

———. *The Four Fundamental Concepts of Psycho-Analysis.* Ed. Jacques-Alain Miller. Tr. Alan Sheridan. New York: Norton, 1978.

———. "The Meaning of the Phallus." *Feminine Sexuality: Jacques Lacan and the école freudienne.*" Ed. Juliet Mitchell and Jacqueline Rose. Tr. Jacqueline Rose. New York: Norton, 1982.

"L.A., New York Homicides Fall." (AP) *Daily Star* [Oneonta, NY] 20 Dec. 1997: 20.

Langford, Gerald. *The Richard Harding Davis Years: A Biography of a Mother and Son.* New York: Holt, Rinehart & Winston, 1961.

Lanham, Fritz. "A Novelist Not at Rest: Thom Jones' Unlikely Success Mirrors an Equally Unlikely Life." *Houston Chronicle* 16 June 1996: 26–27.

Leed, Eric J. *The Mind of the Traveler: From Gilgamesh to Global Tourism.* New York: Basic Books, 1991.

Lentricchia, Frank. "The American Writer as Bad Citizen." *Introducing Don DeLillo.* Ed. Frank Lentricchia. Durham, NC: Duke UP, 1991.

———. "*Libra* as Postmodern Critique." *Introducing Don DeLillo.* Ed. Frank Lentricchia. Durham, NC: Duke UP, 1991.

Lesser, Wendy. *Pictures at an Execution.* Cambridge, MA: Harvard UP, 1993.

Lesy, Michael. *Wisconsin Death Trip.* London: Allen Lane, 1973.

Leverenz, David. *Manhood and the American Renaissance.* Ithaca: Cornell UP, 1988.

Levinson, Daniel J., et al. *The Seasons of a Man's Life.* New York: Knopf, 1978.

Lewis, R. W. B. *The American Adam: Innocence, Tragedy, and Tradition in the Nineteenth Century.* Chicago: U of Chicago P, 1966.

Lifton, Robert Jay. *The Broken Connection: On Death and the Continuity of Life.* New York: Simon and Schuster, 1979.

WORKS CITED

——. *The Life of the Self: Toward a New Psychology.* New York: Simon and Schuster, 1976.

——. "The Sense of Immortality." *Explorations in Psychohistory: The Wellfleet Papers.* Robert Jay Lifton and Eric Olson, eds. New York: Simon and Schuster, 1974.

Longinus. "On the Sublime." *Critical Theory Since Plato.* Ed. Hazard Adams. New York: Harcourt, 1971.

Lorenz, Konrad. *On Aggression.* Tr. Marjorie Kerr Wilson. New York: Bantam, 1977.

Lovett, Kenneth. "Smaller Cities Showing Bigger Problems." *Daily Star* 29 Nov. 1997 [Oneonta, NY]: 5.

Lubow, Arthur. *The Reporter Who Would Be King: A Biography of Richard Harding Davis.* New York: Scribner, 1992.

Lukacs, Georg. *The Theory of the Novel: A Historico-Philosophical Essay on the Forms of Great Epic Literature.* Tr. Anna Bostock. Cambridge: MIT Press, 1971.

Lyons, Bonnie. Interview with Richard Ford. "Richard Ford: The Art of Fiction CXLVII." *Paris Review* 38.140 (fall 1996): 42–77.

Lyons, Bonnie, and Bill Oliver. "An Interview with Tobias Wolff." *Contemporary Literature* 31 (spring 1990): 1–16.

MacBeth, Tannis M., ed. *Tuning in to Young Viewers: Social Science Perspectives on Television.* Thousand Oaks, CA: Sage, 1996.

Martin, Jay. *Harvests of Change: American Literature 1865–1914.* Englewood Cliffs, NJ: Prentice-Hall, 1967.

Martin, Wallace. *Recent Theories of Narrative.* Ithaca: Cornell UP, 1986.

Mason, Theodore O., Jr. "Walter Mosley's Easy Rawlins: The Detective and Afro-American Fiction." *Kenyon Review* 14.4 (fall 1992): 173–83.

May, Rollo. *Power and Innocence: A Search for the Sources of Violence.* New York: Basic Books, 1973.

McCarthy, Cormac. *Blood Meridian; or, The Evening Redness in the West.* New York: Random House, 1985.

McClure, John A. *Late Imperial Romance.* London: Verso, 1994.

McLaren, Angus. *The Trials of Masculinity: Policing Sexual Boundaries, 1870–1930.* Chicago: U of Chicago P, 1997.

McWhorter, Diane. "Cigarettes Rolled from the Bible." Rev. of *Town Smokes* by Pinckney Benedict. *New York Times Book Review* 12 July 1987: 13–14.

McWilliams, John P., Jr. *The American Epic: Transforming a Genre, 1770–1860.* New York: Cambridge UP, 1989.

Mellard, James M. *Using Lacan, Reading Fiction.* Urbana: U of Illinois P, 1991.

Melling, Philip H. *Vietnam in American Literature.* Boston: Twayne, 1990.

Melville, Herman. "Billy Budd, Foretopman." *Shorter Novels of Herman Melville.* New York: Liveright, 1978.

Messner, Michael. "The Meaning of Success: The Athletic Experience and the Development of Male Identity." *The Making of Masculinities: The New Men's Studies.* Ed. Harry Brod. Boston: Allen & Unwin, 1987.

WORKS CITED

Michael, Magali Cornier. "The Political Paradox within Don DeLillo's *Libra*." *Critique* 35.3 (spring 1994): 146–56.

Miedzian, Myriam. *Boys Will Be Boys: Breaking the Link between Masculinity and Violence.* New York: Doubleday, 1991.

Mifflin, Lawrie. "Study Finds a Decline in TV Network Violence." *New York Times* 14 Jan. 1998: E7.

Miller, Wayne Charles. *An Armed America, Its Face in Fiction: A History of the American Military Novel.* New York: New York UP, 1970.

Mithers, Carol Ann. "The War Against Women." *Ladies' Home Journal.* Oct. 1989. Rpr. in *Essays from Contemporary Culture* 2nd ed. Ed. Katherine Anne Ackley. Ft. Worth: Harcourt Brace College Publishers, 1995.

Morris, Mary. Introduction. *Maiden Voyages: Writings of Women Travelers.* Ed. Mary Morris. New York: Vintage, 1993.

Mosle, Sara. "Don't Let Your Babies Grow Up to Be Cowboys. "Review of Cormac McCarthy's *Cities of the Plain. New York Times Book Review* 17 May 1998: 16–17.

Mosley, Walter. *Black Betty.* New York: Pocket Books, 1994.

———. *Devil in a Blue Dress.* New York: Pocket Books, 1990.

———. *Gone Fishin': An Easy Rawlins Novel.* Baltimore: Serpent's Tail, 1997.

———. *A Little Yellow Dog: An Easy Rawlins Mystery.* New York: Pocket Books, 1996.

———. "On the Other Side of Those Mean Streets." Interview with Charles L. P. Silet. *The Armchair Detective* 26.4 (1993): 8–19.

———. *A Red Death.* New York: Pocket Books, 1991.

———. *White Butterfly.* New York: Pocket Books, 1992.

Mosse, George L. *The Image of Man: The Creation of Modern Masculinity.* New York: Oxford UP, 1996.

Mott, Christopher M. "*Libra* and the Subject of History." *Critique* 35.3 (spring 1994): 131–44.

Mulvey, Laura. "Visual Pleasure and Narrative Cinema." *Feminism and Film Theory.* Ed. Constance Penley. New York: Routledge, 1988.

Nealon, Jeffrey T. *Alterity Politics: Ethics and Performative Subjectivity.* Durham: Duke UP, 1998.

Niehoff, Debra. *The Biology of Violence: How Understanding the Brain, Behavior, and Environment Can Break the Vicious Circle of Aggression.* New York: Free Press, 1999.

Norris, Rebecca. "Boxer's Best Friend." *American Health* Dec. 1994: 96.

Oates, Joyce Carol. *On Boxing.* New York: Kensington, 1987.

O'Brien, Tim. "The Vietnam in Me." *The New York Times Magazine* 2 Oct. 1994: 48–57.

———. *Going after Cacciato: A Novel.* New York: Dell, 1978.

———. *If I Die in a Combat Zone; Box Me Up and Ship Me Home.* New York: Dell, 1973.

———. *The Things They Carried.* New York: Penguin, 1990.

WORKS CITED

Ogdon, Bethany. "Hard-Boiled Ideology." *Critical Quarterly* 34.1 (summer 1992): 71–87.

Ong, Walter J. *Fighting for Life: Contest, Sexuality, and Consciousness.* Ithaca: Cornell UP, 1981.

Osborn, Scott Compton and Robert L. Phillips Jr. *Richard Harding Davis.* Twayne's United States Authors Series 289. Boston: Twayne, 1978.

Phillips, Dana. "History and the Ugly Facts of Cormac McCarthy's *Blood Meridian.*" *American Literature* 68.2 (June 1996): 433–60.

Poe, Edgar Allan. "The Black Cat." *Complete Stories and Poems of Edgar Allan Poe.* New York: Doubleday, 1966.

Pollack, William S. *Real Boys: Rescuing Our Sons from the Myths of Boyhood.* New York: Random, 1999.

Porter, Dennis. *The Pursuit of Crime: Art and Ideology in Detective Fiction.* New Haven: Yale UP, 1981.

Potter, W. James. *On Media Violence.* Thousand Oaks, CA: Sage Publications, 1999.

Pratt, Mary Louise. *Imperial Eyes: Travel Writing and Transculturation.* New York: Routledge, 1991.

Propp, Vladimir. *The Morphology of the Folktale.* Tr. Laurence Scott. Austin: U of Texas P, 1977.

Pughe, Thomas. "Revision and Vision: Cormac McCarthy's *Blood Meridian.*" *Revue Francaise d'Etudes Americaine* 17.62 (Nov. 1994): 371–82.

Rendell, Ruth. *The Keys to the Street: A Novel of Suspense.* New York: Dell, 1997.

Rifkind, Donna. "Loot and Consequences." Review of Richard Bausch's *In the Night Season. Washington Post* 28 June 1998: 8.

Rimmon-Kenan, Shlomith. *Narrative Fiction: Contemporary Poetics.* New York: Methuen, 1983.

Ringnalda, Don. *Fighting and Writing the Vietnam War.* Jackson: UP of Mississippi, 1994.

———. "Unlearning to Remember Vietnam." *America Rediscovered: Critical Essays on Literature and Film of the Vietnam War.* Ed. Owen W. Gilman and Lorrie Smith. New York: Garland, 1990.

Rodriguez, Luis J. *Always Running:* La Vida Loca, *Gang Days in L.A.* New York: Simon and Schuster, 1993.

Rogozinski, Jacob. "The Gift of the World." Courtine, et al. *Of the Sublime.* Albany: State U of New York P, 1993.

Rose, Jacqueline. *Why War? Psychoanalysis, Politics, and the Return to Melanie Klein.* Cambridge, MA: Blackwell, 1993.

Rosmarin, Adena. *The Power of Genre.* Minneapolis: U of Minnesota P, 1985.

Rotundo, E. Anthony. *American Manhood: Transformations in Masculinity from the Revolution to the Modern Era.* New York: Basic Books, 1993.

Rubin, Gayle. "The Traffic in Women: Notes on the 'Political Economy' of Sex." *Toward an Anthropology of Women.* Ed. Rayna R. Reiter. New York: Monthly Review Press, 1975.

Saeta, Elsa, and Izora Skinner. Interview with Ernest Gaines (1991). *Conversations with Ernest Gaines.* Ed. John Lowe. Jackson: UP of Mississippi, 1995.

Scarry, Elaine. *The Body in Pain: The Making and Unmaking of the World.* New York: Oxford UP, 1985.

Scholes, Robert, and Robert Kellogg. *The Nature of Narrative.* New York: Oxford UP, 1966.

Sedley, David L. "Sublimity and Skepticism in Montaigne." *PMLA* 113.5 (Oct. 1998): 1079–92.

Sepich, John Emil. "'What kind of indians was them?': Some Historical Sources in Cormac McCarthy's *Blood Meridian.*" *Perspectives on Cormac McCarthy.* Ed. Edwin T. Arnold and Dianne C. Luce. Jackson: UP of Mississippi, 1993.

Shaviro, Steven. "'The Very Life of the Darkness': A Reading of *Blood Meridian.*" *Perspectives on Cormac McCarthy.* Ed. Edwin T. Arnold and Dianne C. Luce. Jackson: UP of Mississippi, 1993.

Sherman, Charlotte Watson. "Walter Mosley on the Black Male Hero." *American Visions* 10.4 (Aug. 1995): 34–37.

Showalter, Elaine. *Hystories: Hysterical Epidemics and Modern Media.* New York: Columbia UP, 1997.

Silverman, Kaja. *The Subject of Semiotics.* New York: Oxford UP, 1983.

Slabey, Robert M. Going after Cacciato*: Tim O'Brien's "Separate Peace."* *America Rediscovered: Critical Essays on Literature and Film of the Vietnam War.* Ed. Owen W. Gilman and Lorrie Smith. New York: Garland, 1990.

Slotkin, Richard. *Gunfighter Nation: The Myth of the Frontier in Twentieth-Century America.* New York: Harper, 1992.

———. *Regeneration through Violence: The Mythology of the American Frontier, 1600–1860.* Middletown, CT: Wesleyan UP, 1973.

Smith, John. "A Description of New England." *The Complete Works of Captain John Smith (1580–1631).* Vol. I. Ed. Philip L. Barbour. Chapel Hill: U of North Carolina P, 1983.

Smith, Lorrie. "Disarming the War Story." *America Rediscovered: Critical Essays on Literature and Film of the Vietnam War.* Ed. Owen W. Gilman and Lorrie Smith. New York: Garland, 1990.

Smith, Paul. "Eastwood Bound." *Constructing Masculinity.* New York: Routledge, 1995.

Smith, Paul, ed. Introduction. *Boys: Masculinities in Contemporary Culture.* Boulder, CO: Westview, 1996.

Smith, Sidonie. *A Poetics of Women's Autobiography: Marginality and the Fictions of Self-Representation.* Bloomington: Indiana UP, 1987.

Solotaroff, Ted. "*Semper fi,* Nietzsche: *The Pugilist at Rest* by Thom Jones." Review. *The Nation* 6 Sept 1993: 7+.

Spacks, Patricia Meyer. *The Adolescent Idea: Myths of Youth and the Adult Imagination.* New York: Basic Books, 1981.

St. Jean de Crèvecoeur, J. Hector. "Description of Charles-Town; Thoughts on Slavery; On Physical Evil, A Melancholy Scene" (9th letter). *Letters from an Ameri-*

WORKS CITED

can Farmer. *The American Tradition in Literature* 7 ed. vol. I. Ed. George Perkins, et al. New York: McGraw-Hill, 1990.

Stanage, Sherman M. "Violatives: Modes and Themes of Violence." *Reason and Violence: Philosophical Investigations.* Ed. Sherman M. Stanage. Totowa, NJ: Littlefield, Adams, 1974.

Stein, Thomas Michael. "The Ethnic Vision in Walter Mosley's Crime Fiction." *Amerika Studien/American Studies* (Amsterdam) 39.2 (1994): 197–212.

Sullivan, Nell. "Cormac McCarthy and the Text of Jouissance." *Sacred Violence: A Reader's Companion to Cormac McCarthy.* Ed. Wade Hall and Rick Wallach. El Paso: U of Texas at El Paso, 1995.

Tabbi, Joseph. *Postmodern Sublime: Technology and American Writing from Mailer to Cyberpunk.* Ithaca: Cornell UP, 1995.

Takaki, Ronald T. *Violence in the Black Imagination: Essays and Documents.* New York: Oxford UP, 1993.

Tal, Kai. "Speaking the Language of Pain: Vietnam War Literature in the Context of a Literature of Trauma." *Fourteen Landing Zones: Approaches to Vietnam War Literature.* Ed. Philip K. Jason. Iowa City: U of Iowa P, 1991.

Tasker, Yvonne. *Spectacular Bodies: Gender, Genre, and the Action Cinema.* New York: Routledge, 1993.

Todorov, Tzvetan. *The Conquest of America: The Question of the Other.* Tr. Richard Howard. New York: Harper, 1984.

———. *Genres in Discourse.* Tr. Catherine Porter. New York: Cambridge UP, 1990.

———. *The Poetics of Prose.* Tr. Richard Howard. Ithaca: Cornell UP, 1977.

Tompkins, Jane. *West of Everything: The Inner Life of Westerns.* New York: Oxford UP, 1992.

Toufexis, Anastasia. "Seeking the Roots of Violence." *Time* (19 Apr., 1993). Rpr. in *Essays from Contemporary Culture* 2nd ed. Ed. Katherine Anne Ackley. New York: Harcourt, 1995.

Trilling, Lionel. *The Liberal Imagination: Essays on Literature and Society.* New York: Viking, 1950.

Twitchell, James B. *Preposterous Violence: Fables of Aggression in Modern Culture.* New York: Oxford UP, 1989.

Wallach, Rick. "Judge Holden, *Blood Meridian*'s Evil Archon." *Sacred Violence: A Reader's Companion to Cormac McCarthy.* Ed. Wade Hall and Rick Wallach. El Paso: U of Texas at El Paso, 1995.

Washington, Booker T. "Atlanta Exposition Address." *Cultural Contexts for Ralph Ellison's* Invisible Man. Ed. Eric J. Sundquist. Boston: Bedford Books of St. Martin's Press, 1995. 33–38.

West, Cornell. "An Interview with Cornell West." *Modernism/Postmodernism.* Ed. Peter Brooker. New York: Longman, 1992.

Whillock, David Everett. "The Fictive American Vietnam War Film: A Filmography." *America Rediscovered: Critical Essays on Literature and Film of the Vietnam War.* Ed. Owen W. Gilman and Lorrie Smith. New York: Garland, 1990.

Whitmer, Barbara. *The Violence Mythos.* Albany: State U of New York P, 1997.

WORKS CITED

Wittman, Sandra M. *Writing about Vietnam: A Bibliography of the Literature of the Vietnam Conflict*. Boston: G. K. Hall, 1989.

Wolff, Geoffrey. *The Duke of Deception: Memories of My Father*. New York: Vintage, 1979.

Wolff, Tobias. *Back in the World: Stories*. Boston: Houghton Mifflin, 1985.

———. *The Barracks Thief and Selected Stories*. New York: Bantam, 1984.

———. *In the Garden of the North American Martyrs: A Collection of Short Stories*. New York: Ecco, 1981.

———. *This Boy's Life: A Memoir*. New York: Harper and Row, 1990.

Wolff, Tobias, ed. Introduction. *Matters of Life and Death: New American Short Stories*. Green Harbor, MA: Wampeter, 1983.

Woodward, Richard B. "Cormac McCarthy's Venomous Fiction." *New York Times Book Review* 19 Apr. 1992, 28–31, 36, 40.

X, Malcolm, and Alex Haley. 1964. *The Autobiography of Malcolm X*. New York: Ballantine, 1992.

Yarborough, Richard. "Race, Violence, and Manhood: The Masculine Ideal in Frederick Douglass's 'The Heroic Slave.'" *Haunted Bodies: Gender and Southern Texts*. Eds. Anne Goodwyn Jones and Susan V. Donaldson. Charlottesville: U of Virginia P, 1997.

Young, Philip. *Ernest Hemingway*. New York: Rinehart, 1952.

Young, Robert. *White Mythologies: Writing History and the West*. New York: Routledge, 1990.

Ziff, Larzer. *The American 1890's: Life and Times of a Lost Generation*. New York: Viking, 1967.

Zweig, Paul. *The Adventurer*. New York: Basic Books, 1974.

INDEX

INDEX